WORK COMMANDO 311/I

American Paratroopers Become
Forced Laborers for the Nazis

Claire E. Swedberg

STACKPOLE
BOOKS

This book is dedicated to all those POWs, living and dead, who were interned at Work Commando 311/I. Without the honesty and unflagging generosity with painful memories the characters of this book provided, Work Commando 311/I *could never have been written. Many thanks are owed to the military historians and soldiers who assisted with the facts of this text.*

———————————————

Published by
STACKPOLE BOOKS
5067 Ritter Road
Mechanicsburg, PA 17055

Printed in the United States of America

First edition

10 9 8 7 6 5 4 3 2 1

Library of Congress Cataloging-in-Publication Data

Swedberg, Claire E.
    Work Commando 311/I: American paratroopers become forced laborers for the Nazis / Claire E. Swedberg. — 1st ed.
        p. cm.
    Includes biographical references.
    ISBN 0-8117-1908-1
    1. World War, 1939–1945—Prisoners and prisons, German. 2. United States. Army—Parachute troops. 3. World War, 1939–1945—Conscript labor. 4. Prisoners of war—United States—History—20th century. I. Title. II. Title: Work Commando Three Hundred Eleven/One.
D805.G3S88 1995
940.54'7243—dc20
                                  94-31223
                                       CIP

PART I

CHAPTER 1

The engines of the C-47 plane roared. The men of the 502nd Regiment sat silently on metal benches inside the dark fuselage, only the lit ends of their cigarettes visible in the darkness. Their faces, camouflaged under thick layers of chocolate, matched the blackness of the night.

The sky was clear, and as they flew across the English Channel toward Normandy, a full moon rose like a beacon for the 101st Airborne.

Nineteen-year-old Pvt. Danzley Jones closed his eyes and let out a deep breath. He enjoyed a feeling of self-confidence that coursed through him as he anticipated the jump into France. Finally the moment was upon him. The days, the months of preparation, then waiting, had played an excruciating, slow tune on his nerves. Now, late this night of June 5, 1944, the wait was over. Within hours he'd find out what kind of soldier he really was. Many of the men seated around him stared silent and transfixed like himself as they flew toward the French shore. Some slept, drowsy from the Dramamine they had been issued before the flight. A few talked together in strained voices over the roar of the engines. One man vomited on the floor between his feet.

The rising moon shone a dim distraction across Jones's closed lids, and he blinked in its glow. The Dramamine seemed to imbue him with a strange calm, and yet he couldn't be sure that it was the airsickness pill and not his own mind that gave him this unconcerned self-assurance.

A few days before, he had written his last letter to his mother, in Coeur d'Alene, Idaho, before the men were forbidden to write. Until then he had corresponded with her through the V-mail almost every day. But he found that he began each letter the same way: "The Invasion should begin any day now." He had tried to leak information about his jump through codes to his mother. He asked repeatedly about his Aunt Frances in hopes that she would realize the Invasion would be in France. He wrote to his sweetheart, Caroline, whom he had met while stationed on the coast in Ireland awaiting this offensive against the Germans. But even his love letters turned repetitious as he grew more and more distracted by the Invasion. Everything depended on it.

Now, with the Invasion upon him, Jones stared at the light that would signal their jump glowing red above the airplane door. He thought of his brother, who had wanted to be a soldier but had been 4-F'd. He wondered what Vern was doing now and if he was thinking of him, sensing that the big moment had arrived. Vern was his closest brother, his greatest rival and best friend.

As the plane coursed above the cold, gray waters of the English Channel, he thought of his father, who had died less than a year ago and would never know of the Invasion of Normandy or his son's role there. He thought of the other friends and family members who had helped him through the past few years. He hoped at least one of them was thinking of him now.

His reverie was interrupted by a voice beside him, and he turned to glimpse the red light's glow in the eyes of Private Holland, a quiet, serious man he had known only by last name since his training in Hungerford, England. The soldier lit a cigarette with unsteady hands and handed another to Jones.

"Are you a religious man?" Holland asked, holding his lit match out to him.

"I guess I'd say I was, yeah," Jones replied. Holland paused in silent pondering, then slid the matches into his pocket.

"I'm not. My parents took me to church for a while, but I never could convince myself to believe. I been an atheist all my life, and I'm still an atheist tonight." They smoked in silence for several minutes before he continued. "But what if I die now? You all got God to save you, but what do I believe in when I'm dying?"

"I got a good feeling that when a man's time comes, he finds out what he believes in, even if he didn't know it until then," Jones reflected, crushing out his cigarette under his boot.

"Yeah, well, I hope you're right."

Two hours passed before the light flashed above the door, alerting the men. They were approaching their drop zone.

CHAPTER 2

"Stand up and hook up!" the jumpmaster shouted, and the men climbed to their feet, each struggling under a hundred pounds of equipment. The plane forged into a sinister gray layer of clouds that now hung densely over the French coast. Jones looked out the door as the pilot brought the C-47 below the clouds in an attempt to identify the proper drop zone. German searchlights beamed up at them through surface fog, swinging menacingly back and forth as they swept the sky for enemy planes.

The men heard their first shots, and the plane picked up speed to avoid flak that sliced through their airspace from an unseen German artillery station. Shots jarred the plane, and the men looked around nervously. The green light came on like a sigh of relief as the men in the plane ahead of them began tossing out hundreds of pounds of weapons, medical supplies, radio equipment, and food.

Jones was fourth on the stick and watched the three troopers ahead of him disappear out the vacuum of the door. He patted Holland on the back as his friend leapt ahead of him. Then Jones took a breath and dove out the door headfirst, letting out a victory holler that cut through the damp air. He saw the taillight flashing between his legs as he began his quick descent.

Jones had jumped at such a low elevation that his feet scraped the upper foliage of a tree before his chute opened, sucking the breath from his lungs. Tracer bullets sliced the air around him as his chute made him a slow and helpless target. He tugged on his front risers, dumping air from the front of his canopy, and it dragged him rapidly past the trees and into the middle of a soggy field.

As he hit the earth, he realized in horror that dark figures were moving all around him. He clawed at the snaps on his harness, panicking until he recognized the familiar mooing of cattle over the rattle of gunfire. The cows trampled the meadow in confusion as parachutists dropped on them from the sky. As the animals circled, they tangled in Jones's chute and cords, tugging him back and forth in the mud like a rag doll. He unfastened three snaps, then was yanked backward with a jolt, losing the mortar baseplate that was strapped to his leg. Several cattle were hit as automatic fire chased him in the mayhem.

The last snap came free as he gave it a final desperate pull, and he leapt for a natural ditch several feet behind him. As he huddled against the mud, the shooting ceased. He saw another parachute in the field, thirty feet ahead, and realized that a man was still attached to it. He had been unable to find his rifle or mortar in the dark field under pressure of heavy fire, and he was now left with only his knife and several grenades. He was frantic over the loss of his rifle, even though for now it made little difference—the men had been instructed not to shoot unless absolutely necessary, ensuring that gunfire could identify the Germans.

An automatic weapon fired overhead, and faster than he could react, a large figure leapt into the ditch beside him. The intruder lay panting for a moment, then spotted Jones and reached for his knife.

"Victory!" Jones hissed. This was the American password, and the man at his side showed his white teeth in a grin in the dark.

"Welcome," he returned. He told Jones he was a corporal with another 502nd company. "Let's make our way back along this hedgerow, where we can get a break from this fire."

"I gotta check this kid ahead of us, who's still in his chute," Jones responded. The corporal shook his head. "He's dead. Probably shot on the way down."

"I have to go," Jones insisted. "My rifle's out there." The corporal seemed to shrug in the dark.

Jones slid out of the ditch and ran toward the parachute, scanning the ground for his rifle. He hunched beside the soldier, taking shelter behind the waving canopy, and turned the motionless body onto its back. He recognized Holland's dead face above the bleeding hole in his neck. A burst of gunfire gave him no chance to mourn his friend, and he scanned the ground around his feet. He located Holland's rifle and grabbed it as he ran, diving back into the ditch. He sat in the mud watching dark shadows and gasping for breath, and realized that the corporal was gone.

He was not alone, however. He could hear the tunes of men's crickets playing a symphony around him. The crickets were metal toys the American paratroopers used to identify one another in the shadows of night combat. Pulling out his own cricket, Jones sounded it several times, then crawled out the other side of the ditch and hurried toward a hedgerow that defined the perimeters of the field. As he crossed into the next field, darker and quieter than the one he'd just left, he tried to concentrate on the direction from which the crickets' *clik-clak* came. He isolated the sound of one, but as he headed toward it, it ceased. Nobody was there. He tried to locate his men this way for what seemed hours, always finding the phantom paratrooper and his cricket gone when he reached the bush or tree where he thought he had heard the sound. His frustration built to a fever pitch as he futilely walked from spot to spot. Cold sweat ran in a stream between his shoulder blades. He sounded his cricket repeatedly and fought the urge to shout to the moving shadows. Finally he heard a voice that he identified as American.

"Psst. You, there. Victory?"

"Welcome!"

The man who approached identified himself as a lieutenant from another company. "One of us is a hell of a long way from his drop zone," he told Jones. They worked their way together across the wet grass and mud, the lieutenant picking up other troopers with his aggressive technique of calling out to the dark shadows. The crickets they discarded as useless. As the group grew in manpower, the men found that few of them were properly armed; many had lost their larger weapons in the jump. One of the men picked up a bazooka he found jutting out of the mud from the impact of its fall and lugged it along.

The lieutenant directed the group toward a cluster of lights shining a half mile beyond their field. The shooting ceased again, and they walked in the open toward what appeared to be a village. The group, now numbering more than eight, worked its way single file, skirting the town. Machine-gun fire cracked the night air dangerously close. The lieutenant, at the front of the line, brought the men to a halt.

"Pass that bazooka and some ammo up front. Two of us will put out that son of a bitch," the lieutenant said. The bazooka was passed to Jones, standing third in the row, who handed it to the private in front of him. The private in turn handed it to their impromptu officer, but the lieutenant waved it aside. "You two go." He gestured at Jones and the hapless private holding the bazooka. Obediently the two soldiers, strangers to each other, crawled ahead of the group and worked their way toward the crossroads where the machine gun spit bullets skyward. They edged along a ditch, peering over its side until they were within twenty feet of the German station. They could see little of the gunner other than an occasional glimpse of his back, but the station made an easy target for a bazooka.

The men worked together hastily, the private setting up the weapon and Jones loading it. The private set his sights in the periscope and fired. They heard the explosion, then both scrambled out of the ditch and raced across the road and away from their target, dragging the bazooka with them.

"Do you think we got 'em?" the private shouted between breaths as they slowed to a stop and leaned against a hedge in exhaustion.

"I don't know, but I ain't goin' back to find out."

They retraced their steps to rejoin the lieutenant and the makeshift squad. When they reached the spot where they had left the group, they stopped in amazement. There was no sign that anyone had ever been there.

"To hell with 'em. Let's just keep moving," Jones said, and they followed their compasses north, through fields that framed the silent French village. The moon glowed through clouds that were spread like gauze over the dimly lit sky. As they neared a road, they found bodies strewn around them in the dark, whether German or American neither of them knew. They eyed the dark figures for movement, always on the alert for some kind of ambush. Jones noticed a farm fifty feet from the road, and they headed for it, hoping they would find Germans sleeping there unawares.

Several cows grazed nearby, looking up with bland curiosity as the American troopers passed. The soldiers tested the front door and found it locked. Jones backed away from the house, sizing up the front window. He reached for a grenade, pulled the pin, and threw with full force, shattering the glass. Both paratroopers watched and waited. The grenade exploded with deafening precision in the front sitting room. Voices came from the second story, and a few moments later a middle-aged couple emerged from the front door, staring in horror at the foreign soldiers with blackened faces. The couple began to shout in French, waving their hands frantically while Jones and the private approached them.

"We're American. Are there any Germans in the house? Hey, shut up! We're on your side!" Their voices frightened the couple further, and husband and wife let out a torrent of French that was completely unintelligible to both Americans. Jones pointed his rifle at them, fearing that they would draw German attention, and the private grasped the Frenchman by the shoulder.

"We just want to know where we are. Where—are—we?" he shouted in the Frenchman's ear, giving him a hard shake for further encouragement. The wife began sobbing, and Jones imagined she would wake every German soldier in France.

"Quit your Goddamn jabberin'!" Jones barked at both of them, again raising his rifle. "Let's get them inside. They don't understand a damn word." They marched the couple into their house at gunpoint, gesturing at them to light a candle.

The husband and wife were in their late fifties, she in a robe, her gray hair tied in a plain scarf, he in a nightshirt and one slipper, the other apparently lost in the scuffle outside. The troopers pointed to the American flags on their shoulders and pantomimed their jump into Normandy. The couple fell silent as the paratroopers gestured their questions: "Where is the water?" "Where are we?"

As the private unfolded a map from his pocket, the Frenchwoman nodded in understanding. Her husband looked over the soldier's shoulder as he spread out the map on a small table. Jones surveyed the French household with curiosity. The grenade had done considerable damage to the front room. The furniture was broken and strewn around the floor; that and a singed rug had been the only luxuries the home had once offered. He could understand why the Germans hadn't bothered with this modest farmhouse.

The Frenchman explained that they had just passed the town of Ste. Mère Église, which Jones could see was some five miles from his drop zone. The beach was an eight-mile walk to the north across farmland.

With this information, they left the house and started trekking across the fields. They became aware of an increasing number of bodies, and Jones held his rifle cocked and ready in front of him as his companion drifted behind, both turning circles as they walked, their eyes straining in the dark.

Jones rounded the corner of a hedgerow and came face-to-face with another paratrooper, who had a nervous expression similar to his own. He began to greet him, then paused. Dread stole upon him like a stealthy cat as he grew aware of the other man's horrified expression and the realization dawned on him that in contrast to every American trooper in Normandy, this soldier wore no chocolate on his face. Jones's eyes moved down slowly to take in the German uniform as both stood motionless, frozen by their mutual discovery of the enemy.

The German soldier moved first, cocking his rifle and aiming at Jones's face. Jones automatically squeezed his trigger and unloaded five bullets point-blank in the man's chest. He watched as the man danced with the rhythm of the bullets then collapsed in his pooling blood. The smell flooded over him as he stood above the body. He heard a strange moaning sound as the rifle shook in his trembling hands, unaware that the sound came from his own throat. He put a hand to his blackened face. He'd never been told in training that the German soldiers were just scared kids, not unlike the Americans themselves—so much like them, in fact, that he would have been more inclined to share a card game and a beer with them than kill them.

His companion grasped his arm and slapped him across the face, snapping his head sideways with the impact. "C'mon buddy, break out of it. Let's keep moving," he shouted in Jones's ear. Jones tightened his grip on his rifle and the two, still strangers to each other, continued on in silence toward Utah Beach. A dark grayish glow broke on the eastern horizon, warning of the coming daylight.

CHAPTER 3

Jones reached Utah Beach alone at dawn. He had left his companion with a group of soldiers drinking brandy from a deserted farm's vat in celebration of their survival. Jones drank heavily from the brandy in his helmet, emptying it before he continued on, his conviction returned.

Full daylight exposed the hardships of the battle over the beach, where American troops were pouring onto the shore. He saw infantrymen under heavy fire fall around him in massive waves. Jones realized that with the infantry already working its way well south of the beach, his own company was long gone. He was now almost frantic to locate his regiment.

From a group of troopers headed south from the beach, he learned that the 502nd was pushing south toward the town of St. Côme-du-Mont, where they were to organize for their next campaign near the Douve River. He and twenty troopers headed after the regiment, their path leading them south.

As Jones climbed over a grassy incline, he stopped short, motioning to the other men to drop down out of sight. Before them sprawled a large meadow and farm, outlining the entire valley below. A group of German soldiers were crossing from the barn to the house, less than a hundred feet away. Twenty or thirty of them walked leisurely, talking and laughing with casual voices that carried up the hill toward the troopers. Jones dropped to the ground and aimed his rifle at one of the men nearest the house. He squeezed the trigger carefully, and instantly all the troopers were firing as Jones watched his man fall. It was a perfect shot.

The Germans, caught completely by surprise, scattered in panic. Although they were armed, returning fire was impossible. Some headed for the house and others for the barn in general confusion, making them easy targets for the troopers to pick off. Jones set his sights on a heavy man lumbering toward the barn and watched him fall with a combination of satisfaction and nausea. The Germans were being slaughtered and already knew that they would have to surrender. Jones paused, watching the carnage before him as dying men pleaded for mercy, and a wave of horror swept over him as if he had just now come to his senses. He dropped his rifle to his side and turned away from the bloodbath with revulsion, looking skyward and taking deep gulps of smoky air.

"Hey, what's the matter?" the soldier beside him shouted.

"I can't shoot anymore," he answered. "Those are human beings. I just can't." The other man nodded in understanding and patted him on the shoulder.

"Go sit down for a minute," he said before turning to fire again at the now-desperate Germans.

"Kamerad!" the surviving Germans called up, holding their hands above their heads in defeat.

Jones's enthusiasm returned as he joined the men heading down the hill in victory to claim their prisoners. He stayed with the newly captured Germans while the others searched the house and barn for survivors, and caught the eyes of a young German soldier looking at him. The prisoner refused to flinch or turn away, his face expressionless, his eyes accusatory. Jones felt a familiar resentment that had been building since his jump.

"What the hell are you starin' at?" He pointed his bayonet at the man, then clipped the brass buttons off his jacket one by one. He was disappointed when the prisoner failed to react. Giving the man a jab in the butt, he walked off, both bored and irritated with his victim.

Several troopers marched the prisoners into the barn, and Jones entered the house, roaming through it as he searched for food or souvenirs. The main room had been refurbished as a crude barracks with several rows of bunks; the rest of the house remained unchanged. A small Frenchman, the owner of the farm, watched them silently from the doorway. His home had been overrun by Germans until this afternoon, and the Americans seemed to be, if not an improvement, at least a step in the right direction.

Chewing on the end of a lump of bread he had scavenged from the pantry, Jones instinctively walked around the side of the barn and found his comrades at the vat of brandy that every French farmhouse seemed to have. Each man in turn held his mouth open under the spout and drank long swallows until he sat up sputtering. Jones waited his turn at the vat and handed his bread around to the other men. With his first gulps of brandy, he felt himself relax and his battle-anxiousness ease. He had killed three Germans already that he knew of, and so far no one had gotten close to him. He didn't dare believe he was blessed, but he respected—and drank to—his good fortune. He filled a discarded bottle he'd found and lifted it high above his head as he drank. A sense of courage coursed through his veins, heightened with each drink. But it was never quite enough.

Dark fell as they drank, and soon the group assembled inside the farmhouse, leaving one man posted behind a machine gun on the porch. Jones took his post at 0300, carrying his bottle of brandy for companionship. The Frenchman was nowhere to be seen. He imagined that the middle-aged farmer had sought refuge in the trees behind the house once the troopers had started drinking. As Jones squinted at the horizon, he saw movements in the fields, and he sprayed the area with gunfire, watching the shadows and listening to the hammering of the gunfire played back to him. Then, seeing nothing more, he leaned back and looked at the ground around him. Not two feet from his boots lay a dead German, shot during their siege earlier in the evening. He nudged the body onto its back with his foot and grimaced as he regarded the soldier's blown-open chest. From the look of the man's face, he was in his late twenties—an old man in comparison to most soldiers—and Jones looked for stripes to indicate an officer.

He had started to turn away when he spotted a large ring on the man's right index finger. It was a German military ring of some kind, molded from heavy silver, and Jones admired it, grasping the cold hand and turning it to and fro. It was a perfect souvenir. Gripping the corpse's palm in one hand, he pulled at the ring with the other, but with the swelling of decay it was stuck fast. He stood above the body and placed his foot on the upper arm, then used both hands to pull on the ring with all the strength he could muster. He had to have it. He would give it to his brother Vern saying, "Sorry you couldn't have been there to get it yourself." Still the ring remained on the finger, sinking deeper into the flesh the harder he pulled.

Jones saw only one option left. Reaching for his knife, he went to work removing the finger at the knuckle, bracing the dead hand on his knee. He sliced through the skin with the pointed tip of his blade, then began sawing through the finger. Almost through the bone, he paused, then dropped the hand as a wave of nausea overwhelmed him. He backed away from the body and ring and sat on the porch step behind the machine gun. He stared directly ahead of him, wiping sweat off his face every few minutes. Frantically he tried to forget what had happened but found the image of the dismembered finger returning to him with unfailing persistence.

"Oh God, I must have lost my mind," he thought, realizing how much he had changed since the night before.

At 0600 he was relieved from his post, and he retched on the ground before wandering into the house and curling under a rug on the floor for the first real sleep he'd had since his jump.

By 0645 he was up and looking for a cigarette. He took a drink from his nearly empty bottle of brandy and walked onto the porch, where the other soldiers were watching the sunrise. The men agreed that it was time to continue on toward their battalions, which couldn't be far ahead.

As the men proceeded on their way, they drank from bottles of wine they'd taken from the farm and tossed them empty on the fields, leaving a trail behind them. They crossed a narrow, unpaved road as the sun beat on them with the heat of midday. They had nearly reached their units now, as was evident by the swarms of military'men and trucks around them. Most of the group sat as they waited for a convoy to pass, and soon they had fallen asleep on the grassy slope beside the road. Jones, the only trooper still standing, looked around him anxiously, his adrenaline not allowing him to get that drunk. He stepped into the now-quiet road to get his bearings and recognized an officer's jeep approaching from the south. Raising his hand in a salute, he backed onto the shoulder to allow the vehicle to pass. The jeep stopped, and the colonel in back glanced at the drunken soldiers' scattered, limp bodies, then at the trooper now standing at attention on the opposite side of the road.

"What are these men doing here, soldier?" the colonel asked over the grumble of the jeep engine.

"They're dead, sir," Jones responded.

The colonel shook his head, looking the bodies over again. "That's a damn shame. What about you, Private?"

"Private Danzley Jones, 502nd Company G, sir. I landed near Ste. Mère-Église and haven't met up with my battalion yet."

"The 502nd? You'd better report. They're half a mile beyond the road. You'll be pulling out tonight."

"Yes, sir!" Jones watched the colonel drive on and cast one last glance at his sleeping comrades. Shaking his head, he picked up more ammunition and headed north to rejoin his squad.

The first familiar face he saw was that of Pvt. Nathaniel Ellis, his mortar partner. Many of the men of the 502nd were still unaccounted for and presumed dead. The remaining troops would soon move out toward St. Côme-du-Mont for an attack engineered by Gen. Maxwell Taylor, commander of the 101st Airborne, scheduled for the next night.

Jones had rejoined Company G as the men were celebrating their victory in a skirmish with the Germans. Happy to be a part of his company again, he laughed and joked with the men as he sat on a dead German soldier, whose body had bloated to nearly twice its natural size. He pulled out his K-rations for the first time. Ellis sat down beside him, and they traded stories of their two days as outlaws and fugitives. Jones's head was now cleared of the brandy and wine, and he was eager to begin their attack.

At sunrise the following day, the 502nd pressed toward the Douve River. Their assignment was to take the strategically vital city of Carentan some ten miles and four bridges to the south. The city was easily accessible during peacetime, a wide, paved highway leading straight through the meadowland and across four rivers, connecting it to the north. During wartime, however, it was possibly the most treacherous approach in combat, a fact that the 327th Regiment, already just past the city, could attest to. The 327th was now poised south of Carentan, ready to squelch any opportunity for the Germans to escape as the 502nd Regiment choked them out.

The causeway stretched dead straight above the flooded meadows. Only a few gnarled trees stood near the road, and their spindly, naked limbs offered no protection. As the men marched along the causeway, the only route to Carentan, they would be visible from three directions, including the air, without solid ground to dig into. The four narrow bridges were the most dangerous. Along the causeway the men could follow the ditches, but on the bridges they would be completely exposed.

The regiment pulled out late in the night of June 9, several thousand men in total, with Jones and Ellis near the front one hundred. Jones carried the mortar base plate, staying close to Ellis, who carried the tube. It was a cool night with clear skies and breathtaking clusters of starlight. The moon illuminated the ribbonlike length of the causeway, which stood out against the dark landscape.

The shelling began before they had even approached the first bridge, a quarter mile down the road. The men hit the ditch and wet meadow to avoid sniper fire.

After several hours, with the majority of the men pinned down and helpless, their commander, Col. Robert Cole, ordered them to retreat back to St. Côme-du-Mont. The shelling followed them back into town, and the men scattered, digging in wherever possible to wait out the night. Jones, chased by a round of machine-gun fire, lunged behind a large, dark object and was overwhelmed by the stench of decay. He discovered his shelter to be a large horse, dead for many days and abandoned on the side of a dirt road. It was the best shelter he would find for the night, and he began crawling under the pungent horse, tucking his legs and most of his torso under the cold corpse's belly. The smell nearly overpowered him as he lay listening to the sporadic gunfire that sprayed around him throughout the night. Occasionally a bullet hit the horse and jarred deep into its meat, far from reaching the soldier lying underneath.

CHAPTER 4

J ones awoke with daybreak, numb from the waist down. He had dreamed he
was back in Idaho, playing football with his high-school team. The dream
had been so vivid that he could still hear the cheers from the sidelines, smell
the grass, feel the wind in his face as he ran with the ball. But the stench of
decomposing flesh dragged him back to reality, and he squirmed and struggled
to free himself. Unable to move his legs, he pulled himself out from under the
horse with his arms, and felt the blood rush into his crushed limbs in a burst of
immobilizing pain. When he finally stood, it was stiffly, and he limped toward
his squad for their second march toward Carentan. As the group collected, he
stamped at the ground to restore circulation. Ellis backed away from him and
laughed with his hand over his nose. "You mind standing downwind?"

Again the troops were plagued with German sniper fire. The narrow bridges
allowed only a few soldiers passage at a time. As Jones watched the men ahead
of him dash across the first bridge, he saw at least a fourth of them picked off
by German fire before reaching the other side. When he approached the bridge,
he took a deep breath and sprinted across, only good luck sparing him as he
dove for the road again as if he were sliding into first base.

It was a grueling and desperate journey the entire distance. The men were
fired on by German burp guns, mortars, and 88s. The enemy stayed right beside them on the opposite side of the causeway. While the Americans made their
way up the ditch on the west side of the road, the Germans lined up along the
ditch on the east, picking them off from across the causeway.

It was dark before the men dug in, and Jones noticed it was as if the sun
had been shut off with a switch very suddenly—one instant it had been daylight, the next it was completely dark. Not even the moon had appeared yet to
provide the dimmest light. Jones dug himself a shallow foxhole and spent the
night up to his chin in cold, muddy water. He didn't dare sleep for fear his head
would slide underwater, so he sat, alert, looking around him and listening, wishing he could see beyond the causeway.

As the moon rose late into the night, it illuminated a clear and quiet sky. The temperature dropped, but he felt nothing, numbed by the frigid water. With fascination he listened to the voices of German soldiers on the other side of the causeway. They conversed casually, almost jovially, so close that if he'd understood the language he would have caught every word. The firing had stopped with nightfall, an unstated truce for the night, and the men waited for the inevitable sunrise, when the fighting would begin and they would try to survive another twenty-four hours.

As the sun rose, Colonel Cole passed among the men, shouting and waving his Colt .45 in the air. Jones understood that Cole was ordering them to cross the field with him toward the farmhouse and to bring their bayonets. He climbed out of his watery foxhole as men around him roused themselves in confusion, uncertain of the orders, and ran out after Cole belatedly. Ellis stopped Jones as he fixed his bayonet to his rifle.

"Stay here. We'll give them mortar fire."

They set up the mortar and fired their shells at the farmhouse beyond Cole and his men. Soon they found themselves the object of sniper fire from across the road as their number of shells dwindled. Jones had crawled farther up the ditch toward an abandoned mortar unit to scavenge more shells when a soldier came running from the field, a crazed expression on his face.

"They need more ammo and grenades up front. It's a hell of a fight up there. Cole's surrounded." He ran past Jones to alert the others, not bothering to wait for a reply.

Jones dropped the mortar shells and scrambled to pick up as much ammunition and grenades as he could carry in his pockets and arms. He waved to Ellis and shouted that he would run the ammo to the front. Ellis waved him on with a frantic gesture. He would stay with the mortar.

Rushing across the field toward the farmhouse, between two hedgerows, Jones was reminded of a football field by its size and symmetry. He heard bullets flying all around him as he increased his speed. The number of dead lying in the field was overwhelming, as many Germans as Americans. He tried to run around the dead, stumbling over them several times and losing ammo on the way. Panting through a rush of adrenaline, his heart pounding in his ears, Jones reached the farmhouse. He deposited the ammunition and grenades on the porch as other ammo runners appeared around him to add to his pile. Colonel Cole himself looked out the front door at the cluster of runners, who waited expectantly for orders.

"Spread out, men. Don't stand there in a group," Cole shouted before disappearing again.

Rapid fire from a German burp gun chased Jones toward a grove of oak trees in the back garden behind the house. He recognized the unmistakable sound of a mortar shell descending above his head, and he threw himself under a fruit tree. The concussion from the shell was so powerful that it lifted him off the ground and pounded him against the tree trunk, then slammed him back to the ground several yards away in a rush of light and then darkness.

As light pounded against his closed eyes, he tried to move his arms then his legs, pain rushing through his body like a tidal wave. Taking a breath was excruciating. He let out a gasp and again lost consciousness, then regained it within seconds. He took shallow breaths and felt blood running warm between his shoulder blades. He was dimly aware of shooting going on around him, a few soldiers running by, but was unable to turn his head to determine clearly whether they were American or German.

He lay waiting for several hours until the shooting suddenly ceased. He heard voices around him and understood one man's shouts: "Temporary truce, clear out the dead and wounded." Jones looked around painfully and realized there were no soldiers to help him. If he was going to survive, he'd have to walk out himself. He struggled for some time in a daze, unsure of the movements of his own body. He was surprised when he found himself standing and taking steps toward the field. He walked forward mechanically in his pain, instinct carrying him while his reason grew weaker.

He reached the bridge and crawled through the gate, then stumbled on toward the next bridge. Large groups of men hurried past without bothering with him. He was still walking; most of the wounded had to be carried. He continued methodically for miles, and the shooting recommenced abruptly. When something nicked his leg, he dropped to the ground. He could no longer bend the joint, and blood poured down his shin, hard and fast. He had taken a bullet cleanly in the kneecap. He pulled himself to a stand desperately, the new wound lending panic to his determination.

When he reached the final bridge, the first bridge from St. Côme-du-Mont, he tried to climb up onto the causeway to cross but found himself instead stumbling down the slope, directly into the waters of the river below.

PART II

CHAPTER 1

Pvt. Herbert Marlowe of the 82nd Airborne had never felt such profound relief as he did in July 1944 watching the miles pass between him and France. He had just survived thirty-three days of combat in Normandy under the bloodiest conditions he had yet seen in his three long years with the military. Standing on the deck of the troop ship among hundreds of soldiers, he was thankful to God and his own stubbornness for surviving to see this day. Recapturing France had been a great victory for the Allies, and he dared hope now that the war was nearly over. Maybe this time, he thought with a smile, he was finished with combat for good. He could marry his sweetheart, Emma Lee Mikell, and return to the United States to start a family.

Marlowe had begun his war experience in northern Africa, fighting through Sicily, Naples, and northern Italy, each campaign ending with a unique sense of relief. But he had never had so much to live for as he did now, traveling back to England on a cool, foggy day.

He had volunteered for the 82nd Airborne Division in 1941 and was positive that it was the last time he would volunteer for anything in this man's army. He had survived a string of bad luck, which had started the day he earned his wings at Fort Benning. He was sent into heavy combat in Africa, where in the deserts he learned that the glamour of the airborne had been left behind in Georgia. It was spring 1944 when he was sent to England. He was twenty-six years old, older than most of the soldiers around him, and he wanted nothing more than to be done with the war.

While stationed in Lancaster, awaiting the Invasion of Normandy, the one happy aspect of the war startled his battle-numbed senses and fed his desire to leave his military career behind him.

He learned that his hometown girlfriend, with whom he had parted three years before, was also in the military. A nurse and a lieutenant, Emma Lee was working in a hospital in Stafford. They were reunited before the Normandy Invasion, and now that the battle was over, Marlowe was going to marry her.

He had first proposed to her in early June, before he had learned that the war had other plans for him. Gen. Dwight Eisenhower had been planning the Invasion of Normandy while Marlowe and Emma Lee were planning their life together. Marlowe would land with the 82nd and 101st Airborne, in a glider, carrying heavy artillery and vehicles.

Now, returning to England war weary and thankful to be alive after the Invasion of Normandy, he immediately sent a wire to Emma. He learned happily that his unit was returned to Lancaster, not far from his fiancée. He needed a pass to marry, but a previously sympathetic captain was no longer with the unit. Marlowe pleaded his case with several officers before a lieutenant agreed to his request, allowing him fourteen days for a wedding and honeymoon.

With a heavy flow of wounded soldiers from France, the new bride couldn't venture far from the Stafford Hospital, and Herbert and Emma Lee Marlowe spent their honeymoon in a nearby hotel, in a tiny room overlooking a narrow cobblestone street.

The marriage of an officer to an enlisted man, while not forbidden, was frowned upon by the military. The union was already the cause of some embarrassment for the young couple. They had discovered the awkwardness of their roles in the military as they walked arm in arm along a Stafford sidewalk. The couple met a sergeant, who immediately saluted Emma and glanced sharply at Marlowe, who responded by saluting the sergeant. As Marlowe and his wife continued, on they looked at each other and laughed. They would surely face such situations again, they knew, and they would have to get used to it.

Now, following the wedding, the doctors and officers of the hospital held a party for the newlyweds in lieu of the honeymoon missed. Marlowe had suffered many jibes from his friends for marrying a woman who outranked him, and at the party he was the only private in the room. Standing with his punch balanced carefully away from his pressed airborne uniform, he was uncharacteristically awkward as officers pounded him on the back good-naturedly. Despite his extensive experience in combat, he had yet to be considered for a higher rank. He accepted this fact with resigned good humor.

Although they were disappointed that their families and friends could not attend their wedding, the couple spent their short time together, ecstatic. But as they strolled through Stratford-on-Avon and visited the home of William Shakespeare, Marlowe's arm wrapped comfortably around his wife's shoulders, the 82nd Airborne was swelling with replacement troops. Another invasion was in the works, but Marlowe waited out his two weeks' leave with deliberate oblivion. He watched the hot, dry weather turn to a gentle English rain as fall came to southern England. On a rainy day he left his bride to return to his regiment with a new and profound reluctance. He was a married man now, twenty-six years old and three years into the war. He was eager to return home to a civilian job and begin his family.

Upon his return to Lancaster, he learned that he would soon be part of the Invasion of Holland—Operation Market-Garden, predicted to be the final breakthrough to Hitler's defeat and the end of the war. It could very likely be the last battle he would fight in. As usual though, his luck seemed to be bad.

CHAPTER 2

In contrast with Private Marlowe, 82nd Airborne privates Stan Watsick and Earl Mickelson arrived in England with youthful enthusiasm. While Marlowe planned a life after the war, the two best friends dreamed of conquest against the Germans. Having just arrived in England from New York, they were thankful to be off the crowded troop ship and still sore with disappointment at missing the Invasion of Normandy. The Invasion was long past now, with the Germans retreating south and east, and they wished earnestly that they had been a part of it.

The two troopers were eighteen. They were inseparable friends and miraculously were assigned to the same outfit.

They found England, in midsummer, a war-ravaged and poverty-stricken country. A desperate and enraged Hitler pounded incessantly on London with his infamous screaming meemies, destroying homes, businesses, and churches. But of greater concern to the two young troopers were the dwindling supplies in the city of London. Beer couldn't be found, nor could most liquor. Food and clothes were scarce. The two friends learned quickly that their salary was at least twice that of most Englishmen, and they were sought out consistently by women and bootleggers.

British bootleggers enjoyed a healthy business with the American GIs, and soon Watsick and Mickelson, like the other soldiers, were pooling their entire wages to buy a bottle of gin. They sniffed it carefully before drinking, and often spent the evening in a hotel room, with British women or other troopers, talking excitedly about the war and their future in it.

In an American airborne base near London, Pvt. Jim Rizzuto sat with a group of friends on a rainy evening playing cards. He was a trooper with Company D of the 82nd Airborne, with Watsick and Mickelson, although he knew the two only by sight. He had grown up in Michigan and, like the two friends, had enlisted straight after high-school graduation. He was a medium-sized man, small for a paratrooper but strongly built, and he carried the weight of his uniform with the easy swagger of the largest men. He had a sharp mind for details and learned the tactical end of his training faster than most. He found the inevitable nightly card games a distraction, the competition of the games feeding his nerves at least temporarily. He had heard the rumors of an imminent invasion and knew that it would take place soon. As he played poker late into the night, he glanced up from his hand at his friend Corp. John Greene and tossed the chips on the table with a wry laugh, shrugging as he tempted his own fate.

At Piccadilly Circle, Pvt. Charlie Chasteen stood smiling easily as an attractive blond girl passed. He was surrounded by a large group of friends but had no trouble catching her eye.

He had been in England for a long time—since early June. He was one of thousands of airborne troops waiting as replacements for those fighting in France, but as June turned to July he had not yet been called, and the war raged on. He accepted the delay with the ease of a shrug. He was in no hurry; he was ready whenever they needed him. In the meantime, the girls in this country kept him distracted. He was a handsome man, with strong features and build and a natural and mischievous glimmer in his blue eyes. He had met several girls that he was particularly fond of, one he even considered marrying, but he loved women in general and found the young British girls irresistible.

He spoke up now, asking the young blond if she would like a stick of gum. She stopped eagerly and waited as he pulled it out of his pocket, his eyes gazing at hers. His friends encouraged him with general laughter and several loud comments. He wrapped his arm around the girl and led her away from the group.

"Don't listen to those fellas. They've just never seen such a pretty girl, so they're a little embarrassed, see. What's your name?"

As Chasteen and the girl walked down the street, he turned to wave good night to his friends. They paused to cross the street, and she laughed brightly at words he spoke into her ear. They disappeared into the night crowds.

CHAPTER 3

Dan Jones looked around him in confusion at a small, tidy hospital room, then focused on the warm smile of a young nurse.

"Well good morning Lieutenant, I thought you'd be waking up soon." Before he could respond, she continued. "Why don't you tell me your name, Lieutenant?"

"Why do you keep calling me Lieutenant?" he asked, his voice raspy. The nurse regarded him with sudden suspicion as she bit her lower lip.

"Because you came in here with lieutenant stripes on your helmet."

"Now I know you must've made some mistake. I lost my helmet when that mortar hit. My name is Private Danzley Jo . . ."

Before he finished pronouncing his last name, Nurse Franklin had rushed out the door. Within seconds he was wheeled out of his private room and into a vast ward, where rows of wounded GIs regarded him listlessly. In the confusion, he wrestled with his memory, trying to recall what had happened to him. His last clear memory was of swimming in the frigid currents of a muddy river, but hazy recollections returned to him gradually. Someone had yanked him out of the water and asked him if he could walk, then plopped a helmet on his head. He thought he remembered trying to walk, but his next conscious thought had been in a Red Cross jeep, pulling out of St. Côme-du-Mont.

Several days passed before a doctor came by to explain his injury. As Dan had already guessed, he had taken shrapnel in his back, and some of it had penetrated his lungs. They couldn't removed all the shrapnel, but they expected him to heal easily. The rest he could tell his grandchildren about.

Dan spent the ensuing weeks immobile on his small bed, heavily sedated, sifting through the events of his five days in Normandy. He heard other men call out in pain in the immense ward, and he sometimes became confused, wondering if he might find himself still pinned down in a ditch somewhere with the dead and dying all around him.

Eventually the lucidity of his thoughts returned, and on a lower dosage of sedatives he managed to sit up, ask questions, and look around him with interest. Several weeks had passed, and his companions in the 502nd still fought in France. Dan asked nurses for information about the progress there, but they knew little or nothing, only the number of wounded and dead that were sent back. He wrote to his mother and Vern indiscriminately about his injury and his experiences in combat. But half finished with his mother's letter, he stopped, then added as a postscript, "I hope you don't mind, Mother, but I don't feel like remembering that so much anymore."

To Vern he boasted that he had shot as many as six or eight Germans, "one for each member of the family," then abruptly signed the letter and folded it up, unable to continue. They couldn't really understand. They wouldn't want to.

He recalled his Irish sweetheart, Caroline, now with fervor, and forgetting all else, he composed a lengthy emotional letter to her, downplaying his injuries and promising to visit as soon as possible.

Jones was eager to get out of bed and return to normal life. He stood and walked around the ward several times, testing his strength. One morning in mid-July, unnoticed by the nurses, he dressed in his jumpsuit and walked out the door, down the stairs, and out into a warm, sunny London day.

Although he was still weak, his breathing shallow, and his knee stiff and sore, it felt good to be free again. He looked around him at the young women of London and could think only of Caroline, each of them somehow reminding him of her. She was the only happiness in his life. He was tired of the war and wished it was over. He knew he would be back in France soon, and guessed that this time he may not be as lucky as he had been before.

Upon arriving at his old barracks, he found a few reserves and other wounded men there ahead of him. Their news was heartening: The 502nd had taken Carentan and would be returning to England in a matter of days. No one knew how many of them were left, but they did know that thousands of new troopers fresh from Fort Benning were shipping in as replacements.

His best friend, Frank Kissner, was absent from the surviving group, as were many of the men he had trained with, and Jones asked around about his old friend. No one had seen him, but they knew he was no longer among the living. Even through his numbness, Jones was struck hard by the news, feeling a wave of sorrow for his handsome, cheerful friend. He hadn't considered before the jump just how hard it would be to lose close friends. He realized now that it had been a mistake to open himself up to such friendships, and he resolved not to make that mistake again.

Jones now focused his attention on visiting Caroline. He tried to remember the sound of her laugh and the tone of her voice as she called him "Wee Donny." He knew that he might not survive the next campaign and felt that this could be his only chance to see her. She seemed to him the only bright spot in his war-time experiences.

Dan had first met Caroline when his troop ship had made an emergency stop in a tiny Irish coastal town. The quiet village had not been prepared for the overrunning of its streets by thousands of restless American soldiers.

He had met Caroline at the local dance hall with her best friend and her sister. Caroline was a dark-haired girl with mischievous brown eyes who had never met an American. By the time he was shipped to London, Dan had fallen in love.

Now, with his first combat experience behind him and unsure of his next role in the war, Dan put in a request for a leave to visit Caroline while he still could. He no longer believed he would survive the next battle.

It was late summer when he was granted his request, and he sent a wire to her family before climbing on a train to Ireland. He reached her town without having heard from her since the Invasion of Normandy. Dan walked several miles to her house from the train station. As he came within sight of her tiny house, he felt an unexpected attack of nerves and paused behind a bush to comb his hair and straighten his tie.

He cleared his throat and wiped his hands on his pants as he waited at the front door, realizing he had knocked louder than he had intended to. He recognized Caroline's mother's voice inside. "Now who would be knocking like that on Sunday?" She opened the door and saw Dan on the step in full uniform. She stared at him for some time before calling out, "Maude, where's your sister?"

"Upstairs, of course. Who is it at the door?"

"Well go fetch her, will you?" She smiled now at Dan, relieving him of some of his apprehension. He waited, turning his hat in his hands and scuffing his feet on the floor uncomfortably as he told Mrs. Boyd briefly of Normandy and his wound. He listened to the clamor upstairs as he spoke, and he heard the familiar voice that made him flush before she came down the stairs, her face calm but expectant. They faced each other, riveted, as her mother looked on with a smile.

"Go on, give your friend a kiss, he's just come back from the war," she said. Caroline kissed him on the cheek. She sat beside him on the weathered couch as he made polite conversation with the family, holding the inevitable cup of tea in his lap. Her mother sat in a rocking chair smiling and nodding approval. Caroline's sister Maude sat on the floor watching Dan with a teasing grin. It seemed hours before the teacup was empty and Caroline suggested they go for a walk. As soon as they were alone, he allowed himself to notice she was prettier than she had been a few months before.

"Why didn't you answer my wire?" he asked, twining a strand of her dark, curly hair through his fingers. Now that he was with her, he intended never to let her go again.

"I wanted to, but I didn't have enough money. Anyway, I knew my Wee Donny would come back. Once you decide to do something, it would take more than me to stop you." She laughed, and he wrapped his arms around her tighter.

"Caroline, I would love to show you America. It's beautiful in Idaho. After this war when I get back there, I want to go back to school and make something of myself."

"I know you can do it, Donny."

"Will you marry me? I'll buy us a house and make good money. You'll have anything you could want."

"I don't know what my Dad would say," she answered, looking up at him with a mixture of confusion and surprise.

"I'll talk to him," he offered.

"No Donny, I'll do it. Right now let's talk about America. And your family, do they like Irish girls?" In a swell of emotion, he pulled her into his arms and kissed her.

The following morning he hurried to his fiancée's house, where he was heartily welcomed by her smiling father. Mr. Boyd liked Dan better than he had her previous beaus and was sure that, like all Americans, he was rich and could provide well for his eldest daughter. She had little future in Ireland, working at a shirt factory. The eligible men in town either were being killed in the war or were factory workers themselves. He liked the idea of his first daughter living in a big house and not having to work to keep food on the table. "God knows I'll miss me gal, though," he said as he led Dan into the sitting room.

Dan's visit ended two days later. His two-week leave was marching fast toward its end, and he had yet to visit his sister-in-law, a military nurse in London. He wrote his mother, asking her to write to her future daughter-in-law. He was eager for them to meet. He planned to buy a house in Coeur d'Alene, large enough that his widowed mother could live with them. The time when the war would end seemed dreamlike to him.

When he finally left, he lingered with his sweetheart at the train station, missing the first train in his reluctance to go. They whispered together and promised each other complete devotion as the crowds passed by them, oblivious of the sad couple.

When Dan finally returned to his camp four days later, and one day late, he was shocked to find his bags packed for him and his jumpsuit waiting. If he had been one day later he would have missed the invasion and been considered AWOL. He climbed into his jumpsuit to catch up with the others. They were informed, however, that the planned invasion, in East Antwerp, Belgium, was canceled. Gen. George Patton had already reached the Allies' objective, and the French were now prepared to liberate their city with their own men. France was once again in the hands of the French.

The new recruits marched into the camp in droves, their naiveté and youthful excitement displayed in their posture like the wings on their uniforms. They stood out from the veterans of Normandy with their enthusiasm, polished boots, and close-cropped hair. Those who had already been in combat had no interest in military appearance and wore their uniforms sloppily. They knew the war, and they knew that polished boots meant nothing on the battlefield. Dan couldn't stand having the new recruits around him, with their excitement, nervous questions, drunken toasts, and late-night bravado. They were walking corpses to him; he knew they were more likely to die than the veterans, who at least had the benefit of experience. Jones chose to avoid friends now and spent most of his free time alone.

In late August the men packed up again for an invasion, this time in Belgium near the city of Tournai, a border town near the northwestern corner of France. The jump would take place over a large insane asylum several kilometers outside of town.

The men were transported to the marshaling area and lined up in their sticks, but General Taylor announced, in a booming voice through several loudspeakers, that the invasion had been canceled. The American 1st Army had beaten them there.

"But don't worry, men, we'll find you another mission soon!"

The booing came in waves of disenchantment with the war; it came from the veterans, and it rang around the field in contest with the words of the general.

But in the meantime, Operation Market-Garden was under way in the depths of military headquarters and the minds of strategic officers. By early September the division unit officers had been briefed, and Jones could feel the tension of another jump approaching. On September 16 the men were briefed for the invasion that would begin the next morning. They would be jumping in Holland, and their task would be to secure a twenty-mile length of road for the British into Germany. They were doled out Dutch currency and sent to their barracks to pack.

Once again Dan Jones and Ellis would be a team, and once again they would be fighting the German airborne, the same men they had met on the causeway to Carentan. Jones packed his jumpsuit with the necessities and didn't bother to polish his rifle or sharpen his bayonet. It was sharp enough to do the job.

They climbed into the C-47s in the full light of a sunny morning. They took no Dramamine this time and sat facing each other on the row of benches in sober silence. A young rookie sat beside Jones and started up a conversation as the plane ascended into the clear sky above the airstrip.

"Did you fight in France?"

"Yep," he replied. He did not want to talk to this kid and hoped the conversation would die there. He believed the rookie could be a jinx.

"That must've been a hell of a fight. I wish I'd been there. Were you nervous before the jump?"

"Look, why don't you shut up and find out what it's like for yourself," Jones snapped at the young man, then stared ahead of him, having successfully silenced the soldier. The last thing he needed was a kid like that to follow him around. This time he knew what death was like; he admired those who had already lost their lives and was convinced that he would soon share their fate. His life was worth little now, and he waited in resolute acquiescence as the plane brought him over his drop zone.

CHAPTER 4

For Dan Jones, the jump in Holland could be compared with that in Normandy only by contrast. The C-47s reached the drop zones unimpeded by enemy flak. They had eluded the Germans as they flew in from the north in the bright light of midday. The men jumped at a comfortable six hundred feet, and Jones looked around him in appreciation of a perfect day as his chute eased him to the ground. As the sky filled with round, bright chutes like mushrooms, not a single shot was fired. They had taken the Germans completely by surprise.

Late in the afternoon they crossed the Best Bridge near Eindhoven, in the tracks of the 506th Regiment. They made progress slowly, drawing occasional sniper fire from the ditches around them. They had heard no news of the battalions ahead and did not know how many, if any, German troops would be gathered to meet them in the city of Best.

The late afternoon sun beat down with stifling heat on the men in heavy jumpsuits and equipment. Jones felt sweat collect on his back and chest from the heat rather than nerves. The land around them was flat, without so much as a mound of dirt raised along the horizon in any direction. The fields were clear, providing little protection, but the regiment soon reached the edge of the Zonshe Forest, a wooded area some six miles from Zon.

Night fell quickly, and a gentle rain accompanied it, providing cooling relief from the heat of the day. The men were instructed to dig in for the night along the perimeter of the forest. They could go no farther on Day One of the invasion. Although they had crossed the Best Bridge, they had still seen little enemy activity and had attracted only isolated sniper outbreaks as they pushed farther behind German occupied lines. Jones and Ellis found a young pine a hundred feet from the road and near a footpath that ran into the forest. Here they dug adjacent foxholes in which to wait out the night.

As Company G settled on the edge of the Zonshe Forest, just a few miles south Company H was in the midst of a bloodbath. Upon joining the 506th, they had discovered too late that the Germans had collected in numbers and strength as the Allies had struggled to cross the numerous collapsed bridges on their way toward Best. They were now pinned down by German mortars, machine guns, and 88s, and more tanks were moving in. They had already lost one-fourth of their men and were desperately calling for backup. But with only the 502nd behind them and the British troops still several days away, there was little hope.

Jones slept easily in the foxhole, taking advantage of one of his few opportunities during combat to sleep. He was unconcerned about the day to follow, satisfied, as a soldier had to be, to have survived another day behind enemy lines.

The men awoke early in the morning, before sunlight had penetrated the forest, to the sound of German artillery. Thinking at first it was just a few stray snipers, Jones and Ellis waited in their holes, their backs planted against the muddy walls, looking up at the sky and the protective branches of the tree in front of them. They had no idea that these German airborne soldiers had already plowed through the 506th and 502nd Company H and were still gaining momentum.

The men waited in their foxholes for hours as the artillery gained force and spewing gunfire slashed through the air above them in a swell of offensive might. Jones watched in fascination as several of the branches above his foxhole were blown off by flying bullets.

It was afternoon before Jones and Ellis looked up to see a Company G corporal running to their foxholes. "Get out of the holes—the Krauts are moving in on you!" he shouted and turned to run on. At that instant, a mortar shell exploded at his feet. Jones dove for the floor of his hole, holding his hands over his head. He reemerged as the dust flew around him and looked over the edge. The corporal was lying where he had been standing at the edge of the foxhole, blood pooling around his knees as the firing heated up, now aimed directly at them. Jones gripped the corporal's hand and dragged him down into the hole with him, seeing now that the man had lost one leg at the knee. The other leg hung alarmingly awry and was bleeding hard. As the corporal lay immobilized in shock, Jones cut loose material from the dangling pant leg and tied it tight around the stump. The foxhole was sprayed with blood. He found a twig blasted loose from the tree above and made a crude tourniquet. With measured satisfaction he watched the bleeding slow to a trickle.

Then he pulled himself out of his foxhole, forgetting the gunfire around him, and ran up the footpath. If he ran deeper into the forest, he was certain he could enlist a medic. He passed several bodies, all of them American, and was shocked to see his lieutenant lying dead, his body full of holes. (Many years later Jones would learn that his lieutenant, David Irwin, had not been dead and had miraculously survived his injuries and the war.) Jones glanced beyond the lieutenant to a foxhole where a soldier named Pvt. Ted Howard hunched anxiously, a desperate expression on his face. He looked as helpless as Jones had just felt, waiting in his own foxhole while those around him were slaughtered. He continued on, finding medics just beyond the injured lieutenant. He explained where they would find the corporal, gesturing and pointing wildly before a machine gun opened up directly behind them.

Jones fled back down the path as gunfire followed his movement. He dove into the closest foxhole, and sat up to look at Private Howard. Howard helped Jones to his feet, anxious to know what was happening at the front. The two troopers spoke with restraint, diving continually for the bottom of the cramped hole, then standing again to peer at the treetops around them.

"Jesus, they'll never let up. What time is it?" Howard asked, as a surprising lull spread temporarily in the forest around them. Jones reached his arm upward, stretching his sleeve away from his wrist, and peered at the face of his watch.

"It's two thir . . ." A shadow fell on the watch and Jones looked directly into the eyes of a German sergeant. He held his breath, as Howard glanced up. Then he heard the cocking of a rifle, and they were surrounded, the barrels of six German guns pointed directly at their heads.

CHAPTER 5

Pvt. Herbert Marlowe leaned forward in the seat of his glider, staring down at the landscape below with growing alarm. He had been briefed before the flight and was well familiarized with the direction and distance of their drop zone mission. He knew without a doubt, as he watched the tree-lined perimeters of green fields passing below, that they were past their drop zone.

The glider format ran with ten gliders on each of two wings, led by one plane at the nose of their formation. The Germans had spotted them already, flying over silently in a blue and tranquil sky, and they opened up with antiaircraft artillery. As flak pursued the airborne noisily, Marlowe leaned toward the pilot, seated directly in front of him. He shouted in the man's ear, straining his voice above the humming engine and exploding artillery shells.

"We're past the drop zone. Radio the lead pilot, he's taking us straight into Germany." The pilot reacted swiftly.

The men seated around Marlowe stirred restlessly. The plane flying adjacent to them had been hit and now plummeted to the ground, the flames from the explosion momentarily rivaling the bright rays of the sun. The troopers broke into a controlled panic, preparing themselves for an unanticipated jump. They were not parachutists, but they could jump and were well trained to do so when necessary. Grimly Marlowe conceded his usual bad luck coming into combat, as the aircraft jolted and shuddered, taking several shells in the fuselage. The lead glider slid downward toward the grassy fields.

"All right, men, we're bailing out. Line up and check equipment." The men threw out what heavy equipment they could before leaping one by one into the gunfire-riddled sky. As the last trooper jumped, just a few hundred feet from the ground, the plane plunged downward in flames, with the pilot and copilot accompanying it to their demise.

The surviving men converged around a quiet pasture, clearly some miles from any town. Marlowe's sergeant, representing the highest rank among the men, led the group back toward Holland, determined to rejoin the division and accomplish their original objective. The downed gliders sent dramatic smoke signals to the surrounding countryside and would have German defenses close at their heels.

The group overtook a quiet farmhouse, taking prisoners of a group of German men who were seated at a table playing cards. They set themselves up for the night in preparation for the worst.

By early morning they were in trouble. The Germans had gathered outside overnight and continued to build strength around the farm. It was the first time the Allies had penetrated the border, and the Germans fought with a determination fed by uncertainty. They could not be sure if these were a few misguided paratroopers or a spearhead to the giant invasion that had been rumored for months. The Americans, in desperation, began to flee out the back of the house.

Marlowe made a frantic dash to a large oak offering questionable protection. He fired his carbine toward the German stronghold but knew that surrender was inevitable. The Americans not only were outnumbered, but were obviously deficient in weapon power, having lost most of their equipment as their gliders crashed.

When the white flag was waved above the house, Marlowe pulled apart his gun, throwing pieces of it across the yard. He stood waiting with dread as several German infantrymen came around the side of the tree and looked him over.

CHAPTER 6

Looking up at the six German soldiers with their weapons trained on them, Jones and Howard dropped their own weapons.

"Comrade!" Jones exclaimed, grasping at the word he had heard so many German prisoners use. The sergeant seemed not to hear and barked at them in German, gesturing at them to climb out of their hole. Mechanically Jones pulled himself up from his shelter to stand among his captors. He left his rifle behind, and Howard followed his example, climbing out unarmed. They stepped away from the foxhole and were immediately surrounded. The Germans formed a tight circle around the prisoners as the sergeant searched their pockets.

The soldiers surrounding the Americans were all members of the German 59th Infantry Division. Their stiff, brown uniforms with tiny swastikas and their well-groomed hair curling below their ears seemed out of place in the battlefield. Their weapons, however, told another story. Jones had never before seen soldiers so well equipped with grenades, rifles, and machine guns. These were the soldiers Hitler was so proud of. But they seemed to have stumbled upon Jones and Howard by chance, not realizing the numbers of Americans still hiding around them. If Jones had not raised his hand when he did, they most likely would have walked past without seeing him.

The Germans now trained their rifles on the two Americans, who held their arms high over their heads. The sergeant stripped them of grenades, bayonets, and handguns. Over the sergeant's shoulder, Jones noticed movement from a foxhole not far from their own, but he was caught by surprise when an American machine gun opened up on the backs of their unsuspecting captors. Jones and Howard dropped to the ground as bullets sliced over their heads.

The firing ceased abruptly, and silence set in as the air slowly cleared around them. No one was left standing. After several seconds, return fire came from a German machine gun. Jones stayed where he was, smelling the musky odor of the ground in his face and trying desperately not to inhale or expand his lungs in any way. If he played possum long enough, he believed he just might escape capture. He waited, listening, but heard only the crackle of firing in the distance. He had no idea who might have survived the burst. He could see light through the crook of his elbow and watched for a shadow or some sign of movement. There was none. He continued to wait, drawing silent shallow breaths, hearing his own heart pound desperately against his ribs. He suspected now that the Germans were dead. His good luck had come through for him more miraculously than ever before.

He had no idea how long he waited. It seemed close to an hour but could have been only five minutes. Very slowly he lifted his head to squint into the light that hammered on his eyes. He gazed straight into the blue eyes of the German sergeant, whose face was only inches from Jones's. The sergeant, lying on his stomach, stiffly pulled his rifle under his arm and pointed it at Jones. Together they climbed to their knees, and the sergeant motioned toward the ground, speaking unintelligibly as he pointed with one arm. Jones followed the sergeant's eyes to Howard facedown on the ground, still patiently feigning death. The other Germans lay sprawled around the area in gruesome pools of blood.

The firefight began now from both sides with shocking suddenness, Germans shooting behind them and Americans returning fire over their heads. Jones tapped Howard on the arm roughly.

"Get up. He knows you're alive."

The sergeant motioned them to follow him back toward the German lines but dropped again to the ground as gunfire heated up on both sides. He shouted, then gestured that Howard should go first, he would follow, and Jones would take up the rear.

The three men wormed their way across the ground now with a single mission—to escape death. Their progress was slow and painful, bullets slicing so close that they left holes in the men's clothing. Whether the bullets were German or American, Jones couldn't tell.

Once past the heaviest trees, the three men neared Jones's original foxhole, but he saw no sign of life there. The place was thick now with German fire. He remembered he had a knife in the secret compartment of his collar as well as a grenade in his pocket that the sergeant had missed in his search. Jones could move up closer behind the sergeant and knife him right through the ribs.

In training, Jones was instructed that once captured it was his patriotic duty to attempt to escape. In fact, to remain a prisoner complacently was an act of betrayal to the unit. But if he knifed the German, he would have no choice but to crawl back away from the Germans and through the lines to his own men. He knew without doubt that he couldn't survive the trip again. He could stand and run back to his men, but he'd probably be picked off by the Germans, and if he wasn't, his own men might shoot, being in a desperate and trigger-happy state of mind. Jones continued on, his face inches behind his captor's boots.

Once the men reached the safety of the road, the sergeant stood, and Howard and Jones hesitantly climbed to their feet, glancing over their shoulders for a sudden rescue or ambush.

The curve of the road offered shelter for a row of Germans. The two GIs stared in amazement. Before them, in the trenches along the side of the road and canal, came hundreds of German troops, moving toward the forest and Company G, having already mopped up Company H and the 506th. Jones clenched his fists in a swell of sorrow and frustration for his company, which he now knew was doomed.

The sergeant shouted at his new prisoners, forcing them to entwine their fingers on the tops of their bare heads.

Now, a safe distance from the front, German soldiers marched on the road itself and in the ditches. Trucks and tanks worked their way forward in a massive crush.

Several German soldiers approached the two prisoners, circling them with violent anger undisguised in their expressions. One soldier cracked Jones across the head with his rifle, and the sound against his skull reverberated between his ears in sudden shock. As he tried to regain his balance, several men raised their guns, and one pressed the barrel against his head. He felt the pressure of the cold metal against his temple but did not react. The sergeant stopped the soldier before he pulled the trigger, arguing with him in a harsh language. The men wandered off grudgingly, giving both prisoners a shove.

Jones felt blood run along his hairline and tried to clear the dull, buzzing sound in his head that had momentarily replaced reason. He now reached in his pocket and pulled out the hidden grenade. The sergeant watched him with narrowed eyes until Jones handed it to him. He would have no need for it now.

The sergeant gestured at them to continue on their march, replacing their hands on their heads. As the road stretched on to the south, they came upon an unmistakably familiar stench. The American Aircorps had clearly been strafing along the road not long before them and had left nothing but devastation behind. So many bodies were sprawled in the road, fields, trenches, and ditches that they didn't seem real. Like dead animals struck by cars, they lay formless and inhuman, a useless testimony to a massive German defensive maneuver. Jones was reminded of his own men, strafed on the Carentan causeway, but felt no sense of vindication now. The smell swelled on the sides of the road in the heat and gathered around the men who marched along it. The stench of death combined with the dust that parched Jones's throat, nostrils, eyes, and lungs made him choke on his own hoarse breathing. He wondered when he had last had a drink of water. On his head, dust clung to the coagulating blood, which hardened and cracked in the September sun.

Several more Germans approached them now, searching through the Americans' pockets as if scavenging from the dead. One young soldier pulled a pack of cigarettes and a deck of cards from Jones's jacket pocket and shouted in conquest, handing out cigarettes for the soldiers who now circled around them. Jones watched helplessly as his only cigarettes were distributed, before the sergeant barked at the men, waving his hand and shouting his irritation.

At first the soldiers paused, then grudgingly they replaced the cigarettes into the pack. One German soldier slid the pack into Jones's pocket along with the cards, giving him a patronizing slap on the cheek as he did so. Jones looked at the sergeant in surprised gratitude. He guessed that their captor was rewarding him for voluntarily turning over his grenade. He exchanged a look with Howard and they both shrugged, a thousand unspoken thoughts in their eyes. Jones handed the sergeant a cigarette and tentatively lit one for himself. The sergeant nodded and lit his own with Jones's match without speaking. A strange comradeship had taken root.

After several hours, they came upon a small sign standing forlornly on the edge of the road. Most signs had been removed by the Dutch to confuse the Germans, but this crooked sign, LIMPI 5 KM, persevered stubbornly, a beacon of hope to Jones, who imagined irrationally that the British would be at their heels to take the small town.

They passed a few quiet and desolate farms, and while crossing before a white farmhouse, the three men were startled by the voice of a young woman. They stopped to watch a girl of nineteen or twenty wave to them from the doorstep, then run across the garden to the road where they stood. She was a strange sight in the war-ravaged area, young and strikingly pretty. Her smile was sweet and generous as she sidled up to the German sergeant. She spoke in his language with soft eagerness in her voice. When the sergeant glanced away, she caught Jones's eye and winked pointedly. She made a quick comment in German and ran into the house.

The men waited, the two prisoners with their hands still wrapped around the tops of their heads. The sergeant motioned for them to lower their arms, and Jones felt numbness give way to pain as blood rushed into his deadened fingers. He felt the side of his head and explored the small gash that now lay beneath a layer of dried blood and dirt.

The girl returned, gracefully balancing a pitcher, a crude metal cup, and a loaf of bread in her hands. Suddenly it occurred to Jones that she had played up to the sergeant in order to bring food and drink to what probably looked like pathetically wretched prisoners she had seen passing.

She poured milk from the pitcher into the cup and handed it to the sergeant. He drank from it greedily, and the Dutch girl waited, scanning the prisoners with sympathetic brown eyes. When the sergeant returned the empty cup to the girl, she shrugged, speaking in German and nodding toward Jones and Howard. They both looked at the prisoners for what seemed an eternity before the sergeant nodded. She refilled the cup and handed it to Jones. The fresh milk tasted better to him than anything he had ever had, and he drained it almost before bringing it to his cracked lips. He wiped foam from his chin as he held the cup out for the smiling woman. He returned her smile as she again refilled the cup, and he handed it to Howard. The sergeant tore himself a chunk of bread and grudgingly passed the loaf to Jones, who had little appetite but forced himself to eat a few dry lumps.

When they marched on, his arms aching as he placed his hands back on his head, he dared a glance over his shoulder at the Dutch girl who watched their departure.

"That's a hell of a sweet girl," he spoke under his breath to Howard before the sergeant shouted at him, jabbing him half-heartedly in the back with his rifle.

Once in the town of Limpi, the sergeant turned his two prisoners in to a group of soldiers converged on the steps of a church and was gone. Jones would never see him again and would never be sure if the man had saved his life or ruined it. The soldiers led Jones and Howard into a convent beside the church, fashioned into an impromptu German headquarters, and left them to stand in a narrow hallway before a closed door.

When the door opened, a middle-aged man in Nazi uniform poked his head out just long enough to motion for Jones to step inside. Howard was left in the hallway to wait his turn.

The room was brightly lit and sparsely decorated. It had once been a Dutch classroom, but the desks were removed and only a large table with several chairs remained in the center. A window at the end of the room was covered by a thick, red curtain, something that appeared to have been hung there since the German renovation, providing privacy to a room that had never before needed it. Another door stood slightly ajar on the opposite side of the room, whatever lay behind it ominously invisible in the darkness.

Three men occupied the room, a high-ranking officer seated at the head of the table regarding the prisoner coldly, and two others standing, one on either side of him. The officer spoke, and as Jones looked about him in confusion, one of the men gestured for him to sit. He sat in a hard, wooden, high-backed chair, his exhaustion forgotten as adrenaline charged through his veins in useless alarm. He looked from one face to another, meeting with impassioned expressions, as if his interrogators were already bored with him. The officer spoke again, and when Jones didn't answer, one of the men standing translated into heavily accented English.

"What regiment are you from?"

Jones told them his name and rank, then stopped with his serial number when one man crossed the table and pulled the chair out from under him. As he tried to stand, the man hit him across the face with his pistol. He lay back stunned, but before the room had completely returned to focus, he was yanked to his feet. He stood shakily as they barked out another question. He knew nothing that would be useful to them, except the size of his regiment and the fact that the Royal Infantry was moving in behind them. But even about this fact he knew no details—their numbers, their objective path, or their time of attack. He remained silent as they asked something in an accent so thick it was hard to understand.

"What is your division's objective?"

"My name is Danzley Jones, serial number . . ."

This time, when he was hit with the pistol, he was expecting it, and he steadied himself to remain standing. How many times he and the interrogator acted out this ritual he was unsure. He reached for his swollen chin, but the German interpreter jerked his hand from his face and held it in his clutches. The man looked up at him from not more than five feet, three inches, but his size was no hindrance for him now. He pulled out his knife as he repeated his question. Jones took a long breath before spewing back the same information. He looked at the officer warily for a response. The officer returned his look with a bland and unctuous sneer. Jones felt pressure on his finger and, without surprise, saw blood. He no longer believed that what happened around him was real. He stumbled, reaching for the back of the chair, then realized it was lying on its side on the polished wooden floor, and he fell hard. His injured hand came down with a splatter of blood near the interrogator's feet. He looked at his hand, unsure of what he saw. Had they actually cut off his finger? His face fell to the floor and he waited, vaguely aware of the commotion above him and the sensation of being kicked, but he was unable to crawl to his knees or feet. He felt his interrogators lift his shoulders and drag him across the floor toward the opposite door. He made no attempt at resistance. The door was kicked wide open, but only blackness stared at him, and he was kicked into its embrace. He felt himself fall, not once but again and again, hoping that each landing would be the last, but he continued to fall for what seemed an eternity.

Jones finally looked up from a small dungeonlike cell with one lighted bulb straining in the gloom to provide light. He had fallen down a long, narrow flight of stairs and was now unable to move. Sprawled helplessly with his feet still on the last step, his chest flush against the basement floor, he lost consciousness, aware only of occasional bodies slamming against him throughout the night, waking him with a fresh flash of pain and annoyance before he slipped easily back into sleep.

CHAPTER 7

Pvt. Jim Bruton gazed over the friendly faces of the cheering crowd lining the streets on both sides of him. They gathered to welcome the American 82nd Airborne as he marched with his squad through the narrow roads of Nijmegen. They had been in Holland only twenty-four hours and already had become heroes. Nineteen-year-old Bruton grinned at the faces around him as many of the younger people shouted good wishes in English. From the windows, and in the hands of many people, waved the bright orange color of Holland, displayed by jubilant Dutch citizens confident that Holland was once again a free country.

Bruton noticed some of the prettier girls in the crowd, which consisted mostly of women and children. He shared a smile with several young girls, winning a giggle or a wave in response. A tall, sinewy man, he'd reached his full height of six-foot-three and was easily recognized in a large group of soldiers. He'd been an athlete in high school, lettering in every sport offered. Upon graduating, his future looked bright. He had a choice of athletic scholarships from universities around the country. He was already being considered for three major baseball leagues. He was well known in his small town in Kentucky and was expected to be a great star.

But instead he was drafted and forced to put his opportunities on hold. He joined the airborne, the most challenging of the armed forces, where he could put to use his athletic talents. His outgoing personality was his trademark, and he was true to his nature now as he flirted with the girls around him.

Since his jump into Holland the previous afternoon, he had seen little combat, most in the latter half of the past evening. He'd jumped easily with his squad and immediately intercepted a group of German soldiers on bicycles, whom they'd taken prisoner. It had been unnerving, the almost uncanny ease with which they had come into the town of Nijmegen from their drop zone, not a single shot fired.

Within the following days, Bruton experienced the worst of combat fighting. As the Germans moved in, his squad resecured the drop zone through a painful inch-by-inch battle across three hundred yards of open field. It had been a grueling struggle, but the men had had little chance to catch the rest they needed. They moved on immediately, pushing toward Germany.

The morning brought defensive maneuvers by the German Red Beret. The forty-five Americans moved into the countryside to maintain an impenetrable line while waiting for backup.

Bruton set up his machine gun with determined optimism, sure that they could hold the town. He and the other men secured themselves at the base of a hill, facing the road, where they watched for German movement. They would keep in front of the hill at all costs.

They were sheltered only by low hedgerows, and they took cover behind them, digging into foxholes where they could. Bruton dug himself a hole and watched as his closest friend stood in full view above ground, too crazed and bitter to worry about safety.

Within several hours, anxiety pervaded the air around them. They hadn't expected the fight to last this long, and there were no reinforcements.

The ammunition could last only another hour and the squad's number had dwindled to twelve. The sergeant shouted to them, the grim prospects clear in the strain of his voice.

"All right, men, do we want to fight it out?"

"Yeah! Fight to the end," they responded.

But within a half hour, they retreated up the hill as it was stormed by the Germans. As a group they surrendered, holding their hands up in bitter defeat. They destroyed their weapons before appearing in the open, walking down the hill single file, their hands up in clear sight of the Germans.

Before they were halfway down, Bruton heard the Germans open fire, and he dove for the ground. Instinctively he tumbled the rest of the distance down the hill. When the burp gun had fallen silent and the German shouts had quieted, Bruton looked around him. Only one man remained unwounded as the Germans approached. Bruton carried a minor flesh wound in his leg.

As they entered city limits, their hands on their heads, their uniforms covered with blood, they were an object of hostile curiosity from German civilians. Bruton felt their eyes on him, hating him, as they stood beside the road to watch the procession. Several young women walked in front of him and stopped to shout insults before spitting in his eyes. He could only guess what was ahead for him.

The troops were locked in an unmarked brick building with several English and Polish prisoners. A Polish man, who spoke no English, practiced medicine, and the prisoners accepted his administrations thankfully. He examined their wounds carefully in the straining light, dressing them with sulfur and shreds of their own clothing. The window was barred and the large room they waited in was unlit. In the late night, the men gathered at the window to look at the moon rising through the bars.

The following morning, the Germans found a jump map in Bruton's pocket. It was a map he'd carried throughout combat showing the path they had already traced, with one point of interest marked. While still in England, he had circled one small building, east of their jump site. This building, he had been assured, was a school for teenage girls. He hadn't wanted to forget this spot, should he have a chance to sightsee in Holland.

Now the guard examined the map and the circled building with great interest. He shouted to another guard, who looked over his shoulder at the map. They discussed it for several minutes before approaching Bruton. He shrugged when they pointed inquiringly at the mark. "Girls, you understand girls?" He gestured the shape of a woman, and they looked at him skeptically. After speaking with several officers on the matter, he was released suddenly with disdain and sent marching to the train, headed for his first stalag. He left with a large group of Americans he had never seen before. With regret he climbed aboard a train with the other prisoners.

The train stopped in Linburg, and here they climbed off to begin a fast-paced march into the country, several miles down an unmarked road. They came to a stop at Stalag XII-A, their temporary new home.

CHAPTER 8

S tan Watsick glanced back at Earl Mickelson through the noise and smoke of the machine guns. They stood their ground in the country farm that their company had overtaken the night before, fighting desperately to stay alive. The farm was strategically located overlooking the intersection of two major roads. The building stood under the questionable shelter of a thick thatched roof, which absorbed the noise of artillery. The walls and doors were ravaged with bullets, and Watsick saw scattered bodies where his men had stood hours before. They had been in Holland only a few days, and already their situation seemed desperate.

"Hey Stan, you hungry?" He heard the voice of his friend behind him and grinned through his set teeth.

"I can't say it's the first thing on my mind." He heard a German mortar fired from behind a rut in the ground and fired his own weapon in response.

Mickelson shrugged and stood by the door, surveying the area before making a lunge outside. He headed for an apple tree not far from the house. Watsick ceased his firing to watch in horror. Mickelson plucked a ripe apple off the tree and took a bite from it as he returned to the semi-safety of the building.

"What the hell do you think you're doing, you crazy bastard? You pick now to be a daredevil?"

"Hell, I'm no daredevil. I'm just hungry," Mickelson replied with a shrug.

As the day progressed, the Germans of the panzer division worked their way up toward the intersection of the two highways. Jim Rizzuto had dug in on a hill several yards from the house with another trooper and, from his vantage point, had been watching the Germans advance since the night before.

The CO had chosen the house fully aware that the Germans were close behind them. He was confident that they could hold the enemy back the following day until reinforcements reached them.

But over the course of the night, the Germans had overtaken the regiment's drop zone and set fire to the abandoned gliders. As the gliders burned, the bright flamelight had kept Rizzuto awake and edgy, his instinct telling him that the regiment was in a lot of trouble.

Now, as he and Pvt. Edward Rhinehart waited helplessly in their foxhole, 88s pounded all around them. When the firing waned, Rizzuto took advantage of the quiet to scan the area, glancing back at the large house and the frantic movement of the Americans near it. When the shooting recommenced, it came from all directions, and it was now chillingly clear that the farmhouse had been surrounded. Rizzuto crawled out of his foxhole and, rifle in hand, backtracked toward the house by weaving in and out of a series of trees and haystacks. He took refuge behind a haystack near the house as he reloaded his rifle. Under fire from all directions, he hugged the hay, peering over it to shoot at the German silhouettes that passed between the apple trees.

Even before he saw the flames on the roof of the house or the white flag that the lieutenant waved bitterly over his head, Rizzuto knew that they had no more chance against the German artillery. He was prepared to die in this, his first battle, and his emotions ran the gamut from relief to horror when he learned that the men were surrendering. The war was over for them.

Mickelson and Watsick heard an explosion, followed by shouts of alarm from their men. The thatched roof had caught fire. The men streamed out of their protective cover, and for the first time they saw the CO waving a white cloth wrapped around his bayonet. They marched into the open, seeing Rizzuto come from around a haystack without his weapon. Behind them the house burned red hot, casting a strange glow in the pale afternoon light.

The Germans piled the wounded into trucks and drove them to a nearby hospital, while the rest of the captured soldiers, including Watsick, Mickelson, and Rizzuto, were force-marched along the road for fifteen miles toward the Rhine River.

During their first night as prisoners, they huddled in a German stockade in the small town of Emmerich, cold and nervous. They awaited their move to the massive prisoner compound Stalag XII-A in Linburg, Germany.

CHAPTER 9

In the confusion of his surrender, Herbert Marlowe saw now the body of his sergeant, then looked down into the eyes of the German soldiers. He was considerably taller than the other men, and several years older than most of them. He realized that with the sergeant now dead, the Germans might assume that he was company commander. They marched him toward a row of poplars, and an officer looked him over briefly before asking him in English, "What is your name?" Marlowe hesitated, recalling the Italian he had learned during his short time in that country, and responded in that language, hoping to confuse them.

"I'm talking to you in English, American."

Marlowe relented, sounding out his name, rank, and serial number in English. Shots broke out around them as they spoke, and the new American prisoner watched in amazement as the officer buckled and fell to the ground, bleeding from the lower chest. Marlowe waited in horror for German retribution, but instead the firing stopped, and he was marched down the road with a dozen remaining troopers to a small, abandoned schoolhouse. His mind flashed back to his new wife, Emma Lee, now waiting for him in an army hospital. They had been married less than two weeks. Would she hear that he had been captured? Would they say he had been killed or was missing in action?

The troopers were herded into a covered truck where several other prisoners already sat, miserable and silent. The truck drove through the afternoon and night. None of the men had eaten since their jump, but thirst, more than hunger, began to plague them as they waited helplessly. Marlowe had been equipped with a Red Cross package, but now he sat stripped of everything but his uniform, staring at his feet as the truck bore them farther into Germany. Two days later, as they were ushered from the truck to a crowded train boxcar, Marlowe had lost any remaining sense of where he was. It was September 20, three days after his jump into Holland.

On the third morning of his captivity, Marlowe climbed off the train with a crush of prisoners, and the Germans locked the large group of men in a fenced yard in which stood a shack. They were surrounded by other buildings exactly like it, each separated by barbed-wire fences. A row of Russian prisoners lined the fences watching through wire, their baggy uniforms hanging loosely off their emaciated bodies.

Despite their own hunger and sickness, the Russians seemed to regard the new American prisoners with sympathy, and several of them tossed cigarettes one by one over the fence to the Americans. Marlowe scrambled with the others in the dirt yard, picking up what he could and stuffing them in his pockets. The Russians also threw several chocolate bars over the fence, and Marlowe recognized them as being from the Red Cross. The guards shouted warnings at the Russians, waving their rifles at them with violent curses, but the prisoners ignored the guards, and Marlowe collected several more cigarettes off the muddy ground.

No one expected the guards to open fire, and when they did, the Americans shrank away from the fence in horror. But the shooting was directed at the Russians, several of whom fell dead as the others piled backward to safety. Still a cigarette flew over the fence in Russian defiance, but the Americans backed away from the barbed wire, retreating into the building rather than have the guards fire again. The final cigarette remained on the ground until a prisoner sneaked out later and snatched it from the mud.

The next morning they were again marched to the train station. As they climbed off the train a day or two later, Marlowe noticed a sign at the station that read "Linburg," and for the first time he had a vague idea where he was in northern Germany.

Stalag XII-A, located outside the town, was a massive overcrowded prison compound consisting of tents and tin huts on one side of a wet, muddy field. Across the field stood a cluster of permanent barrackslike buildings that had at one time been the entire stalag. They looked luxurious in comparison with the hasty lodgings the Germans now forced the prisoners into.

Several latrines stood overflowing and stinking nearby, drains plugged and human waste spilling over the length of the field. A soft drizzle hung in the air as if to cleanse the filthy camp, while the new group of several hundred prisoners marched into their temporary home. Their captors squeezed the men into a hut, tin walls and a concrete floor framing their confinement. The building was nearly sixty by fifty feet and sheltered six hundred men from the rain. They each were given a small bowl of runny soup and each split a loaf of bread with twenty other men. They lined up for delousing, which Marlowe endured with waning patience.

Each passing moment seemed to mean less individuality for the prisoners. He knew no one around him and saw little interaction of any kind among the men. Hopelessness was rife throughout the building. It was impossible for the men to lie down in the small space, and many huddled along the front of the building to avoid the crowd, standing under the edge of the rafters in hopes of staying at least partially dry. A few smoked the cigarettes they had gotten from the Russians. Though some of the men had come from another compound, many had come with Marlowe from his previous camp, but he was unable to discern or recognize faces. He didn't doubt that they soon would be moved on again.

CHAPTER 10

Dan Jones stood on the platform of a train station near Limpi, Holland, blinking his eyes in the early morning light. He was dimly aware of a train screeching and grinding to a stop before him as the smell of the massive oiled wheels permeated his numbed senses. Around him stood rows of American prisoners, lining the tracks in tight groups that extended across the train station and down a hundred feet of track. They all were tired, beat up, and sick. No one spoke; the silence was striking. Without turning to look, Jones knew that Howard stood beside him, had been beside him for some time, the only friend he now had in the world.

Several days had passed since the interrogation in Limpi. The train station where they now stood appeared to be some distance from the convent where their captivity had begun. He could remember nothing of the time since the interrogation.

When the train had come to a full stop, the guards began barking orders, lining the prisoners in even numbers in front of the train cars. Jones hurried to the nearest car door, pulling Howard along by the arm. Those who had been slower were hit on the head or between their shoulder blades.

"Dummkopf! Schnell!" he heard shouted all around him. Howard moved apathetically, and Jones surveyed his friend's haggard form and gray face with concern. Howard seemed to be hurt worse than he was, and he feared that the trooper might not survive without his help. His own hand ached badly, and for the first time he remembered in horror the blood splattering from his finger as he fell during interrogation. He raised his left hand to his face and was relieved to see that his middle finger was mostly intact. Only the tip, along with most of his fingernail, had been hacked off. He shoved his hand into his pocket.

The German train consisted of passenger cars turned prisoner transport. The guards herded the men inside the car, along the narrow hallway, and into square compartments. The compartments were designed for four passengers each, with facing benches on either side and a now boarded-up window between them. A door shut to the hallway with a small window overlooking it. The passage ran along the train's left side and was lined with a row of windows looking out onto the train station. Jones walked into a compartment with Howard and eighteen more men were shoved in. The benches had been folded up to the walls to allow the men to squeeze into the eight-by-five-foot room. Each prisoner, as he climbed into the train, received a hunk of bread the size of his fist, a rank yellowed sausage, and a large tin cup filled with a tepid, stinking brown liquid that the guards called "kafee."

After the men had been shoved into compartments and the doors shut, guards were deployed before each door with rifles. Those prisoners who stood near the door watched them cautiously, while the others looked helplessly at another prisoner's chest or face, or a wall. Their shoulders were pressed tight together, and there was not room to move or adjust positions.

Not knowing how long they would be on the train, many of the men tucked their bread and sausage in their pockets for more desperate times. Howard, too weak to consider eating, nearly dropped his food before Jones rescued it for him, putting it in the soldier's loose pockets. He ate his own bread before the train pulled out. The last time he'd eaten had been when the Dutch girl intercepted them with milk and bread. All he cared about now was obviating his own starvation for another day.

The bread was made of sawdust, and at the time unaware of the ingredient, he wondered over the strange flavor and texture. The ersatz coffee, made from grains synthesized to replace coffee beans, tasted as bitter and loathsome as it smelled. Too thirsty to care, he drank the whole cupful, then shuddered at the aftertaste.

Before taking a bite from his sausage, he held it to his nose and then immediately dropped it, sucking in his chest to allow its free fall to the floor, where someone beside him trod on it. As desperate as he was for food, he couldn't imagine eating spoiled meat, which probably would kill him anyway.

The train pulled out of the station and proceeded toward Germany at a sloth's pace. It stopped every few hours to allow another train past, change guards, or load up more prisoners. Some of the men in Jones's compartment were already so sick they couldn't stand on their own. Like Howard, they leaned on someone else and slipped in and out of consciousness. The men pulled one of the benches down, squeezing into an even tighter space to allow those badly hurt or sick to take turns sitting or lying down.

Those still healthy enough to stand on their own tried to rotate slowly, allowing everyone a turn at the door window to look out at the guards and the passing countryside behind them.

The time passed in spurts for the first two days, sometimes each minute passing so agonizingly slow that Jones couldn't see how he'd make it. He tugged at his collar and leaned back from the body in front of him, vainly trying to feel fresh air against his sweating chest and shoulders.

"If you don't get your elbow outta my ribs you sonofabitch, I'm gonna throw you out to the guards," an irritable voice commented from another part of the compartment.

"Blow it out yer ass," was Jones's hostile response. Within minutes he was provoked into a shoving match with the lanky trooper beside him, whose sweaty, vomit-stained shirt had been in his face for days. The other prisoners shouted in outrage as they were jostled and smothered by Jones and his antagonist.

"I'll see you when we get off this train!" Jones shouted at the tall man, knowing that his threats meant nothing. They had no idea if they would ever climb off the train alive.

At the dawn of the third day of the trip, Jones noticed that Howard still carried a fair-size bulge in his pocket where he had stashed the food several days before.

"Hey, Howard, you ever gonna eat that bread?" he asked. Howard shook his head with a shrug, his head lolling to the side where he leaned against the wall.

"I can't."

"You mind if I eat it?" Jones pressed.

"No, you can have the sausage too if you want it." Jones pulled the food out of his friend's pocket and smelled the meat again for a possible change of heart, then vehemently tossed it on the floor before tearing off a piece of bread.

As he chewed on the bread, the train stopped with a sudden jolt, the men slamming against the wall. They weren't surprised by the stop; they had grown accustomed to repeated delays, even in the most remote areas, such as the beet field they now overlooked. Jones glanced up when he heard the buzzing sound of distant approaching airplanes. The men watched through the window as the guards threw open the train door and ran into the fields, stopping a safe distance from the train. The guards turned and dropped to one knee, their rifles trained on the prisoners, who stood helplessly in the compartment, staring out like confused cattle. As the guards kept their weapons on the men, they repeatedly looked over their shoulders for the fighter planes. If a prisoner panicked and tried to escape from the train, he would be gunned down at once.

Through the window Jones watched the engineer, a small Dutch man with a round, bald head, run into the fields and continue toward the woods beyond, determined in his fear. Jones realized the engineer had no intention of coming back, and he almost laughed at the sight before looking up to see the planes that barreled toward them. They were American planes, descending on the German train. The pilots seemed to have no idea that it was full of their own men. He counted four planes in formation, and they approached so low that Jones could see the faces of the pilots before the strafing started. The men dove for the center of the compartment in sudden terror. Those in the middle dropped or were shoved to the floor and were smothered with leaning bodies. Bullets flew through the train and bounced around them, ricocheting off the wall and ceiling before sinking into the bodies of the exposed prisoners. Jones tugged Howard and himself down and had his face ground into the wet floor as panicking men stomped on his cheek, shoulders, and back. So much weight pressed down on his ribs that he was unable to breathe, but as the planes circled and returned for more, he tried to crawl even farther underneath the protective cover of the other men.

As the planed departed, their sound gradually yielded to moans of fresh pain and fear. Jones pushed at those on the top, now sensing a real chance of suffocating on the floor of the compartment.

"Come on, git the hell up! We can't breathe!" he hollered in a choked voice he hardly recognized.

At first, as the men picked their way off the pile, it was hard to tell who had been hit and who had not. Blood spattered on the walls, ceiling, and window attested to the damage that had been done, and the men pulled limp bodies onto the floor where space could be made. When Jones and Howard finally stood again, both uninjured by the strafing, they were drenched in blood. Awkwardly the men stood around the dead and wounded, trying to sort through them but without enough space to be sure. Those who remained on the ground as the others climbed to their feet were trampled, assumed to be already dead.

The guards climbed back onto the train and opened the compartment door to survey the damage with distaste. They directed those who were able to remove the dead from the compartment and throw them off the train.

The train soon ground back into motion with its reduced cargo. Whether the Dutch engineer had returned or someone else had taken control, Jones didn't know. Although the prisoners' numbers were smaller, the compartment seemed even more cramped than it had been before. Fewer men stood straight, and the leaning became overwhelming in the tight space.

Over the following days, the only relief offered the prisoners was refills of ersatz coffee, which Jones accepted and swallowed reluctantly. He wished eventually that he had eaten his sausage or had saved Howard's for later. Now the trampled sausage on the floor was indistinguishable in the accumulated blood and filth. His uniform was caked with dried blood, and it chafed against his flesh, his neck red and irritated from his collar.

On the fifth day of the journey, Jones watched as they pulled into their final stop, just another train station in the light of dusk with a small sign saying "Linburg." He no longer cared to know his fate or wonder about this new place. He watched with tired apathy as the guards opened the compartment door. The prisoners were to begin their internment in the sprawling POW camp known as Stalag XII-A.

CHAPTER 11

Over the following weeks, Jones and Howard stayed close together in the camp quarters they shared with Allied prisoners from all over the world. Since his capture, Jones had come to think of Howard as his best friend and ally, the only person he trusted. After having so recently vowed to avoid friendships in combat, he now found that one trusted companion was a matter of survival. Much of the camp was comprised of such partnerships in which prisoners would defend each other at all costs. They survived by sharing food and protecting each other from punishment, starvation, and theft. They were put to work in the nearby gardens, and Jones learned to get by on extra vegetables that he secreted in his soiled uniform when the guards turned the other way. But the two friends' time together was soon to come to an end.

After three weeks, the men were called to the yard in front of their barracks for inspection. They lined up in long, sloppy rows, looking like a homemade quilt in their assortment of military uniforms and colors. They were examined by a German officer Jones didn't recognize. The officer began picking out men, all members of the airborne, pointing with a long, gloved finger as he shouted for them to step out of line. Each man reluctantly came forward to form a group. Jones's nerves drew taut as he and Howard were approached and then looked over.

"Du!" the officer said, pointing directly at Jones. Jones stepped toward the group, his friend Howard at his side; the two were inseparable. The officer snapped at Howard, "Nein! Nicht du!" and Jones turned to see his friend pause, then reluctantly return to the rows of men, his shoulders hunched. Howard was fortunate enough to remain at Stalag XII-A, until the next recruiter arrived.

The men immediately were moved out toward the train station. Jones carried his cup and wooden shoes but had to leave the mattress behind. He was unable to look back at his friend as he and the small group of men were herded to the road. He knew that Howard stood in the yard watching them go. He had written his friend's name and home address in his green address book, but he doubted they would see each other again. Despite himself he was sad, and he shook his head severely. As a prisoner, he couldn't afford to get emotional.

After a five-day journey, Jones disembarked at Stalag II-A near the city of Neubrandenburg, a temporary stop before his final placement in a work commando.

CHAPTER 12

Pvt. Charlie Chasteen of the 505th Parachute Infantry Regiment ran ahead of his commander down a fifty-foot bed of gravel. The landscape around him was flat and wet, and the only rises in the land, like the one he now reached the bottom of, were man-made supports for the railroad. Below the railroad tracks stretched a large, winding road, which Chasteen and his company planned to secure, effectively blocking any German movement toward the city of Groesbeek.

Chasteen was an experienced demolition man but now carried a Browning automatic rifle, one of the American weapons the Germans hated most. Chasteen settled in to reload, watching a fifteen-foot American roadblock with wary eyes. He had been in Holland for only twenty-four hours and even the intensive demolition training could not have prepared him for this. His casual days in London were now behind him for good.

As the day had passed, SS paratroopers has gathered along the ditch of the road in swelling strength. "Potato mashers" came over the blockade and exploded among the troops, killing and wounding with steady precision. The fight had become desperate within a matter of hours, and the men looked behind them at the steep incline leading to the railroad. This was their only path to escape. By this time their commander had been killed, as had most of the men. Chasteen was left to make decisions. They were running out of ammunition fast, and the Germans shelled them with ever-gaining momentum. Chasteen glanced at his friend Pvt. Bill Lindsey, and they saw their fears reflected in each other's eyes.

"We ain't gonna make it, Billy," he shouted, looking around him to see that only he, Lindsey, and a soldier known only as Private Wilson were still standing, all three of them carrying flesh wounds from flying shrapnel. Lindsey nodded in reluctant agreement, and the three troopers ceased their fire.

"Comrade!" Lindsey's voice echoed across the roadblock, and he stepped into the open, his hands above his head. Throwing their weapons aside, the other two survivors followed, Chasteen tearing his BAR apart before discarding the pieces in the grassy canyon. One German sergeant came over the side of the roadblock, a rifle in his hand, and gave the Americans a wry smile.

"It's a long way to Tipperary," he said with a heavy accent, his finger wagging at them. Lindsey and Chasteen were marched away from their battalion at gunpoint, their future unknown. Wilson remained behind them, more severely injured, and his companions did not see him again or ever learn of his fate.

The Germans marched them, without stopping for rests, toward the Rhine River, where they bore witness to the multitudes of troops now being sent toward the front in Holland. Chasteen looked around him in disbelief as thousands of German troopers marched past the tanks, armored trucks, half-tracks, and 88s, as well as an immense entourage of smaller weapons.

"These guys really mean business, don't they?" he commented to Lindsey.

Several days later Chasteen was sent out alone with a private guard. Placed in a sweatbox on a train with his guard, he moved at top speed to an unknown destination.

After a day, several British POWs were thrown into the boxcar with him, and Chasteen was pleased to have companions who spoke his language. He talked to them with the openness he had learned growing up in South Carolina. The British received him with cool politeness, and he shared his last D-Bar with them. The British ate his chocolate willingly but soon broke out their own rations and huddled in a corner away from him as they whispered among themselves. He watched them with hostile irritation but refused to be bothered for long. He had had a bowl of barley soup and a piece of bread, and after picking the insects out of the soup, had eaten it eagerly. He wouldn't starve today, he knew that much. He fell asleep in a back corner of the car, crawling under a pile of straw, determined to get the rest he had yet to enjoy since he'd jumped at least ten days before.

When he awoke he was surprised to see that something had changed around him. Although he was still buried in a pile of hay, the rest of the boxcar had been swept clean. The British prisoners were gone; he was entirely alone. When he stood and walked to the open door, he caught the attention of a guard, who took one look at him and let out a surprised shout. The guard called for assistance, holding his rifle on Chasteen as if the prisoner had threatened him. Chasteen watched in stunned confusion as German soldiers rushed back from the train engine, shouting angrily as they came. Soon an officer strode toward the group with authoritative determination. They yanked the prisoner from the car and shook him, shouting in his face. All Chasteen could do was shout back in English. "What the hell's the matter? I just went to sleep in the hay!" He wondered now how long he had been asleep or whether the Germans had noticed him missing.

The following day he was hurried across the camp to the American compound of Stalag XII-A in Linburg.

It had been raining for several days, and he sank ankle-deep in mud as he
walked. Where the latest American prisoners were housed, he found latrines
running over and clogged drains. Water and human waste pooled around the
prisoners, accompanied by disease and misery. The compound consisted mostly
of tents with walkways down the middle, separating tiny straw-filled cubicles,
just long enough to accommodate a grown man. Water flowed underneath, soaking the straw, and ran through the passageways like muddy rivers. These were
the prisoners' beds.

Chasteen was left there with hundreds of other American prisoners, tired
and hungry like himself, and many sick. The prison camp was at its most
crowded, and only the fortunate prisoners, those of several weeks before, slept
in regular barracks across the compound and worked in a neighboring garden.
Chasteen tried to sleep but found the straw so cold and uncomfortable that he
instead stood beside it, looking around him in restless exhaustion. None of the
men spoke, few knew anyone else, and all were isolated in their discouraged
depression. The rain pattered harder against the canvas roof as the day passed,
and the rivers inside the tent surged.

An American sergeant from the 101st was placed in their command, one
of many Americans in charge of the prisoners. He was a stern and unsympathetic
man who spent more time with the German guards than with the Americans,
and Chasteen hated him instinctively. He watched him give orders and punish
men, and he kept his resentment to himself with growing bitterness. There was
little food—some soup, bread, and occasional cheese or salt-cured meat, generally spoiled. The conditions were worse than anything he'd imagined in training, and although he tried to distract his thoughts from the stench, hunger, disease, and wet cold around him, he often felt he would lose his mind in this place.

He sat near his cubicle one morning, only half-heartedly trying to avoid a
large area of the tent that had been sprayed with feces by a dysenteric soldier.
He watched as the sergeant in command walked into the tent with two German
guards and paused to overlook the situation in disgust.

"Who shit all over the place?!" the sergeant demanded, waiting for an ad-
mission from the apathetic and miserable faces. He didn't suffer from dysentery, or the cold; the Germans put him up and fed him properly for his service.

Chasteen stood without thinking, his temper taking over. "Just who in the
Goddamn hell do you think? You come in here hollerin' at your own men—
just whose side are you on, anyway? You one of the Krauts yourself now?"

The sergeant looked at him in silent rage, and turned in response to the questioning of the guards. He spoke to them in German, then walked over to Chasteen.

Within minutes Chasteen found himself standing with his nose touching the barbed-wire fence, his shoulders back and his chest out. He was to stand at attention for ten hours with his nose against the fence for insubordination. It was a punishment the American sergeant had determined, and the Germans had nodded in agreement, allowing him the luxury of deciding the man's discipline.

Three days later, the men were gathered from the tents and shacks, all Americans to be reviewed by several German officers. The men chosen were called out in large numbers, as many as three hundred in a group.

Chasteen was one of the first selected. He watched as the Germans chose a tall blond man in his mid-twenties out of the ranks to be leader and sent him to the front of the group. Chasteen watched curiously as the tall man hollered at the prisoners to move out and walked ahead with a group of Germans, although he did not speak with them. Slowly Chasteen shouldered his way ahead until he had broken ranks and stood beside the leader.

"Where are we going?" he asked the tall impromptu leader.

Herbert Marlowe looked at Chasteen, at first surprised to see this audacious trooper who had broken ranks to ask him a question, then shrugged with a smile as he answered honestly: "All I know is we're fixin' to board a cattle train for a place called Neubrandenburg."

PART III

CHAPTER 1

On October 17, 1944, four dozen prisoners stood waiting at the Neu-brandenburg train station in a dirty collage of uniforms, coats, and hats. They were all members of the 82nd and 101st Airborne from Stalag II-A, and all had been captured in Holland. Four armed guards watched them carefully as they waited for their train.

Since their capture, the paratroopers had been shuttled from one place to another, farther and farther from the main stalags. Now they were being sent to a small farming town to work. This was in large part the result of their bad reputation among the Germans. American paratroopers were considered little more than hoodlums by the Germans, who wanted them out of the way and kept busy.

Dan Jones felt the bottoms of his pockets as he exchanged a glance with Jim Bruton. Bruton was tall and athletic looking, and Jones thought he remembered seeing him somewhere at the stalag before. He tried to recall where, and his mind skimmed over the details of his arrival at II-A several weeks before.

At the time, Jones had fallen out of the train compartment to the sight of a mass burial. A bulldozer roared by as he tried to move his stiff legs. What he saw in front of the bulldozer made him forget his legs. The rolling bodies being plowed toward an open grave would have reminded him of any other refuse but for the heads that rolled to face him, limp arms and legs that spun to dance and wave at him. The sight horrified him, and he summoned a will to live that he had thought he'd lost. He couldn't tell if these dead were Allied soldiers or German civilians of some kind. He took it as a message and determined not to end up with their fate. Now, weeks later, at the station again, there was no sign of the dead or their graves.

Charlie Chasteen, standing just behind Jones and Bruton, also recalled the first time he had been in the train station. There was no sign of a grave now, but when he had been brought to the stalag, some time before Jones, the guard had forced him to walk in the shallow trenches filled with layers of bodies, the only passage toward the road to Stalag II-A.

He did not dwell on this recollection now, however. He was excited because he was reunited with his friend Bill Lindsey. They had met again at II-A and were now being shipped together to their final stalag, 311/I. He shared a joke with his friend and a small, tough Bronx kid named Rodney Spivey. Chasteen and Lindsey laughed now at Spivey's accent and stories.

James Rizzuto, Earl Mickelson, and Stan Watsick stood in a half circle around Marlowe, a man who by nature seemed to be in charge. At Stalag II-A, Marlowe had been assigned leader of the unruly bunch of troopers. The men now turned to him automatically with their questions.

Rizzuto was happy to be moving away from II-A. It had been Corp. John Greene who had arranged the transfer for him. Greene, a friend of Rizzuto's from the 508th who was captured with him in Holland, acted as records officer and "assistant camp leader" at the stalag. Greene tried to look out for his friends and had been happy to tell Rizzuto that he had found him a healthy assignment at one of the work satellite stations. Greene had explained the work as the Germans had explained it to him. It would consist of farm work with other troopers, picking potatoes and vegetables.

"It's good work—whenever you're working on the farms, you can always get enough to eat. It'll be a helluva lot better than this place." He extended the fountain pen and document for Rizzuto to sign, and Rizzuto eagerly signed his agreement to the work detail. He was eager to get out of this stalag where he and the other men were slowly starving.

The train took the men through northeastern Germany, through the city of Rostock, and finally to the small town of Dettmannsdorf. Here four guards herded the prisoners off the train and down a country road. Dettmannsdorf was a farming community, and fields of turnips and beets lined the road they walked down.

Their destination was a small, abandoned farm, claimed by the German government and transformed into Arbeitskommando (Work Commando) 311/I. After the crowded and active conditions they had known at both XII-A and II-A, the lonely, dark, and decrepit barn they were now being ushered toward seemed the very symbol of bleak despair.

Stan Watsick saw the structure and felt his spirits drop. He had determined to keep his hopes up, and now, seeing this solitary dilapidated barn in the heart of German obscurity, he assured himself that this would not last long. The war would be over soon, everyone agreed—another month at the longest.

The barn, their new prison barracks, sat off the road, a mile from any city. It had several purposes, housing not only prisoners but also some livestock. The west end of the building was fashioned into a kitchen and bakery. Had there been a house once, it was long since destroyed, leaving only the barn as reminder of a once-active farm. The fences surrounding it were wrapped with barbed wire in hostile twists above face level; this effectively set the atmosphere for the place they now entered. The barn was black, a large, square building with a tiny door on each corner and dark windows lining the edge of the rafters.

The men marched through the dark doorway and up a narrow flight of stairs along the north wall of the building. They reached a dark, narrow loft lined with two rows of bunks.

Jones tripped as he entered the dim room, and looked down at a large milk can fashioned into a chamber pot. The chamber pot and the bunks were the only furnishings in the atticlike loft. In the center of the room, between the bed rows, sat a squat potbellied stove, its pipe extending through the ceiling. Some of the bunks were covered with mattresses already; others waited bare for the prisoners who now arrived. Several prisoners already occupied bunks and watched with apathetic eyes as the large group filled the tiny loft. In the evening gloom, the newcomers were issued new mattresses—limp potato sacks, like those at the stalags—and a thin, rough blanket. A dim bulb dangled between the beams above the bunks and cast a pale yellow light in the center of the room. A window at the end of the room could have admitted moonlight but for a thick blanket hanging over it for the German blackouts. Short, blackened windows lined the walls at knee level where the angular roof nearly touched the floor.

As the men awaited their next instruction, a tall, grossly disfigured guard joined them in the loft. He appeared to be in his early thirties, but his expression reflected the mind of a child. His one good eye stared at the men blankly, while his mouth hung limply open. A fresh and angry scar slashed across his face from his left eye to his mouth. The left side of his face was paralyzed, and his lid fell shut around the hollow of an empty eye socket. He made stabbing motions in the air as he barked orders at the men, waving at them and the empty bunks with a large, freckled hand. As he shouted, a small stream of drool trickled from his displaced mouth.

Jones helped himself to a bottom bunk near the center of the room, close to the potbellied stove. Another prisoner already occupied the bunk above him and watched him without comment. Chasteen took a bunk beneath Spivey and beside Bill Lindsey, and Watsick and Mickelson found two across from them. Rizzuto and Bruton claimed beds in a hurry as the four guards barked at them in the dim light.

The guards took a noisy inventory of the men, walking between the bunks and marking off names on a yellowed piece of paper. Jones watched them silently, cold and hungry. He understood a few of the German words now, having heard all the orders before. The guards left abruptly and locked the door behind them with loud ceremony, leaving the prisoners alone together.

The young trooper in the bunk above Jones looked down at him over the side, then disappeared from view again. Nobody spoke in the small room, and the air was thick with tension and hostile suspicion.

One prisoner unscrewed the light bulb, and only coughing broke their silence in the black night. But a foreign sound came from beneath the floor. Jones listened to the high-pitched squealing and stomping for several minutes before whispering loudly to his bunkmate.

"Hey, you got a name?"

"Turner. Doug Turner."

"Turner, you hear that noise?"

"What, you mean the hogs? You'll get used to it."

Jones at first listened to the pigs curiously, but as the noise persisted into the night he tried to shut it out. They seemed to have been fed recently, fighting for their food in grunts and squeals.

He lay awake all night, trying to hear sounds from the guard posted out front, who he was sure must be there. The pigs gradually fell silent. He would have liked a cigarette but had run out several weeks before, and he lay chilled and worried, wondering how he'd survive this depressing pig barn. He longed for the end of the war more than ever before.

Several hours before sunrise, the guards burst into the loft. "heRAUS!" the one-eyed man bellowed. They obeyed lethargically, climbing off their bunks and wandering toward the stairway like zombies. The guards chose one man from the group to remain behind to help around the compound—a young 82nd Airborne private named William Kalkreuth.

The remaining forty-five or so prisoners standing in the morning dark were less fortunate. Jones looked at the men lined up beside him and, except for Bruton and Marlowe, didn't recognize anyone from Stalag II-A. He had never bothered to look at faces.

They marched down the road with four guards, in the direction they had come from the previous night. They had eaten little since leaving the stalag, and they dwelled on their hunger pangs. The guards issued them each one cup of ersatz coffee before going to work, plus a small bowl of soup that tasted of strained potatoes. The soup, they would learn, was produced from the runoff of the pigs' cooked potatoes. Jones consumed it greedily, savoring the bland taste. Jim Rizzuto exchanged a glance with him as he tried to pull the maggots out of his cup.

Upon reaching the train station, the men stood waiting in the early morning silence, stuffing their hands into their pockets and frowning against the cold breeze. The station was devoid of even the early German commuters, and Jones looked at his watch to see that it was just past 5 A.M. He showed the time to Stan Watsick, who nodded thanks, while a heavyset guard looked on with curiosity.

They had walked several miles to the station, and Rizzuto fought a strong urge to sit on the platform. He knew now that he and the other men had been double-crossed. It was not farm work they were headed for, and this was not a better life he had agreed to. They had been chosen for their big shoulders and heavy frames, for hard labor: railroad work. He knew nothing of this kind of work. He wondered, now, how many times the Germans had misled Greene as he encouraged men to join labor camps.

After a half-hour wait, he watched the train approach with a mixture of relief and apprehension. He had no idea where they were going, but he could think only of sitting on the train and of the possibility of being fed again somewhere along the tracks.

On the train, however, the prisoners were forced to stand while the four guards sat. Several older German women stood and hurried to another car, one spitting on the last prisoner she passed. The one-eyed guard, whom the other guards called Leeps, laughed as the prisoner wiped a clot of spit off his face.

"That Leeps, he's as crazy as he is ugly," Turner whispered to Jones.

They stood on the train for a half hour before climbing off at another small station. The guards hurried the men inside the station and down a set of stairs, locking them in a basement room. Another hour passed before the guards unlocked and opened the door and marched them down the tracks, where they were met by two German men. One was an unarmed older man in his fifties or sixties, with a round face and balding head, who looked more fatherly than dangerous. He was the railroad superintendent. The other, the chief foreman in charge of their labor, was a stiff-looking man in full Nazi uniform, large swastikas displayed on his dark cap and on the shoulder of his jacket. As the guards stepped aside, the foreman looked the men over with contempt. He was eager to get started.

The men began their labor at a gaping hole in the railroad tracks. The rails had been blown apart by Allied bombs the night before and needed to be repaired before the 11 A.M. train arrived with supplies. The men learned the work through trial and error, helping each other when necessary. Turner and Jones worked together with unspoken bunkmate camaraderie. Jones had found a new ally, and the two became fast friends. They avoided the other prisoners as they learned the pattern of the job.

The basic element was simple. The men unloaded new rails from boxcars and carried them on a handcar to the work site along with the proper tools. They then cleared the tracks of scrapped metal and debris from the bombing, and hacked off twisted ends of rails, throwing them to the side. Next they laid the ties, then screwed the rails into every other tie with a swivel-like manual drill. To secure the remaining ties, they hammered the rails with a sledgehammer and eight-inch steel spikes. When they had properly secured the rails, they shoveled gravel underneath and smoothed it out, and the tenuous patchwork track was complete.

They worked slowly and awkwardly with the giant rails and heavy equipment. Jones was familiar with some of the tools from his childhood on the farm but struggled physically with the heavy labor. His weakened back ached with exhaustion, and his stomach groaned from hunger. Often he stopped his work and stood motionless to ensure that his unstable legs would not collapse. The other men worked in the same fashion, and the foreman leaped up from the rock where he sat beside the tracks.

"Los! Los! Dummkopf! Donnerwedder!" He walked to a prisoner who labored several feet from Jones. The man struggled with obvious pain, tugging at his hand drill uselessly, unable to budge the bolt. He caught the eyes of the foreman, then looked away, ignoring him.

"Schweinhund! Was machst du, hast du einen Stein für den kopf?" He gestured at his head, implying stupidity, before hitting the prisoner across the side of the face with the barrel of his rifle. The young man fell onto the tracks, then stumbled back to his feet, wiping blood from his mouth with his sleeve. The foreman walked away, glancing over his shoulder at Jones and Turner, who stood watching. They returned to their work with zealous alacrity, turning their backs to the Nazi. The foreman strode back and forth in front of the men, occasionally grabbing a guard's rifle to intimidate the prisoners. Jones recalled the life he'd led at Stalag XII-A and wondered if Howard knew how lucky he was there.

As the sun gathered heat at midday, the guards and foreman seated themselves together on the ground, taking off their jackets and rolling up their sleeves. They pulled sandwiches out of stiff leather satchels. Before eating, the foreman removed his hat and displayed a smooth bald head and large, drooping ears. A young woman came by the tracks to speak with him and offered him a kiss on the cheek before hurrying off with a laugh and cheery good-bye. The men looked furtively in their direction, more interested in the food than the foreman's attractive daughter.

The sandwiches consisted of hard, brown bread smeared with a layer of goose grease, or so the prisoners guessed from the strong smell that wafted toward them in the warm breeze. Jones raised his arms high over his head, bringing the sledgehammer down hard on the spike between Turner's hands. He had shed his jump jacket in the heat, and his sweat-soaked shirt clung to his back. He hands split open and bled, making his grip on the hammer dangerously slick. Turner held the spike low, watching his bunkmate warily, his hands and arms at the hammer-wielding man's mercy.

The section of track they worked on was several miles from any town, and other than the foreman's daughter, they saw no German civilians. In the fields that extended in both directions around them, women prisoners worked on the sugar beets that grew in narrow rows. They didn't appear to have feminine forms, buried in shapeless burlap dresses that hung heavily in the dirt. They sang melancholy choruses as they worked, and Stan Watsick recognized the Polish folk songs he'd heard his grandparents sing in Minnesota. He called out a greeting to the closest women in Polish but was silenced by one of the guards.

The workday lasted for hours beyond the men's endurance. The 11:00 A.M. train had not been able to pass until well after 3 P.M. because of the prisoners' slow progress. Now they repaired another track a hundred yards down from the first. The damage to the rails was too extensive for possible repair in one day. Night fell, and the guards wrapped themselves in their coats as a dark chill rose with the moon. Jones saw his breath mingling with the clouds that emerged from the lungs of the other prisoners. It had been dark several hours, and Jones put his jacket back on over his wet and clammy shirt, moving trancelike, unsure of what he did or whether he actually was still working or even standing.

The foreman gathered the guards at 9 P.M., and they shouted at the men to stop. Jones dropped his shovel with immeasurable relief. As he stood straight, his hands on the small of his back, something lashed out at him and he ducked, pain slashing across his neck. He turned to face one of the guards, who stood with a riding crop in his hand. The guard, in his late thirties, had only one arm, the empty sleeve of his shirt folded underneath his armpit so that it flapped wildly in the wind. He shouted at Jones, pointing anxiously at the shovel that lay at his feet. Jones stooped to pick it up and, with the others, began loading the tools onto a train car several hundred feet down the track. "Is this really happening?" he wondered, not for the first time, in disbelief.

By the following day, Jones realized he could not survive on the food he was given. He watched the others around him growing weak and ashen with hunger and wondered at a way to either escape or steal food. As the morning train passed cautiously over their clumsy repairs, he noticed one of the prisoners following alongside the slow-moving cars and examining their contents. The cars were filled to the top with sugar beets.

Jones watched in fascination as the prisoner quickly looked around for guards, then raised his shovel to the top of the car and chucked a beet onto the ground. As he bent to recover the vegetable, the foreman appeared suddenly from around the train. He rested one boot over the beet. The prisoner straightened slowly as the foreman shouted for the guards. They dragged him to the train station, and the group disappeared from sight. The foreman watched them go, then picked up the dust-covered beet and pitched it into the fields, out of the prisoners' reach. Jones returned to work.

CHAPTER 2

E arly in the morning, the prisoners gathered at the train station in a heavy fog. Marlowe glanced sharply to his right as he heard one of the prisoners speak out with antagonism in his voice. "Just stay the hell away from me, you asshole."

Marlowe remembered the young trooper's face and knew how much trouble someone like him caused for everyone. All the prisoners were airborne men, with strong opinions and chips on their shoulders, even in this camp. He hated to see them fight each other, but they did so almost constantly. They were not taking to prison life well.

He hadn't asked to be leader of anyone, especially such a sorry-looking group of prisoners of war, and he knew that he would win no rewards for his efforts. Now that he had been placed in charge, however, he felt a natural responsibility, which he realized the Germans had counted on when they'd chosen him. He watched now as the two hostile prisoners drifted away from each other. This time a fight had been avoided.

Several German commuters had arrived in the station now, waiting for the same early train. Marlowe noticed that many of them wore black armbands to mourn the death of a family member. The prisoners stayed huddled close together, finding some safety in one another as the Germans glared at them. Leeps watched the confrontational anger in amusement. He seemed to have no intention of interfering if any violence should break out. Two other guards stood nearby and ignored the people around them as the train pulled to a stop in their midst.

After reaching the work site, Jones and Turner pumped a handcar down the tracks to load up the tools and rails from a waiting boxcar. They were accompanied by the heavyset guard, a suspicious and war-weary man in his thirties named Henry, who sat on the car and rested his rifle in his lap while the two men pumped. The railroad was damaged near the town of Sanitz, where bombs had hit the day before. Henry watched them struggle with the hand pump, irritated with their slow pace, and barked orders and insults at them several times before their momentum got the car moving at high speed.

The foreman and Marlowe had already taken an extreme dislike to each other. The foreman had been a railroad man for years, and he seemed to relish his new assignment. Although he flushed with frustration and shouted and paced, his fists waving anxious patterns in the sky, the glint in his eyes revealed his enjoyment. Whenever he removed his hat, his ears seemed to flap free and valiant in the breeze, like wings on each side of his bald head. His appearance was comical, but the men didn't dare laugh. He carried a large blackjack in his leather-gloved hand and snapped it in front of the men constantly as they showed their exhaustion.

The noise from the work drowned out the conversations and laughter of the German guards and any civilians who happened by to watch. Occasionally Marlowe glanced up to see the malicious eyes of a German woman or child trained on him, ready to hurl a rock at his head. Some of the men working closest to the station wound up with spittle running down their necks and the backs of their heads, but they continued to work, attempting to ignore the abuse. Several prisoners looked with hostility at the civilians, but they were almost immediately beaten in front of the others while the women and children jeered. Marlowe noticed that though most German men walked past, the women enjoyed stopping to harass the prisoners and seemed to harbor more anger against them.

Jones glanced at his watch every few hours. Henry took a great interest in Jones's Swiss watch. He approached him several times during the day to take the prisoner's wrist in his hand and admire the watch and band. Jones worried that the guard intended to take the watch from him forcibly. It was the only possession he had managed to save through his capture, besides his address book and deck of cards. If Henry did take it, there was little Jones could do about it. But the guard only walked away, then returned again to examine the watch more closely.

The train scheduled for 11 A.M. showed up at 1:30, ten minutes before the men had completed the rails. Although the tracks were slapped together in a crude fashion, they were secure and evenly tamped underneath to support the tons that passed over them. The train waited as they finished at their tired and clumsy pace. After it passed, they continued on with another set of tracks.

At 8 P.M., after the sun came down, they put their tools away and began to trudge to the station. At the Sanitz train station, the foreman and one older guard walked away with Leeps, headed home for the night, leaving two guards with the POWs.

They marched the men down a narrow set of stairs behind the station and into a small basement in which coal and other materials unloaded from the trains were stored. The basement was divided into two rooms by a row of two-by-two slats with six-inch gaps between them. In one room the prisoners stood waiting as they looked through the slats into the other room, where a mountain of coal briquettes towered hopelessly out of their reach. As they waited in the basement, the temperature dropped and rain fell outside. They stuffed their hands in their pockets, jumping and running in place or just tolerating the cold irritably. Several men exchanged insults, and a shoving match broke out. Marlowe quelled it with Watsick's and Mickelson's help. When the train arrived, they were released from the basement and filed into their train car listlessly.

They walked back to the camp in the dark, a downpour of rain squelching any energy left in the men. There was no chance of escape, even in the darkness. The guards carried lights trained on the prisoners and could shoot anyone who bolted before he was an arm's length toward freedom.

By the time they had climbed the stairs of their small barracks and heard the door slam and lock behind them, it was nearly midnight. They each had been allowed a brief turn at the latrine in groups of six, their only turn for the day. Then the guards sent them into the pig barn with a cup of tepid potato soup and a small piece of war bread each. The pigs living with them in the barn grunted and squealed restively below. While the pigs ate potatoes, the men ate their leavings. They finished their soup in silence, hating the pigs and relishing the occasional peeling that still floated in the watery mixture.

Jones crawled under his coat, sacrificing what had served as a pillow to try to keep warm. His clothes and hair were soaked. Some of the men stripped out of their jackets and pants. Jones kept his on, knowing his only chance of drying them by morning was wearing them overnight. Kalkreuth had started a small fire in the wood stove from twigs and scraps of wood he had scavenged around the compound. Within a few hours, however, the fire died out as the men slept, and the cold night air set in.

When Jones awoke to Leeps's "heRAUS appel!" he found the front of his jacket and mattress freshly wet. He placed his hand curiously on the wet spot, then looked up at the loosely laid slats of Turner's bunk. Turner climbed off his bunk, forcing his right leg into a cold, wet pair of jump pants, groaning as he shuddered into them.

"Hey, you pissed on me last night," Jones said irritably, crawling off his bunk to move toward the door. Turner hopped after him, buttoning his pants and shivering violently.

"I never pissed in my sleep in my life," he retorted defensively before Jones showed him the evidence dripping down his shirt and into his pants. "It's that ersatz coffee. I never know when I gotta take a leak. It just comes on out."

Jones nodded, knowing his bunkmate was right. The men urinated in their pants as they worked, only aware of what they were doing after it was too late. Jones was beginning to suffer diarrhea along with several others, but there was nothing he could do about it. He couldn't wash his clothes, hadn't done so or even been out of his uniform since his capture, and he no longer cared what he looked or smelled like. Despite his increasing kidney problems, Jones drank his morning cup eagerly. It was always better than nothing.

CHAPTER 3

Chasteen watched as his bunkmate, Spivey, carefully ran a small, black comb through his hair.

"I can't believe you still got a comb after all this," Chasteen said in his slow southern drawl, and Spivey glanced at him between strokes with a grin.

"What the hell's so difficult about carryin' a comb? Looks like you could've stood to hang on to yours." His voice was defensive, and Chasteen leaned back on his bunk without comment. They had all managed to keep what was most important to them. Spivey had his comb, Chasteen had his address book, and Jones had that watch as well as an address book. Marlowe had saved a beat-up picture of his new wife.

Spivey was a good-looking kid, just turned nineteen and proud of his appearance. It was contrary to their lives in this place, but whatever kept a man sane Chasteen figured was all right with him. He knew most of the prisoners now, some better than he wanted to. Most of the men, coming from the same division, knew each other or friends of friends in the regiments, but still they chose not to talk among themselves.

Spivey looked at his comb with revulsion and shook it out onto the floor and bed. Chasteen watched the movement on the floorboards as tiny, white bugs squirmed off in every direction. Spivey could comb his hair twenty-four hours a day but still wouldn't get the better of the lice or the fleas that leaped and crawled from man to man in the night.

The critters bothered Chasteen, but not as much as they did Spivey or some of the others. Even the hunger that seemed to burn holes in his empty stomach was somehow more tolerable for him than the others. Chasteen had undergone survival training in the States. He knew that only with the right attitude could hardship be endured and survived. Concentrating on anything other than food, he kept his hunger to himself. He imagined that the others suffered worse than he. Most of them complained and whimpered a lot more than he did. He was stronger than they were. He fought with himself constantly to control his fears, his discomforts, his pains, and he was largely successful.

But several of the men very nearly pushed him to his limit. It bothered him to hear prisoners crying in the dark at night, or complaining during the day. He tried to remember that they were mostly just young kids, some not more than eighteen and straight out of school with little or no combat experience. One of the prisoners, a featherweight boxing champion from New Jersey known as Ralph Pombano, often fought among the men, always beating them soundly. He tried hard to lure Chasteen into a fight, but Chasteen brushed the boxer off in bad humor, knowing he was outmatched. He knew he had a short temper, and it was another part of him that he now found hard to suppress. He knew Marlowe didn't like to see the men fighting, and he respected Marlowe. He was thankful he wasn't in his place, but he admired him all the same.

On the third day at the tracks, a Saturday afternoon, Chasteen paused from his work, leaning on his shovel to watch the 11:00 train pass, nearly three hours behind schedule. It groaned with steel reluctance, slowing, stopping, then continuing cautiously over the newly repaired tracks. The tamping underneath the tracks was imperative for a secure railroad, and if the ballast wasn't spread evenly the result would be disastrous.

This train, like the ones before it, carried red beets and sugar beets, picked by Russian and Polish girls, to Berlin. The day before, Chasteen had seen several beets rattle loose from the cars, and a tall prisoner named Bruton had gathered them up while the cars still blocked the guards' view. He'd stashed the beets in the side pockets of his jump pants, and they went undetected by the foreman. Bruton had gnawed on one of the beets the night before in the barracks while the others had watched enviously. The other beet he'd hidden under his bed, but it was missing the next morning. He'd accused someone, but it couldn't really be proved.

On that same day, Chasteen had seen a man nudge a beet loose from the train with his shovel, only to be caught by the foreman. It was still clearly worth the risk. Now Chasteen waited, standing close to the slow train. But the beets, which he could see piled well above the top of the open car, remained secure as the train rattled by. He lifted his shovel slowly, looking around him for German uniforms, then gently snapped a beet loose with an easy movement of his wrist. As the large, round vegetable pummeled down, he caught it in his right hand and stuffed it in his pocket casually, walking back into full view toward the foreman, who now watched him with suspicious eyes.

The foreman didn't like any of the prisoners and had beaten several of them badly with the butt of his rifle or his blackjack. But already within a few days he had singled out those he hated most, and he was now looking at one of them.

Chasteen stared him in the eye, challenging him to approach. He knew that any patronizing look from a prisoner infuriated the Germans and generally got the prisoner beaten. But Chasteen found himself challenging the Germans anyway. He couldn't control himself.

He'd noticed the foreman also carried a grudge against Dan Jones, a stocky, jocular kid from Idaho. Jones possessed an uncanny talent at avoiding excess work, appearing to work hard while actually getting almost nothing done. The other prisoners were amused, but the foreman was infuriated and gave Jones a shove with his rifle between the shoulder blades at any opportunity.

Now the foreman sauntered toward Chasteen slowly, his large ears standing prominently from his bare head. He stopped before him and stared into Chasteen's eyes, his face hovering inches away, and the prisoner was bombarded with the smell of grease and tobacco as the foreman shouted at him.

"You got some kind of problem . . . Flop Ears?" Chasteen asked, confident that the foreman didn't understand a word of English. The foreman brought his rifle around, snapping it against the side of the prisoner's head. Chasteen was only dimly aware of his marching away as he tried to clear his ringing head and control the pain. Despite the throbbing between his ears, he was well satisfied with the encounter. The foreman hadn't discovered the beet, and he hadn't backed down. He knew he wasn't finished with his German adversary but was pleased with the minor triumph anyway.

Over the course of the day, several other men learned the skill of stealing beets and turnips from the passing trains. When a train lurched or shuddered, prisoners scrambled along its shanks in the dirt, snatching up rolling vegetables. Several men were caught and punished, the beets confiscated and their daily rations reduced or cut off entirely. It was still worth the risk, and by the end of the day, a dozen or more men walked home with at least one beet or turnip.

Once in the barracks, the men sat by the wood stove, with burning twigs popping and crackling inside. Jim Rizzuto pulled a small beet from his pocket and placed it on the stove experimentally, watching it crack and steam as it cooked. Soon all the men had followed his lead and carried their beets to the stove to be cooked to a softer and more edible meal.

Chasteen set his beet on the middle of the stove. He had chosen it for its size before pulling it from the train. It was the largest, most succulent beet in the bunch. He waited on his bunk, talking with Spivey and Lindsey while the fragrance of baked beets filled the loft as if to overpower the pervasive pig smell. He tried to relax the tired muscles in his back as he talked to his friends, and he agreed to share his dinner with them.

Ten minutes later he returned to the stove to retrieve his beet but froze in anger before it. His beet was gone—all the beets were gone—and only a small, tired-looking turnip remained on the edge of the stove as men sat around it eating contentedly.

"Who in the HELL has my beet?!" he challenged, as those eating watched him with cautious curiosity. He walked by the men, looking at their beets before stopping in front of a small kid, barely eighteen, who shifted his eyes away as he chewed, his guilt displayed in his nervous hunched shoulders.

"That's my Goddamn beet. Stand up."

The boy stammered a denial, holding the vegetable away from Chasteen before he jerked him to his feet, grabbing his collar and demanding through clenched teeth, "You're eatin' my beet, ain't ya? Admit it, that's the beet I brought back with me from the tracks." The boy started to shake his head, and Chasteen's mind went blank with rage. The impact of his fist on the boy's jaw brought him back, and the beet rolled under Jones's bunk as the young trooper fell to the floor, stunned.

"Why'd you do that Charlie? He didn't mean anything, he's just a scared kid," one of the men commented as they helped the boy to his trembling feet. Chasteen retrieved his half-eaten beet and dusted it off before speaking to the young trooper.

"Hey kid, I'm sorry. I shouldn't't've hit you. This place gets to me sometimes, you know?" The boy nodded, turning to walk toward his bunk, his hand pressed against his chin. "Forget it," he mumbled. He'd been scared more than hurt.

Spivey eased Chasteen's feelings of guilt. "Don't worry about it. Anybody would've done the same thing. It's life or death here. You got to fight for what's yours or you'll never make it."

Although Spivey's words were spoken sincerely, he acted on them less than many others of the group. Fighting had broken out everywhere and grew worse daily. Men stole food overnight and bickered over duties on the tracks, and most commonly, bunkmates fought because the prisoner in the top bunk lost control of his bladder during the night.

Pombano and a French-American known as "Duperry" were the men most often involved in fights. Both had hot tempers and aggressive natures, antagonizing other men.

Chasteen retrieved the small turnip left cooking on the stove and handed it to the prisoner he'd hit. He vowed to himself to control his temper at all costs.

CHAPTER 4

"Her DA! Jude!"

Mickelson turned as he followed five men out of the latrine and looked into the eyes of a guard. It was Henry. He turned and continued walking. The guard couldn't be talking to him.

"Du! Bist du ein Jude?" Mickelson again looked at Henry, seeing that Leeps had now joined him. They seemed to sneer as he met their gaze, and he realized they were addressing him. A chill ran through him as he stopped, letting the other prisoners walk on without him. The guards shouted and waved for him to come the twenty feet to stand with them. He moved toward them quickly. He had recognized one word unmistakably.

"I'm not Jewish," he exclaimed, looking from Leeps to Henry and back for a reaction. They exchanged a look, then turned to him with patronizing laughter. Henry nodded as he waved his finger at him. "Ja. Du bist ein Jude."

"Nein! I'm Danish. You know, Danish? Ich bin Danski."

"Danski?" Henry asked, as both he and Leeps laughed.

"Ja, ja! Danski. Mickelson is a Danski name. Mick-el-son, Danski, nicht Jude." They looked him over skeptically. Mickelson was a strongly built man of medium height, with handsome features and blue eyes. He met their looks with an honest, unflinching gaze. When they shrugged and turned away from him, he hurried after the prisoners toward the barracks, mulling over this disturbing occurrence.

Ironically, although he was not Jewish, another kid named Phillip Kleppe, who'd come with them from II-A, was. He looked like he could be Jewish, too, Mickelson thought, but Kleppe had been smart since his capture, avoiding trouble, being polite and unobtrusive, and the guards rarely noticed him.

In contrast, Mickelson and Watsick had been the cause of problems since their arrival, talking while they worked, taking breaks, stealing beets. Mickelson resolved to avoid these guards at all costs, and to no longer draw any attention to himself if possible. He'd heard what the Germans did with Jewish American soldiers and doubted there would be any way to prove his heritage if they decided he was a Jew.

As the men lined up to enter the pig barn for the night, Henry stared at Mickelson and spoke in his ear as he passed. "Vorsicht, Jude." He made a warning gesture with his finger.

Watsick watched the exchange and looked at his friend questioningly. "What was that about, Mick?"

"Henry thinks I'm Jewish."

Watsick shook his head in disbelief. "You must've misunderstood."

"How many meanings does *Jude* have, then?" Mickelson asked his friend, and they entered the barracks with new apprehension.

The following morning, Mickelson and Watsick made their progress toward the tracks, walking beside a good-natured old guard the men had nicknamed Pops. Pops was a decent man to the POWs, sympathizing after having been a prisoner himself to the British in World War I. As they walked, Pops looked at the two friends and grinned.

"Seid ihr Brüder?"

"Brothers?" Watsick asked with a laugh. "Nein."

"Ihr seht aus wie Brüder," Pops insisted.

"He's Polski, I'm Danski." Mickelson replied, motioning as he spoke, emphasizing himself as Danish. Pops looked at the two of them with an amused nod.

"Polski . . . Danski," Mickelson repeated, pointing at Watsick then himself several times.

"OK, Danski." The old guard laughed with a shrug, convinced.

The men were surprised to discover that the Jewish prisoner Kleppe spoke fluent German. He was the only prisoner who spoke more than a few words, and they encouraged him to act as interpreter. It was a dangerous move, putting Kleppe in the German spotlight, but Marlowe was convinced that he could get away with it.

Marlowe was anxious to bring some order to the group. He pondered now the challenge of building camaraderie among the men. He wasn't happy to see that the men were fighting more among themselves, and he couldn't always be there to break up quarrels. Several men were the main instigators, and the rest followed, hungry, tired, and irritable.

It was clear now that they would remain in this place for the duration of the war, and they would probably starve on the food they were rationed. Marlowe knew that several men were actively stealing from the others. A piece of food wasn't safe unless it was in your mouth, although none of them had come to the point of stealing openly. He had seen one man rat on another prisoner to avoid punishment. That had to be stopped. Marlowe knew how desperate the men's state of mind was becoming. They grew hungrier daily. Most suffered the symptoms of dysentery, and diarrhea was a rampant problem. The raw beets and turnips, mostly beets, were now a staple for the men, but they did little more than fill their stomachs with gases. Many men began to bloat up, their faces and necks swelling and turning a dull, dark red like the vegetables they ate.

"If I ever get outta here, I'm never eating another beet as long as I live," Bruton had said, and Marlowe agreed, feeling the burning sensation of the beet he'd eaten the night before swelling in his stomach. The lack of solid food contributed to the diarrhea, and many men grew weaker and more miserable as their condition worsened. Those who had retained their sense of humor competed in the barracks at night, one man dropping his pants as another lit a match behind him. When he cut loose with a fart, the flame was thrown several feet across the room as the men cheered and laughed.

Some of the POWs had already gone off to the doctors in the nearby town of Marlow and had not returned. Marlowe noticed that Jim Rizzuto was not looking well, and after the trooper had nearly collapsed twice at work, he asked him how he felt.

"I'm all right. I just feel a little sick lately. I can't sleep nights, no matter how hard I try," the trooper responded. Marlowe could sympathize, but little else.

On the sixth day of the internment, Henry intercepted Jones again as he passed onto the tracks. He pointed to his wrist, asking again to look at the prisoner's watch, and Jones sighed, wondering when the guard would take it from him.

"Ich gebe Ihner Brot für diese Uhr," the guard said, and Jones paused, trying to understand. He recognized the word Brot, meaning bread. Henry held his hands apart, measuring a large, imaginary loaf of bread, then pointed at the watch. Jones hesitated. He was hungrier than he could stand that morning, desperate for anything to eat other than a beet. An entire loaf of bread to himself could last for days. He couldn't see what good his watch was to him now. He could tell time by the sun. He didn't really need to know the exact time, anyway. The guards regulated their entire day, so what good was a watch? He unfastened the clasp and handed it to the eager guard.

"Can I have bread tonight? Brot heute abend?" The guard nodded in agreement, "Ja, ja," and walked off cheerfully.

That night, Henry handed him a loaf of bread after the other guards had left, and Jones tucked it under his coat before entering the barracks. He inhaled the smell, savoring it, and when he concentrated it seemed stronger than the smell of unwashed bodies, human waste, and pigs. He would eat a small section that night, then save the rest for the next day, tucking it under himself as he slept, to fend off thieves.

He bit off a portion in full view of the other men and ignored them with heroic effort. They could sell their own valuables if they were hungry. He did, however, hand a piece of bread to Turner, his closest friend and the only prisoner he completely trusted.

As the prisoners slept fitfully in their cold loft, an American soldier traveled toward them by train to be one of the few non-Airborne prisoners at 311/I. Railroad work required heavy labor and a strong constitution, and Pvt. Lou Fisher of the 109th Infantry, 28th Division, had the large frame Germans sought to undertake the job.

Until his capture on September 12, he had been making strong headway into western Germany and had reason to believe he would soon have the war behind him. It was alone in his foxhole at night when all that changed. With the slightest drizzle soaking his face beneath his poncho, Fisher looked out his foxhole at the dark sky. He was alone in his hole and knew that the rest of his division sat around him waiting, although there was no sign of them now.

Fisher had a lifetime's worth of fighting behind him that had started months before with the Invasion of Normandy. His fight across Omaha Beach had been more painful than he cared to remember. He had fought his way through it, losing his buddies and learning the value of human life in combat, until August, when the infantry arrived in Paris. Paris had been his reward. The French people had crowded around his truck, happily offering gifts of flowers and food and wine, and his regiment had marched twenty-four abreast down the Champs Élysées past the Arc de Triomphe, the sound of their boots pounding the street, echoing through the city, signaling the end of the German era in France.

He wrote to his wife on German stationery, telling her of the parade, relating to her openly, for the first time since joining the army, what he had been through. He worried about her when he sat in his foxhole near the German border, on the night of September 12, waiting without enthusiasm for the sunrise or the end of the fall drizzle.

He didn't have to be here. He was an old man to be in the infantry, having celebrated his twenty-seventh birthday in combat several months before. Most of the soldiers were just out of high school, while he had a job waiting for him at home, a wife and three children, and a jazz band he'd been playing with professionally for five years. He had sacrificed it all to be here now. He'd wanted to do his part for his country and his president, and his wife, Marie, had agreed without complaint. He didn't like to think of her struggling to raise their family alone, but at times like these, when all around him was quiet, cold, and unpleasant, memories of the comforts of home came creeping into his mind.

After his capture that night, Fisher spent a month in Neubrandenburg before his latest train ride into the fields of northeastern Germany. He was on his way to join the barn-dwelling prisoners of 311/I.

CHAPTER 5

As the barn door opened and harsh guttural orders came up the stairs, Jones awoke and sat forward, reaching under the mattress for his bread. He had groped for it several times during the night, feeling with comfort its dry edges, crumbling against his mattress. As the other men now crawled off their bunks and wandered down the stairs, Jones tried farther down the mattress by his feet, his hands scraping against bare slats of wood. He took apart the entire bunk and finally looked on the floor underneath it, but found nothing.

Accepting the loss of his bread, he sat on the floor shaking his head and mumbling, "I'll kill the son of a bitch," as the loft emptied of men.

He walked to the train station with conspicuous and murderous rage, looking the men over, trying to guess the thief. He had eaten only a few pieces from the loaf; someone else had gotten five men's rations from what remained. He suspected several prisoners but couldn't be sure. If he had to, he was prepared to whip every one of them.

At the station he stood staring, his fists clenched in his pockets, his eyes squinted nearly shut as they flitted from face to face. Even Turner stayed away from him. The men could easily guess what had happened. Jones had been an obvious target, with more bread than the rest of them had eaten over the past week.

He singled out a prisoner who had been in numerous fights about stealing in the past. He easily cornered the culprit, who was taller than he but not as muscular. The man was a Texan with a direct brazen stare, and he now regarded Jones with a mocking smile. Jones sucked air into his lungs before spitting out his anger.

"Where's my bread, you son of a bitch?"

"I don't know what you're talking about. Get the hell outta my way," he replied, and Jones lunged for him, mad enough to kill him, before Marlowe pulled him away with Rizzuto's and Bruton's help.

"That yellow asshole stole my bread! I traded my watch for that bread; the watch my father gave me."

"You don't know it was him. Forget it. Do you want to entertain the Krauts?" Marlowe answered.

Jones looked around him at the guards and several German civilians who stood nearby watching in amusement. A guard turned to a middle-aged woman and made a comment, to which they both laughed heartily. Jones felt his cheeks burn. His anger redirected itself from the prisoner to the Germans, then gradually dissipated. He stood alone with despair, watching as the morning train chugged toward them. His hunger could only get worse. But worse yet than the hunger was his humiliation.

As the train came to a full stop and the doors opened, the German people climbed aboard. Several children turned to stare at the prisoners, who were shoved back by the guards to make room. Jones felt like both a zoo animal and a slave; the token enemy; a scapegoat for German anger. He imagined how much better off he would have been if he had been killed instead of captured. Death couldn't be worse than this. Stan Watsick pounded him on the back good-naturedly as they climbed aboard the train, and he resolved to forget the bread and the watch.

Rizzuto stood in the train with his shoulder braced against the door. Heavy waves of pain hit him from his pounding head and cramping stomach. His temperature seemed to rise and fall constantly, and he wished that he were anywhere that he could lie down. The night before he had lain awake in his bunk, his shoulders and ribs tired and sore from night after night on the hard wooden frame. The straw mattress seemed to grow thinner every day and was so limp and soaked through from rain and urine that it was nearly useless.

At night he could hear the pigs grunting as they moved about peacefully in their pen, occasional scuffling and squealing the only sign of discord in their world. Closer sounds were less distracting: the movement of other men around the loft, the sound of someone using the giant chamber pot, groaning as he lost more diarrhea. Rizzuto's own bad health had pursued him from II-A. He knew that the food he ate made him sick, but without it he would starve. His choices were clear, and he lay night after night trying to think of better times and places, trying to ignore the sound of men crying, whimpering in a muffled way, or calling out in their sleep during nightmares of combat and captivity.

Throughout the day he walked through his work like a sleepwalker, an automaton. That was the way his days passed, and he tried hard not to notice anyone, or to allow anyone to notice him. He didn't fight with the other men; they were in the same position he was, and he knew it was pointless to take out his frustration on his own men.

Some of the guards actually liked Rizzuto, or at least respected his ability to mind his own business. Pops often talked and joked with him on the tracks. As his dysentery grew worse, he appreciated the mild-mannered Pops, who never bothered the prisoners. Once Rizzuto stopped his work to catch his breath, resting his arms across the giant hand drill, and looked up to see Pops watching him with a wry grin. Pops raised his rifle and aimed it at Rizzuto's head, his eyes squinting with amusement. He made a small popping sound with his teeth, as he pretended to fire the weapon. Rizzuto was compelled to laugh, and determined further to weather out the war. He knew if he was unable to carry his load, he would end up at the doctor's office in the city of Marlow, and from there he could only guess where they would send him.

At least a week passed since the paratroopers had arrived at 311/I, and each day was exactly like the other. They didn't have a day off; every day meant work, from Sunday to Saturday. The Geneva convention stated that prisoners of war were to work only as many hours as a German laborer was required. Unfortunately for the 311/I prisoners, Germans under Hitler worked long hours, as many as sixty a week or more, often seven days a week.

Watsick stared in horror as his urine ran from him bright red. He wondered if he had internal bleeding of some sort, a bad kidney infection from the ersatz coffee, which he'd heard rumored to contain flak. Comparing notes with Mickelson, however, he reassured himself that it was his diet. He now ate three or more red beets a day. They had become childishly simple to steal, and he was good at it. They fell from trains, and could be knocked loose if they didn't fall. Already a thin man, he now saw himself growing gaunt, while his stomach bloated out from the gaseous beets. He wasn't surprised when the diarrhea started. Without much solid food, it seemed as if the beets were running from him at both ends, equally liquid, and he often told himself he'd stop eating them. There were other ways to steal food. He had noticed the bakery and small dairy on the other side of their barn, adjacent to the pigpen, and questioned Kalkreuth as to the best way to steal food and avoid notice. It was watched only by an old Frenchman as they returned from work each evening, but they had to somehow evade the eyes of the guards.

Jim Bruton's mind ran along a similar path, determining to steal coal for the stove. Already the temperature plunged far below freezing each night, while the stove sat frozen without fuel and they slept with only their damp coats and a thin blanket to keep them warm. A few men had carried Red Cross–issue blankets with them from Stalag II-A, but he had no such luxury. He would wrap his heavy Polish overcoat around his body at night, his long legs exposed to the weather through his jump pants.

Coal was scarce in Germany. It was used not only to heat stoves, but also to fuel trains and even cars. He had seen the piles of coal in the basement of the Sanitz train station, and he imagined there had to be a way to get at them. He stared through the two-by-two slats, watching and waiting for an opportunity.

One small Frenchman came and went into the coal room from an outside door, and Bruton watched him speculatively. Some French and Polish prisoners had been in captivity among the Germans for so long that they were awarded a degree of freedom to come and go. They managed tasks that required less supervision and often lived in private houses, with small gardens in front to grow potatoes or other vegetables. This Frenchman enjoyed such freedoms and moved silently, glancing at the American laborers, then turning away, ignoring them with a deliberate frown. Bruton pressed his face between the wooden beams and called out to the middle-aged man before he could slip back out the door.

"Hey there, Frenchman, parley anglaise?"

The Frenchman shook his head nervously, uncomfortable around the prisoners. He had earned enough freedom to ride out the war, and like many French prisoners, he didn't want any trouble. Bruton summoned Duperry, a prisoner who spoke fluent French.

"Tell him to hand us over some of them briquettes," Bruton said. The Frenchman listened to Duperry's translation, then shook his head violently and turned toward the door.

"Hey, wait! What's it gonna hurt? No one'll know," he called out as the door shut behind the man. He tried to reach a lean arm between the beams, but his fingers were easily a foot from the closest briquette. He accepted temporary defeat with a sigh.

Each night grew colder as November approached. The rain had begun to fall more regularly, and often they returned to find their loft drenched. Kalkreuth, commissioned to assist compound cooks and maintain the farm, collected odd twigs and sticks around the compound when he could but was able to build only meager fires with his findings. Most of his day was occupied cooking in a bakery located in the camp. The lukewarm stove couldn't begin to dry their clothes, and the men bickered over the limited space on which to lay their sodden pants and jackets. The men tried to help Kalkreuth's efforts by searching out wood along the tracks for the fire. Occasionally they found coal briquettes that had bounced beet-style from the open cars of passing trains, but it was never enough. Most nights they slept with no fire and no heat.

As sick, injured, and defiant prisoners disappeared, a new replacement now joined them, the first non-airborne man in the compound, appearing one day in late October. 311/I had been home to the others for nearly two weeks. A soldier from the 109th Infantry, Lou Fisher joined their ranks and was well liked by the men. He was close to Marlowe's age, and the two men compared backgrounds as they stood for interminable hours every day at the stations. Fisher had a wife and three children waiting at home, and his concern for them was his foremost preoccupation. Marlowe shared his worries. It was painful to think of their families waiting for them, worried and without any certainty. Fisher told Marlowe of his family with a glow of pride, describing the way his small children had greeted him after a day's work, before he'd left for training. He stared ahead of him as he spoke, visualizing his home in Warrensburg, New York, instead of the barren railroad where they stood.

"They used to come at me all at once, all three kids, like an ambush. Sometimes I'd have candy or some kind of surprise in my lunch box for them that I'd picked up on my way home. So every day for them it was a game, to see what I had in my lunch box. Now my wife, Marie, is expecting our fourth." The two men shared a cigarette butt as they spoke, and Fisher gazed beyond the tracks and into the fields before him. "I sure do want to be home before the baby comes." They fell silent considering their young wives, trying to remember every detail of their features, and momentarily forgetting the discomforts around them.

CHAPTER 6

On the first day of November 1944, the men shuffled up the barn stairs toward their quarters, exhausted after another miserable and wet day. Before they could climb into their bunks, Marlowe called for a meeting by the stove. They looked at him with skeptical surprise. Most were eager to get to bed for four or five hours' sleep before returning to work. They'd been at the compound for at least fourteen days and had completed as many days of labor on the German railroad. Their spirits had plummeted to an all-time low.

Obediently they gathered around the stove, accustomed to following orders. Marlowe watched the silent, hollow, and apathetic men as he waited for them to assemble. Jones and Turner sat on the edges of their bunks a few feet from the stove, making room for several others to join them. The group was smaller than it had been two weeks before.

Jones glanced around at the assembly and guessed that there were fewer than forty prisoners left. Where the others were, he didn't know. He'd noticed that a few sick prisoners had gone to the hospital in Marlow, a town eight miles away. He didn't recall them coming back. Several men at the railroad had been dragged off somewhere for a beating, and he didn't recall their returning either. He hadn't been much concerned with the comings and goings of others.

"It seems to me we're gettin' to be a pretty sorry bunch of soldiers," Marlowe said, looking at the wan faces around him. "The Germans are working this situation just right. They get free slave labor outta us, and free entertainment too, because we fight worse than we did with the enemy. It seems to me if we're going to survive this war, we're going to have to adjust our attitudes. Now I don't see that there's any reason why we should make things easier on the Krauts. We're stuck here for now, until we think of a way out. But we can make those Jerries squirm." The men shrugged and nodded vaguely, unconvinced.

"First of all, though, we got to work together. Nobody here is the enemy— they are. We're stuck here together, and we ought to help each other out. If we all try to work together, we're more likely to survive than if we keep being concerned with our own personal problems.

"We're all pretty much the same, tired and hungry and missing home. But we can make this tolerable. I hear from Kalkreuth, here, that there's a good supply of bread in that bakery next door. If a couple men got the attention of old Leeps, someone could get down in there for a second."

"There's an ol' Frenchman out there working every night," one prisoner pointed out, and Marlowe shrugged.

"Sure, he's real old; he wouldn't even notice if you moved fast. And I've seen chickens a couple times running around the compound. Those'd taste pretty good. And I hear there's a plentiful supply of food at the doctor's office in Marlow, if you can get there and come back." He looked around at the men, who were listening attentively, forgetting for the moment to hack and cough, scratch at the boils on their necks, or pick at their itchy scalps.

"The point is, we got to work as a team—cooperate. If we agree to share all the food evenly, keep a pile of turnips and beets and whatever else we could get, and divide it fairly, we won't have much to fight about."

"Aw, that's no fun," Pombano said, cracking his knuckles with a wry grin, and Duperry let out a hoarse laugh. Marlowe glanced at them and continued.

"And we got to do something about these Goddamn Krauts. They been beatin' us down, just havin' the time of their lives picking on us, seeing us scared and hurt. And look at you all, we're most of us airborne and all of us damn good soldiers. The Krauts are scared of us, that's why they gather around starin' at us at the train station. They think the U.S. Airborne is a pack of bloodthirsty killers. They think we killed their kids or husbands and smiled while we did it. That's what kind of a reputation we got. So they stand around and watch us fight and whimper and complain, and they love it. We don't have to give 'em that satisfaction. Hell, we're still alive, we still got a right to fight. We're Americans, ain't we? We can't let them see us break down, we shouldn't give 'em the satisfaction. Don't you hate to see that foreman, ol' Flop Ears, so pleased with himself? Who the hell is he, anyway? He's not even a military man, he's no better'n a 4-F; any one of us could as easy kill him with our bare hands as look at him. We got to just keep things in perspective and try to make life a little easier for us and harder for them. We can't fight any more of this war with a gun, but we can do whatever we can to hurt the Germans from here."

"We don't have to work so fast," Jones volunteered. "It's real easy to turn the swivel once one way and twice back the other without the Krauts even noticing what you're doing. You can work for hours looking real busy without making any progress at all."

"And we don't have to take such pains in tampin' under the tracks. Supposin' a train derailed 'cause we didn't know how to do the job right? What are they going to do to all forty of us?" Bruton offered.

"Cut back our rations," someone responded.

"Then we steal more food, always have something around for hard times. If the Germans keep losing this war, they're going to run low of what little they give us anyway. We should be ready for that," Lou Fisher pointed out.

"We could get more beatings, too."

"We're already gettin' beat for nothing. What's worse about gettin' beat 'cause you really did somethin'?"

The men began to plan together with enthusiasm. A buzz of conversation broke out in the loft as men who had never spoken to each other now shared ideas. They had all considered a way either to escape or to steal food or tobacco but had never shared their plans. Now together they began to come up with workable objectives.

In the morning they assembled, tired but with boosted spirits. Some men joked with Leeps and the guards as they drank their rations of ersatz coffee.

On the tracks, the foreman barked orders and insults at the prisoners. Once again the morning train had arrived on schedule and they hadn't completed the tracks. Only two sections of rail were needed to allow it passage, but the men worked with newfound ineptitude. The infuriated foreman paced and hurled his fists in the air in vain.

"Dummkopf! Schweinhund!"

"Am I mistaken or is he callin' me a pig dog?" Bruton asked Jones with a grin. "What the hell is it, a pig or a dog? I can't be both."

After waiting thirty minutes, the engineer jumped out of the train to speak curtly with the foreman. He smoked a cigarette and tossed the butt in the gravel before climbing back into the engine. One of the prisoners scrambled to retrieve it and tucked it in another prisoner's pocket. A cigarette butt was a valuable commodity. The guards and foreman crushed their butts out when they were finished smoking, to ensure that they couldn't be smoked again. Only Pops occasionally saved a half-smoked cigarette for the prisoners.

The engineer nosed the train to within a few feet of the men working below, and continued to inch forward as they worked. The prisoners concentrated on their slow progress, deaf to the threatening shouts. Stan Watsick slowly tamped the gravel under the newly fixed rails, knowing full well that the tamping had already been done at least once. He painstakingly smoothed over gravel that was already secure with the appearance of great concentration. He looked up as the foreman faced him, barking orders in a guttural language. The foreman's face and large ears flushed red, and the cords in his neck protruded dangerously as if ready to explode from frustration. Watsick took in the grim sight, then glanced at Mickelson and shrugged. He turned his back on the foreman and continued what he was doing.

Mickelson looked at his friend and laughed. "You crazy asshole," he said.

Watsick looked at him and shrugged again. "I can't understand a Goddamn word he's sayin'."

When the train finally heaved into motion across the repaired tracks, it had been delayed another forty-five minutes, and the prisoners watched it pass with a feeling of accomplishment. Several cheered, while the Germans could only assume the prisoners' joy was due to finishing the track, not delaying the train.

That evening they were given a firm lecture, which Kleppe translated for them simply.

"Keine Suppe diesen abend. No soup tonight."

As they trudged home, they pondered this new problem. Without soup, they were surviving the day on one piece of bread.

They lined up in front of the latrines and looked around with impatient eyes. Only one guard, Henry, watched them lazily. He as usual kept one eye suspiciously on Mickelson.

Chasteen got Spivey's attention with a tap on the shoulder and pointed. "I just saw the most beautiful sight of my life," he said, and Spivey followed his eye. A scrawny chicken ducked around the side of the latrines. They glanced at Henry, then slipped behind the latrines, disappearing into the darkness.

The chicken bobbed its head, moving cautiously as if aware of its pursuers. The latrines emptied into a large gully sprinkled with lye, and Chasteen and Spivey skirted it, cornering the chicken easily. It was a skeletal, unhealthy bird with muck-caked feathers and cloudy eyes, but it could make a decent substitute for the soup they would be without that night. As Chasteen reached for it, the bird squawked and ran between Spivey's legs. They lunged backward at its retreating form, then began scrambling in horrified alarm. Together they fell backward into the latrine gully. The substance they now swam in was largely liquid, and they sank to their shoulders as they floundered in panic. Stifling groans of disgust, first Chasteen then Spivey dragged free of the muck. For several minutes they sat looking at each other without comment. When they returned to the other prisoners to be counted, Henry looked them over with disbelief, then waved his hand in front of his face and continued past. The other prisoners backed away.

"What the hell have you two been doin'?" Bruton asked, laughing outright at their grisly appearance.

Spivey used his drinking water that night to clean what he could of his clothes, and eventually, over the course of the weeks, the smell faded into the fabric of their clothing and the pores of their skin.

That Sunday the men enjoyed their first day off. Rain pummeled the roof above them, and the pigs below grunted and stirred restlessly in their confines.

The men sat locked in the leaky loft, sleeping or playing cards and smoking cigarette nubs as they discussed food and women. Chasteen had the best stories. He had a history with women that left the other men in respectful awe.

One of the younger troopers approached Marlowe in the afternoon, suggesting that they conduct a prayer meeting. He offered a Bible he'd brought with him through combat and his capture. They set up a group around the stove, and most of the men joined in, their faith in God and religion at its highest point since they'd been inducted. Several other men refused to participate and kept to themselves throughout the session, while the men prayed for their families and for their own survival.

Monday morning Duperry refused to be roused from his bunk to work. The steady rain had grown to a storm overnight, and the men had hoped dubiously that they would be spared another day's work if the downpour continued. But now they listened to the familiar "heRAUS!" and climbed to their feet with sore reluctance. Duperry remained where he lay, and they watched as Leeps approached him.

"Bist du krank?" They all recognized the German word for sick.

"Ya, real crank," he answered, his face screwed up belligerently. He was a man who didn't like rules, and as he opened his mouth for Leeps's thermometer, he winked at the men. Leeps ushered the other men down the stairs, and they glanced back at the smug prisoner in his bed as they left, wondering how he could get away with it. If he was sick, he would have to walk to the doctor's office, which was eight miles away, but an eight-mile walk in the rain was a luxury compared with the workday they were about to put in.

The men left without Duperry and envied him as they huddled under a roof edge at the station in a vain attempt to stay dry. When civilians hurried toward the station, protected by umbrellas and raincoats, the guards forced the prisoners out into the downpour to make room. The guards made several comments as they regarded the wet prisoners and laughed, earning an amused murmur from the German commuters. Kleppe translated reluctantly for the prisoners: "Maybe the rain will wash away some of their smell."

Mickelson looked into the face of a new guard as he was jerked away from the awning, and for the first time he noticed his tormentor's absence. He asked Pops where Henry had gone.

"Russland," Pops said, making a slashing motion across his throat.

Mickelson was overwhelmed with relief. He had become more and more convinced that he would be sent to a concentration camp, as the guard continued to call him "Jude," often in front of German civilians and other guards.

Most of the guards were recently off the Russian front and recuperating from injuries until they were fit again for combat. They were hard and bitter men, and the new guard, Herbert, older but not unlike Henry in appearance, was gruff and unfriendly, treating the prisoners with hostile impatience.

The men laughed and exchanged jokes in the rain, despite their miserable condition. They were resolved to be in high spirits. Several scrubbed at their hair and armpits as if bathing in the rain shower, laughing and winking at the German civilians.

Work was almost impossible. The prisoners had not been issued raincoats, and the wool coats that most of them wore soaked up the German rain and weighed down on their shoulders as if there were rocks in the lining. They worked in muck, often losing their footing and stumbling. It was a dangerous situation for those who drove stakes held by another man, trying to keep their stability as they heaved with the sledgehammer.

Rizzuto watched the rain fall as he shoveled wet ballast and wondered over Duperry's luck at being sent to the doctor. Yet, as sick as he was, he continued to work. He had never considered trying to avoid it, and he was now more determined than ever to continue with his share of the work. His dark hair lay plastered against his face as he bent over the rails, and streams of ice water ran down his face. He wiped his eyes repeatedly with a sodden coat sleeve. As he glanced up, he noticed the one-armed guard approaching under a large raincoat. With his right hand, the guard pulled the inevitable riding crop loose from his coat and brought it down on several men's backs, but the weapon was useless against their numb skin.

Chasteen stood near Rizzuto with his sledgehammer in his hand and shouted over the wind and rain as he pushed rivers of water out of his hair. "This kinda work can't be allowed according to the Geneva convention. It's one thing we get no Red Cross packages and not enough food, but this is too Goddamn much."

Mickelson nodded in agreement, blinking hard to clear the water from his eyes. With Henry gone, he felt his rebelliousness resurface.

"Hey, Marlowe, do we gotta do this work?" Chasteen asked their leader.

"Well, now, if we ain't going to work in this rain, we got to all quit together," Marlowe answered, standing upright and blinking at the dark sky. The guards and foreman watched them from covered seats by the train station, raising their rifles in preparation for trouble. Several men beside Marlowe and Chasteen put down their tools and looked up expectantly, following Mickelson, who had already thrown his hand drill aside.

The foreman stood and raised his rifle. He pointed it at Marlowe's head. All the men on the tracks froze, staring at the foreman then Marlowe. After several seconds, Mickelson reached again for his drill. Gradually and bitterly the men returned to their work, and the foreman sat down. The prisoners were not prepared for a confrontation.

CHAPTER 7

Two days had passed, and the rain with them, before the men returned to their barracks to find Duperry sitting by the stove comfortably, a fire lit and a grin on his face.

"Look at the lot of you, what a mess. I just got through washing up and had a nice, big dinner." The men surrounded him, pressing for information, and he lay back on his elbows, taking his time to explain.

"I fooled ol' Leeps with that thermometer. It showed me with a 103 temperature. All I did was wait till he turned the other way and rubbed that little old thermometer against my blanket. Practically caught fire before I put it back in my mouth."

"Shit, that's the oldest trick in the book." The prisoners broke into laughter, and Duperry sat up, holding his hands toward the stove.

"It worked, didn't it? You should see some of the food the doctor's got in the pantry. I brought back some cheese and eggs. And the sheets were fresh and clean, and I got water to clean myself up like a king. That's the life. I wouldn't be back here if I hadn't been so excited they could see I was well again and sent me."

The men cooked Duperry's six eggs and carefully split them forty ways. They broke the cheese into chunks and put them on their rations of bread, then melted them on the wood stove. It was the best meal they'd had in months, and the smell of cheese and eggs lifted the barracks into a level of fragrant ecstasy that set the pigs to grunting below.

As they ate, Chasteen told the men about a German woman he'd noticed walking along the tracks several days in a row. "She's a schoolteacher, and the prettiest gal I seen in a long time. She gave me a look this morning, and I know what that look meant, too. I can't believe none of you queers noticed her."

"Sure, we saw her all right, that big, fat toothless woman that threw a rock at Bruton. She may've given you a look all right."

The men laughed as Chasteen responded, "That wasn't her. She's a hot, little blond gal, and I'm going to give her a ride to work tomorrow on the handcar."

The men were highly skeptical. Most of them had lost interest in women as their hunger had increased, and they seldom gave women a glance.

"OK, Charlie, you just ask old Flop Ears if you can take that German gal for a ride; maybe he'll give you the keys to his car."

"I'm still holding out for Flop Ears' daughter, myself," Lindsey said with a chuckle, falling back onto his bunk.

The following morning the men worked in Sanitz, across a space of track in the center of town, beyond the schoolteacher's route. Disappointed, Chasteen allowed Bruton to take the handcar in his place. Bruton and a new young replacement prisoner took the new guard, Herbert, with them several miles down the tracks to a boxcar holding their rails and tools. It took both prisoners all their strength, each grabbing an end and heaving, to pull the rails down one at a time and drop them onto the handcar. Each of the ten-foot strips of steel weighed several hundred pounds. Herbert watched as the prisoners struggled with the third rail. As the two men dropped it onto the handcar, Bruton let out a scream that sent the guard leaping from his seat. The rail had landed on Bruton's thumb, crushing it beyond recognition. Pulling his hand loose, Bruton ran circles around the tracks in pain. The guard silently watched his dance for several minutes, then shouted for him to get back to work. The railroad couldn't wait for his thumb.

"Hell, you all right?" the other prisoner asked, and Bruton summoned a wan smile, for the first time unable to crack a joke. He carried the remaining rails with one hand, the other useless and throbbing sharply from the end of his thumb up to his wrist. They required twice the usual time to load, and Herbert waited, a look of tolerance if not sympathy on his plump face. He didn't dislike the tall prisoner, who had shown a good sense of humor despite the conditions of the weather and the work. Herbert offered to look at the thumb, and Bruton extended it to him, turning his head away from the sight. He felt as if it were three times its normal size, and it had turned several colors of red and blue. He flinched when the guard touched it. Herbert muttered a comment to himself that neither prisoner could understand. Bruton shrugged and retrieved his thumb, determined to put it out of his mind.

After three weeks of imprisonment and hard labor, the prisoners were a hardened and filthy collection of men. Their own mothers wouldn't have recognized them. A coughing and hacking symphony accompanied the group everywhere, while men continually ran for bushes or even, forgoing modesty, dropped their pants along the tracks. Nearly all suffered from diarrhea associated with dysentery.

They were desperate by this time to steal food other than beets. Almost as important as food were cigarettes, and the prisoners constantly combed the ground for butts. Every guard was aware of a dozen eyes on him each time he lit up a cigarette, as the men waited for him to drop it.

The men in bunks along the far wall of the loft fell asleep each night to the fragrant scent of tobacco. They finally stuck their heads against the wall and, staring through the narrow slats, realized that on the opposite side hung pounds of drying tobacco. Lindsey, Spivey, and Chasteen began searching the tracks for wire and secreted a piece back to slide through the narrow gaps in the wall. Chasteen lay on his back as he moved the wire against the tobacco, gently breaking small sections free until he finally was rewarded with a few dried leaves. They rolled the tobacco tightly in a section of newspaper and relished the smoke, as Mickelson took the wire and began fishing.

They spent most of their days in Sanitz now, where they found a growing number of angry civilians gathered along the tracks to harass them. At least a dozen more men had gone to the hospital and hadn't returned. Some looked like they were going to die, while others were probably sent on to another camp, unfit for detail. Now the replacements were trickling in—a new man in the barracks, then a strange new face on the tracks. Most were paratroopers, and the veteran prisoners pumped them for news of the war. What they heard from the Germans was always bad—the Allies were always losing, Hitler had always made more progress.

Rizzuto continued to feel worse as time passed, and a guard eventually sent him to the doctor. He was back in the barracks the same night, lying in his bunk awake and miserable. Several weeks of almost no sleep, added to a bad case of dysentery, made him a sorry case, and the men offered to save him the easier work on the tracks, but he stubbornly refused.

The men's boots were thinning on the soles and did little to protect their feet from the frozen ground. Watsick began wrapping his feet in newspapers found at the station and bits of cloth torn from his blanket. At night the cold got to him more than ever, as his feet, even with their wrapping, became frostbitten. Although Mickelson laughed, Watsick ripped a slat off his bunk, leaving a four-inch gap under the small of his back, and cut it up for stove fuel. They had exhausted the small supply of wood they had gathered for the stove, and often it stayed unlit overnight as the frosty night winds blew in through the gaps along the windows and walls of the barn.

As the prisoners waited each evening in the basement of the train station,

Bruton stared through the slats separating him from the coal briquettes, piled so high but so out of reach on the other side. He watched the Frenchman enter and considered speaking to him, but remained silent as the man came and went. After the door was shut and locked behind him, Bruton tested the strength of the closest beam, then another, until he felt one that gave slightly in his hands. Jones, one of the brawniest of the men, helped him work on the top and bottom, trying to ease it loose. Before their progress brought them reward, the guards flung open the door, and they jumped away from their work before Leeps ordered them to come out.

As the days passed, Dan Jones began plotting an escape with Doug Turner. He had thought of escaping almost constantly since his capture, and now the idea consumed him, his planning and certainty of success the only thing that made his days bearable. He had no concrete plan. Already two prisoners had escaped from the tracks on one of the first days of their internment; none of the other prisoners had even noticed at the time. Within a day, however, they were caught, and the guards informed the prisoners that the two men had been shot. The risk didn't worry Jones or Turner. Jones approached Marlowe with his plans, and Marlowe shook his head with a skeptical smile. He was dubious, given that they were so deep into German territory. There was little in any direction that would lead to freedom. East would take them to occupied Poland; south led farther into Germany; west would mean weeks of walking to reach Allied lines under constant risk of capture; and north offered only the Baltic Sea, immense, stormy, and ice cold with another German winter looming just weeks away. Marlowe understood Jones's desire to escape and his feeling of invincibility. He was a nineteen-year-old kid and thought he could do anything. He was fool-hardy. Marlowe told him as much but agreed that if they could think of a way out, he would support and assist them any way he could.

As Marlowe and Jones discussed this plan in the loft, another day's work finished, Mickelson and Watsick were sent for water with Herbert. Every night two prisoners were appointed to fill a large water bucket for the men at a communal pump located in Dettmannsdorf. As they neared the water pump, Herbert tersely ordered them to slow down. They heard loud, boisterous laughter and moved forward to see a large group of soldiers in the dark, standing around the pump. They were dressed in SS uniforms and smoked and joked in the dark casually with an air of arrogance and confidence that was not unlike that of the American paratroopers before combat. Herbert froze, his nervousness apparent even in the dark. He was a regular army man and was clearly intimidated by these German supersoldiers. They moved cautiously toward the pump, Herbert warning them to be quiet. The prisoners pumped water into the bucket as Herbert hung back in the shadows, his hands gripping his rifle. Watsick looked at the guard in surprise, then abandoned the pump and wandered over to a pair of SS men leaning against a brick wall. He broke into their conversation abruptly.

"Haben Zigarette? Tabak?" he asked, looking from one to the other with a smile. Mickelson looked at Herbert and could almost hear the guard's gasp of horror. But the guard remained where he was, watching in silence. Watsick waited hopefully for a response, turning to several other SS men, but they only stared at the prisoner in disbelief, then waved him away, more amused than annoyed. Watsick shrugged and returned to the water pump, grinning at Herbert, who clutched his head in outrage. They hurried away from the soldiers with a bucket of water only half full, Herbert hissing, "Schnell, schnell!"

Watsick walked silently, brooding over his bad luck with the SS men. He hadn't had a smoke in several days, and he had hoped a drag off a cigarette would help appease his hunger. As they returned past the bakery, with an elderly Frenchman working in front, he dropped behind Herbert. Instinctively, Mickelson engaged Herbert in conversation. Mickelson spoke a broken and Americanized version of German, grammatically butchering the language. But he enjoyed speaking it, and all the guards found great amusement in his stories. As Herbert and Mickelson spoke, Watsick darted through the front door of the bakery and grabbed a loaf of bread from the kitchen table, tucking it in his coat. When he rejoined the guard and prisoner, he realized that he had managed to pull off the feat without being noticed. He could hardly control his triumphant pride as he carried the loaf safely into the loft, his first real success against his captors.

The prisoners' good luck extended into the next day, as Jones and Bruton felt the two-by-two beam give way and slide loose from its position in the train station basement, leaving an eight-inch opening. Bruton tried to squeeze through, with the men cheering him on, but was stopped short, his chest unable to clear the narrow space, even after he exhaled and pushed with all his strength.

"Who's the smallest man here?"

Spivey came forward and managed to slide through after several moments' doubt, and he raised his arms in triumph before the piles of coal briquettes.

"Move fast, Spivey, the train'll be here any minute."

He went to work stuffing coal in his pockets. He then handed briquettes out in fistfuls for the men to shove into any and every empty pocket. All the men joined in, caught up in the excitement, and as the door opened, Spivey slid through and moved the beam back into place, wiping his hands on his pants. The black smudges would not show on any of the other men—their clothes were filthy anyhow—but Spivey, who was fanatically clean, was conscious of the striking black smudges. He held his hands loosely at his sides, sneaking past the guards without detection. That night he used his drinking water to clean his pants.

The fire burned hot throughout the night, and Spivey hung his pants near it to find them warm and dry in the morning. Turner and Jones, sleeping closest to the stove, basked in the warmth luxuriously as a light snow fell outside.

When Leeps came for them in the morning, he paused at the top of the stairs. The loft was warmer than any home in Germany. He looked at the hot burning stove, then shrugged and continued past it. He was in a bad mood that morning, and the men hurried out to the front yard for roll call, avoiding him until his temperament changed.

When the men reached the work site, Pops pulled Jones and Turner out of the ranks and motioned for them to climb aboard a handcar. Pops explained that the two would be spending the day chopping wood for him in his back garden. He lived in a small house not far from 311/I in Dettmannsdorf, a quiet and stern farming town of no more than a thousand residents. The civilians were hostile to the prisoners, but less so than the people of Sanitz or Marlow. Most Dettmannsdorf residents had worked hard all their lives. Many had been born in the same house they would die in, and their style of living had not changed noticeably from that of their grandparents. They were far removed from the modern world of Berlin and Hamburg and had not been as closely touched by the war as some of those that now were bombed commonly by the American Aircorps and the RAF.

Pops lived with his wife, a quiet, portly woman in her sixties. As the two men went to work with their axes, he walked into the kitchen and sat in the window reading a newspaper. The job was easy and they managed it leisurely, the relief from railroad work lifting a heavy weight from their shoulders. It was a warm afternoon for November, although the ground was frozen and a cool wind had begun to pick up from the Baltic Sea, some twenty or thirty miles to the north.

By late afternoon they had stacked several neat piles of firewood, and Pops hurried them back to the train station. He left them there for a minute, walking into the station office to speak with a railroad man. They stood suddenly unattended, knowing they could escape anywhere, yet each direction led through an active street where they would surely be noticed. They watched as a truck driver unloaded his cargo, setting a stack of boxes beside the back door of a brick building. Within several minutes he drove off. Jones exchanged a look with Turner and moved casually toward the boxes, glancing around him as he went. They were completely alone in the quiet back street, and he and Turner pried open the top box. It was filled to the top with orange marmalade. They stared at their find in disbelief and opened the box wide, plunging their hands in and sliding gobs of jelly into their pockets. The sounds of footsteps and young voices came around the corner suddenly.

Jones and Turner slammed the box shut, trying to wipe their sticky hands clean as they walked back to the doorway where Pops had left them. They were intercepted halfway there by a large group of boys, who circled them hostilely. Most of the boys were between the ages of eight and twelve, and all stood below Jones's and Turner's shoulders. They were all dressed alike, not unlike American Boy Scouts, but in brown and black shorts and shirts and swastika armbands. All were blond and blue-eyed and shared the same hateful expression as they formed a tighter circle around the two Americans. The boys were armed with rifles, and some were already pointing their weapons at the men. Jones held his hands over his sticky, sweet pockets, terrified of detection. Both men circled helplessly, looking at the faces around them and willing Pops to come back as the boys began shouting abuses. Several boys kicked the men in the shins and ankles, as the prisoners now searched the door of the train station, desperate for Pops's return. The boys' shouts grew riotous, and a larger boy reached up and shoved Jones backward. Once on the ground, Jones knew that both he and Turner were done for, and he scrambled for his footing as several boys behind him kicked at his feet. He raised a fist and fought the temptation to strike the boy before him in the jaw.

They heard the sound of an adult shouting with a flood of relief, and the boys hesitated, then turned away. The man who rushed to the group was dressed similarly to the Hitler Youth, and they obeyed him immediately, falling away from the men reluctantly and walking down the street in the other direction. When Pops returned he found the prisoners so pale and shaken that he guessed they were both sick and hurried them back to the compound.

CHAPTER 8

E ach morning, Jones awoke anticipating Leeps's shouts and started scratching the boils that lined his neck. Every day they were more swollen and painful than the night before, while new ones seemed to fill with each hour. The pain of these boils was one of the most intolerable aspects of his captivity, taking a secondary position only to the constant humiliation of their daily lives. Since his and Turner's close call with the Hitler Youths, he had become more resentful and restive than ever. The daily disgrace of the work, the constant insults from the guards, the spitting and kicking by the civilians were all nothing compared with being ridiculed and ruled over by children.

Bitterly he scrubbed at the boils with his hand at night, at the station, and especially at work. The collar of his shirt rubbed against them so relentlessly on the railroad tracks that he thought he'd lose his mind.

On a November day, the first heavy snow fell, and the prisoners stumbled out into a bitter, white landscape. They worked with bare hands cracked and unnaturally purple. A newcomer joined them at the tracks, a small German boy of ten or eleven named Sylvester. Sylvester was a pale, thin boy without the blond hair and blue eyes that would have allowed him the superior status of the Hitler Youth. He was an apprentice to the foreman, there to learn the railroad trade so that one day he could take over the operation of a railway station himself. His superiority over the prisoners was immediately apparent. He marched up to Mickelson, his eyes defiant, his hands held behind his back in imitation of the foreman. He watched the prisoner for several minutes before announcing, "I speak English very well."

Mickelson straightened and looked the boy over as he rubbed his raw hands. "Do you? What's your name?" he asked the boy, who hesitated and grew confused.

"You are son of bitch!" he shouted, and ran off in his small leather shoes.

He learned to torment the men in a gradual childish way, watching them in his spare time, of which he had a lot. Occasionally he would watch for as long as an hour while a prisoner tamped gravel under the tracks neatly and evenly, as if studying his technique. As soon as the prisoner moved on, he snatched the shovel and dug the ballast loose again, then called the foreman over to see the shoddy job the American had done. They learned quickly that the boy spoke no English at all, save for a few obscenities, which he used as often as possible. None trusted him, but all were too preoccupied with their own tired shoulders, sickness, and hunger, as well as the increasing cold, to give the troublesome boy much notice.

On Sylvester's third day at the tracks, Jones reached for his shovel and felt the handle stick to his hands. Peals of laughter came from the boy, and Jones looked up through waves of rage as he realized that the boy had smeared tar on the handle of his shovel and had been waiting for hours for him to pick it up. He didn't dare follow his instinct to bash the child with the shovel or at least shout at him. Instead he wiped his palms uselessly onto his sticky pants. Deliberately he turned his back on the boy, and the laughter died to a disappointed murmur.

News of the war was not good. More than a month had passed, and their hopes of being on a ship home for Thanksgiving waned, then died. Patton was making no progress, and the guards reminded them of this daily.

Jones was desperate to get out. His health was good, other than the boils and a case of diarrhea. He sympathized with some of the men who were worse off than he. As more and more of the sick disappeared, younger and greener kids replaced them. How these kids had gotten into the airborne he couldn't imagine, but he considered it another bad sign for the state of the war, if seventeen-year-olds were jumping into combat. Now there were few men who were as seasoned as he, Lou Fisher and Marlowe being the two oldest. Of all the men, Jones was the one who could escape, who had a chance. He believed it, and the men began to gather by the stove at night, considering ways out. They drew up crude maps and guessed at the distance to the ocean from Rostock. Sweden or Norway seemed an ideal escape route. They doubted Russia would be safe. They'd heard rumors from the Poles that the Russians and Americans were not so friendly as they had been.

Turner insisted on joining him, and Jones agreed. Turner was his closest friend at the compound, and he trusted his judgment. The third prisoner to join them was another volunteer: Duperry. He'd been anxious to escape ever since his return from the doctor's, when Leeps had taken a sudden and violent dislike to him. Duperry had been cocky, pleased with himself for his skill at fooling the Germans. His attitude toward Leeps, as well as the foreman, was often insolent, and they punished him often. Leeps's childish and unpredictable temperament focused all of its rage on this French-American.

So one evening, the three most determinedly impatient men of work compound 311/I began making plans. They examined and reexamined their map, looking over the railroad and the fields around them, the busy train stations, and the compound yard itself. Everyone agreed that a successful escape would have to take place after dark. The cold temperatures were deadly now, especially at night, and they gathered pieces of blankets and cloth to use as scarves and extra socks. All the prisoners chipped together to save up pieces of bread, enough to last the three men several days. They put together three compasses from the metal buttons off their paratroop jackets, attaching two together so that the top could spin easily when tilted.

They found their means of escape through a process of elimination. The only time that the men were not watched at night, but were still free from the confines of the barracks or a train station, was during the evening latrine run. The latrine was a small shack, with a ten-foot board inside extending above a six-foot hole, and a thin wall behind it. The shack seated six men at a time, and one guard stood in front, hurrying them through in groups and watching them come out only casually. If they could pry one or two boards loose behind the toilets, the men could slide out the back, into the free countryside behind the latrine. There, if they were careful, they could walk right out of the compound without being noticed. The other men would bunch up as they came out of the latrine, one man leaving from each of three groups, so that their absence would be distributed less noticeably. They worked on their plans late into the night in their loft, kept awake during the day by their excitement.

Upon securing a plan, the men went to work on the tracks the following day, singing raucous songs and joking together with uncommonly high spirits.

As Jones and Chasteen pumped the handcar down the tracks in the early morning, they sang in booming voices, "I've been workin' on the railroad, all the livelong day. I've been workin' on the railroad, just to pass the time awaaaaay." The guard sat on the edge of the car with the loose sleeve of his armless shoulder flapping in the icy wind, regarding them unamusedly. They passed civilians, who stopped and stared, dismayed to see the prisoners enjoying themselves. Chasteen smiled and waved at the young schoolteacher, who passed with her books in her hand, and she gave the handsome prisoner a cautious smile. He called out to her in German before the guard silenced him.

Kalkreuth had located a crowbar while dumping the chamber pot and had hidden it in the latrine behind the toilets. At night each group of men took a turn prying at the farthest plank along the wall, then quickly tucked the crowbar back into the shadows.

After a week of preparation, the three prisoners were ready to make good their escape. They worked breathlessly on the tracks through the day and stood with impatience on the train returning them to Dettmannsdorf. Before they disembarked, Marlowe shook hands with each of the three escapees. He harbored serious concerns about their chances of surviving in the dead of winter in the middle of Germany while being hotly pursued by the entire country. But he understood their desire to take some action, no matter how risky.

"You three better make it, 'cause I ain't covering for you all for nothing," he said with an easy grin.

CHAPTER 9

Jones had watched both Duperry and Turner enter the latrine consecutively with the first and second group of six. He stood with the fourth group, waiting for the third to emerge. As the men in the first two groups had returned from the latrines, Jones had looked away, too nervous to count them. He glanced at Herbert, to see him standing ten feet behind him with a phlegmatic expression as he listened to the bantering of a young prisoner. The prisoner had been posted to distract the guard until the third man had escaped. Those who'd already been in the latrine huddled in clusters, moving constantly in a confused pattern. How many of them there were would be hard to guess even if someone tried. They moved toward the barracks, past Herbert, who paid little notice. He'd been through the same routine with them dozens of times, and it was bitterly cold on this night, the layer of snow crusted and frozen in the yard to a dangerous slick.

Jones concentrated on his nonchalance, exchanging a few short words with Chasteen standing beside him. Chasteen spoke to him with his usual easy southern manner. "You just keep on goin', buddy, and bring back the whole Goddamn airborne, and every tank you can find."

Once in the latrine, the men surrounded Jones, pounding him on the back jubilantly and offering words of encouragement. It was the first time the prisoners had accomplished anything, and they felt good. They stood watching as he climbed behind the toilet seat and slid through the narrow space, sacrificing their day's turn at the latrine to cheer him on softly.

Once through the hole, he looked around him to see that he was hip-deep in muck. He pulled himself out onto the frozen ground, and shivered in the smell of human waste as snow whirled around him. His legs were wet, but the cold wind would dry them eventually. He felt nothing but his own desire to run. Instead he paused, holding his breath as he listened to the voices on the other side of the latrine. Herbert barked at the fourth group of men to hurry it up as they came out. Afraid to hear if Herbert noticed him missing, he started to move, recklessly fast, trying to stick to beaten paths and avoid leaving new footprints in the snow. He had arranged to meet the other two men just off the road in front of the compound. They would be safe there in the shadows for a few minutes.

He glanced behind him as he walked, stopping several times to throw himself on the ground, listening for guards in pursuit, then hearing nothing but the blood hammering frantically in his ears. Before he was out of the compound, he paused and pressed himself against a tree, and he watched Herbert lead the last men into the pig barn. He would have to move fast, because Herbert would be counting the men now, as he did every night before locking them up. The men had planned for this as well, prepared to mill around the loft in such a way that Herbert's count would be thrown off. He was cold and tired; he would give up on it until morning, if they were lucky. Jones picked up his speed and broke into a run when he saw the road before him. He heard Duperry's voice with a flood of relief.

"Hurry up, Jones! We thought we'd lost you back there!" They converged together as shadows, verifying that they had all made it, and struck out walking northeast in the ditch of the road. As they walked, the snow blew around them and a dark eerie silence pursued them. They moved fast, crossing from the road to the railroad tracks, jumping at every sound, hurling themselves to the ground at every flash of light or movement in the shadows. Because of the blackouts, they could move in utter darkness, even while passing near town. As Jones's nerves relaxed the farther they got from 311/I, the cold made its impression, and he gripped his fingers. He realized that they were nearly frozen. He blew on them, while squirming his toes in his shoes, always trying to keep his senses clear for any sign of danger. They didn't speak until they had five or six miles between them and their guards. They had little plan from this point, but agreed, as the temperature fell and they became more concerned about Herbert noticing their absence, to find a safe hiding place for the next few hours.

They soon spotted a large, frozen mountain of a haystack, recently erected and several yards from the road, and moved easily toward it through the snow. It seemed that there were numerous tracks in the white field, but they couldn't be sure in the dark. They agreed not to stop long, then climbed into the haystack, breaking through the hard outer layer and shaking straw back around them. Breathing was no problem through the loosened hay, and they sat comfortably, waiting and listening, not completely sure that they weren't being followed. Turner insisted he had seen someone behind them on the tracks, who darted into the shadows every time he looked back. The moon, which had been their only source of light, disappeared behind heavy clouds. Several dogs barked in the distance, and planes flew over but they could hear no bombing.

They pulled out their handmade compasses and discussed their plans in hushed voices, constantly interrupting themselves to listen for sounds. They agreed to head north—as far north as they could get—to reach the Baltic Sea. From there they would think of something.

After several hours, they decided to move on. Sitting in a haystack so near the compound had played on their nerves, and Jones's muscles were so taut he walked at a stiff, frantic pace, controlling the urge to run. They kept their stride fast and steady. Their boots squeaked in the snow, and the sound seemed to echo across miles of fields and into the homes of German SS troopers.

By the time the sun cast a light on the horizon, the men's nerves had given way to cold and exhaustion. A hazy blue color spread along the eastern meadows, and they knew that by now the guards would be waking the men, probably already had done so several hours ago. They were definitely being hunted now, if they hadn't been all night. Jones felt nothing in his feet and held his frozen hands against his chapped face, trying to summon heat.

"Let's stop soon. We've got to be a good safe distance now, if we hide ourselves right," he said. They agreed and left the road, weaving to confuse their footprints. They found another haystack a hundred yards into a field, a safe distance both from the road and the farmer's house. This looked like a safe place to hide through the day, and as gray dawn light streaked the sky, the three fugitives, trembling uncontrollably from the cold, disappeared into a pile of hay no more than ten by twelve feet. For several hours they slept.

They heard nothing as the day passed. They had chosen their hideout well, and no man or animal came near them as the sun passed overhead, the sky cleared, and a warm sun melted the top layer of snow.

They began to discuss their plans again, scratching straw out of their eyes. Duperry stuck his head out of their camouflage several times to scan the area, and let out a bellowing laugh. "We made it! We actually got those son-of-a-bitch Krauts this time. Hell, we're halfway home!"

The two friends laughed with him, exuberant with the heady realization that they had finally escaped their tormentors. They talked eagerly about going home, and how they could help the men who were still in the camp. Their confidence soared so high that they all stepped out for a few minutes to stretch their legs in the sun; then, blinking in the bright light, nervous at their lack of caution, they climbed back in and straightened the straw around them. They had only to wait now for the sun to come down, and they would lose themselves again in the dark countryside.

After sunset they emerged from the haystack, their anxiousness sending them out in the rosy gray light that glowed off the snow. Jones had eaten his two and a half pieces of bread and now cursed his lack of restraint. Turner worked on his second piece as they walked straight north, their nervousness now only dim impressions in the back of their minds. Their compasses directed them away from the road, and within an hour the strong smell of seawater convinced them that the buttons had worked. They were headed straight for the shoreline of the Baltic Sea.

When they reached water, they found a peaceful and quiet seashore, houses scattered along its edge, German families inside eating dinner with dim lights, their windows covered with heavy drapes and blankets. The water was rough; waves lurched toward the snowy shore with frantic foaming maneuvers. The men wandered toward a set of docks, trying to avoid homes where tied-up dogs could give them away with a bark. At the first dock they found a lonely dinghy tied up and banging determinedly against the dock in the black water.

"That's it! That's our ticket outta here. We got a boat, we're home free!" Duperry exclaimed, as his two companions tried to quiet him.

"We can't just climb in this boat and head for Sweden; what the hell's the matter with you?" Turner retorted.

"He's right. We need to find supplies for a trip like that, or we'll never make it. We need warmer clothes, and definitely more food. It could take us a week to hit Stockholm," Jones said.

"You think so?"

"Hell, yes, with water as rough as this?"

As Jones and Duperry spoke, Turner was shaking his head with open skepticism.

"That's a long trip for a rowboat. What if we hit a storm out there—have you ever considered that?" he asked.

Duperry wheeled and glared at the pragmatist, his eyes squinted furiously in the dark.

"What if we just stay right here and wait for the Krauts to come get us—would you like that better?" He spat the words in Turner's face, acrid and impatient in his stress.

"You think all three of us can fit in that little tub?" Jones asked.

"Sure, we're more secure with extra weight," Turner answered, as if afraid that Duperry might suggest leaving him there on the shore. The three agreed, then, that they would be on the boat for Sweden as soon as possible. Their main concern was that the boat might be gone when they returned with supplies. Looking around them furtively, Duperry climbed onto the boat and Jones and Turner untied it and dragged it farther downshore, their wet feet slipping in frozen sludge. Duperry was tossed in the boat and doused by each surge, but they concluded it was worth the risk to take the boat out in the rough waters.

Danzley Jones joined the service immediately after graduating from high school in Couer d'Alene, Idaho. He was eighteen years old when he returned home for a visit after completing basic training. Courtesy of Danzley Jones.

James Bruton (tallest in back row) was a high-school athlete, excelling in basketball and baseball. He earned several college scholarships before he was sent to war. Courtesy of James Bruton

James Rizzuto jumped into Holland with the 508th Regiment of the 82nd Airborne during Operation Market-Garden, accompanied by Earl Mickelson and Stan Watsick. This picture of Rizzuto was taken the day before the invasion. Courtesy of James Rizzuto

Herbert and Emme Lee Marlowe married in England, near the Stafford hospital where she worked, only weeks before he was captured by the Germans.

Earl Mickelson joined the 508th Regiment of the 82nd Airborne for the glamour, challenge, and higher wages that lured thousands of young soldiers. Courtesy of Earl Mickelson

Stan Watsick joined the military with high-school friends at the age of eighteen and spent most of his wartime career with his comrades at 311/I.
Courtesy of Stan Watsick

Jones and his Irish sweetheart, Caroline Boyd, found only brief interludes together before Jones jumped into Normandy. Courtesy of Danzley Jones

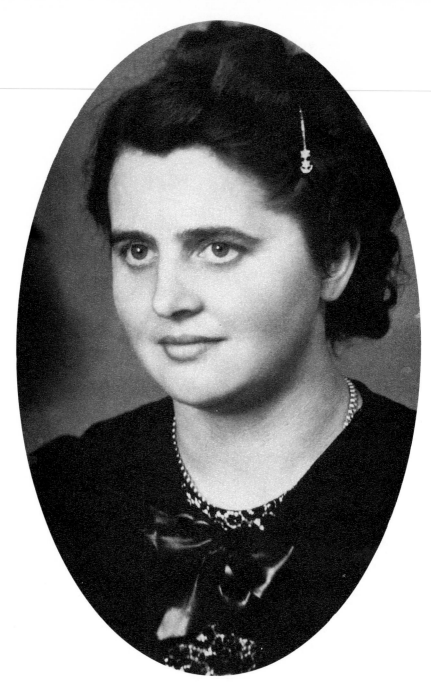

Jones and Howard had a respite from their march into Germany under guard when a young Dutch woman brought them milk and bread. Mrs. Fick used charm and trickery to convince their guard to allow them the food. This photo was taken of her about that time. Courtesy of Fick family

Jones was thrown into this schoolhouse basement in Limpi, Holland, after interrogation by German officers. He returned to the basement forty-five years later to take this picture. Courtesy of Danzley Jones

Troops of the 1st U.S. Army liberated American, Russian, and French prisoners from Stalag XII-A after the fall of Hitler. Twenty miles north of the Rhine, Linburg was first entered by elements of the 9th Armored Division. The next day 1st Army Infantry units cleared the town. Courtesy of the estate of Paul Johnson

Many prisoners at Stalag XII-A slept on the floor with straw for bedding, as pictured here. Charlie Chasteen was one of many who slept in the piles of soiled straw while awaiting assignment to a satellite work commando.
Courtesy of the estate of Paul Johnson

Chasteen was captured during Operation Market-Garden and shipped to Stalag XII-A. This identification picture was taken in early October 1944. Courtesy of Charles Chasteen

Lou Fisher was captured in Germany after helping to liberate France with the 109th Infantry, 28th Division. He wrote a jubilant letter home to his wife only days before his capture. He is shown here in an identification picture taken at Stalag XII-A. Courtesy of Marie Fisher

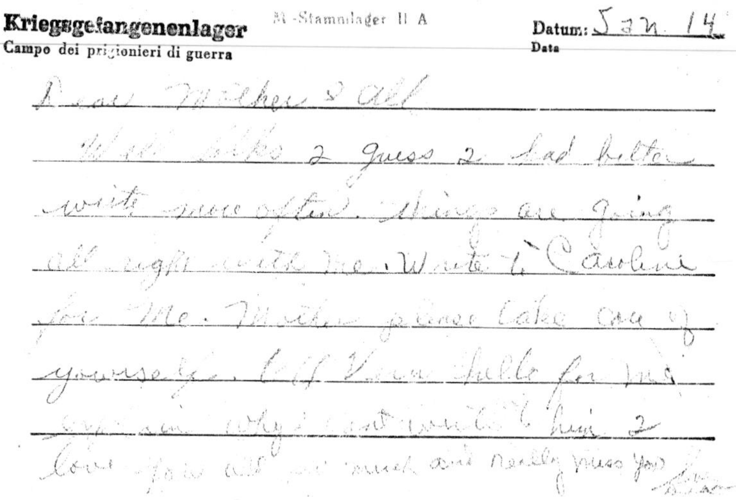
Kriegsgefangenenlager M.-Stammlager II A Datum: Jan. 14
Campo dei prigionieri di guerra Data

Dear Mother & all
Well ... guess I had better
write more often. Things are going
all right with me. Write to Caroline
for me. Mother please take care of
yourself. ... hello for me
...
Love you all so much and really miss you

311/I prisoners were allowed to send letters home. Since their letters were strictly censored by the German military, POWs learned to keep their messages general. Courtesy of Danzley Jones

Bruton brought back souvenirs that he had scavenged on his way across Germany after his liberation. He is pictured here (right) *with two friends and the Nazi flag and rifle he retrieved.* Courtesy of James Bruton

Fisher returned to the United States, like other POWs, suffering from severe malnutrition. The twenty-six-year-old father of four survived influenza, hepatitis, and bronchitis at 311/I. Courtesy of Marie Fisher

Jim and Betty Bruton now reside in Kentucky, where Jim is a clown for Shriners circus.   Courtesy of James Bruton

Jones was reunited with Mrs. Fick, the woman who brought him bread and milk, forty-five years after the war. She assisted many POWs who happened past her house.   Courtesy of Danzley Jones

Chasteen today still takes pride in the airborne but suffers physically from numerous beatings that took place at 311/I. Courtesy of Charles Chasteen

311/I reunions have become a family occasion, allowing wives to share their own experiences of marriage to a former POW. Pictured at a recent gathering is Jones with Virgil and Stan Watsick. Courtesy of Danzley Jones

Rizzuto still jumps from planes, including a jump at the fiftieth anniversary of the Normandy Invasion. Courtesy of James Rizzuto

Herbert and Emma Lee Marlowe celebrated their fiftieth anniversary in 1994.

Courtesy of Herbert Marlowe

Best friends Mickelson (left) *and Watsick* (right) *were separated for nearly forty years before they reunited. They have now revived a close friendship.*

Courtesy of Claire Swedberg

Ex-prisoners of Work Commando 311/I meet yearly to share memories and offer each other support. After fifty years they find camaraderie still links them together. Front row: Jim Novak, Herbert Marlowe, William Kalkreuth, Marion Bell, Claude Arnold. Back row: Stan Watsick, Jim Bruton, Earl Mickelson, Dan Jones, Charlie Chasteen, Jim Rizzuto. Courtesy of Danzley Jones

They dragged the boat several hundred yards from the dock. Duperry climbed out halfway there after being soaked in the frigid ocean. They were again unconcerned with the cold, excited at the prospect of their journey and warmed with the exuberance of newfound freedom. They tied the boat underneath a thicket of bushes and hurried back toward the farm where they had spent the day in a haystack. They now faced the task of finding food and clothing, a challenge they hadn't before considered. As the night passed, they circled the small farmyards and outlying houses, unsure of their next move.

Long before the sun rose, a light shone dimly from a small shack, a typical POW home for a Pole or Frenchman who helped on a German farm. They lay in the snow, watching the house and waiting, until a small man emerged, carrying a lantern and blowing steamy breaths onto his hands. They watched his movement toward the nearby barn and looked at each other in agreement. He was French. Duperry spoke French fluently, and they discussed now whether they were safe to come out in the open. Duperry stood and walked slowly toward the barn, Turner and Jones waiting anxiously in the snow. He made a bizarre figure in fragments of his American Airborne uniform and English flight jacket. They watched as the Frenchman came out. Duperry waved, then spoke to him for several minutes. He made demonstrative gestures as he spoke, and the Frenchman listened and nodded his head. After what seemed hours, Duperry looked back and waved to Jones and Turner, and they stood, looking around them cautiously, then hurried over to meet the Frenchman.

He was a friendly prisoner from southern France, a former freedom fighter who told Duperry that he'd been in Germany for several years. He invited them to have some coffee inside his shack while he looked around for some of the supplies they needed for their journey.

CHAPTER 10

O nce inside the Frenchman's hut, the three refugees eagerly took seats around a small, wooden table. The tiny home consisted of one room, with a makeshift outhouse in back. A small stove heated the room from one corner. The table where they sat, with four homemade chairs, was the only piece of furniture and took up almost the entire floor. A thin mattress leaned against the wall with several moth-chewed blankets draped over it.

As the Frenchman spoke with friendly animation to Duperry, he heated water in a bucket on the stove. He and Duperry laughed and spoke with amiability that came from like nationalities, while Jones and Turner looked on hopefully. The Frenchman had little to share with them, Duperry translated, but whatever he did have he was more than happy to donate for their journey. He sat down at the table with a kerosene lamp and listened to their plans for escaping across the Baltic. He looked from one to the other with dark, intelligent eyes, nodding as Duperry explained. He drew a crude map of Germany and Scandinavia for them on a dirty scrap of paper, his hands cracked and swollen from working in the subzero weather.

They had a long trip ahead of them, he said. The waters were treacherous this time of year, so their progress would be slow. But he shrugged and smiled and said he admired the troopers' conviction. Conviction alone might get them to Sweden. Maybe if he were a few years younger and without a family to worry about . . . he laughed and tossed up his hands in a foreign gesture. He was surviving here in Germany, and soon, if the war went the way he expected, he would be home in France with his wife and three small children. The men ate bread and cheese, which he produced from a cupboard, while he tucked more away for their journey. It was the same bread they had eaten in the compound, but somehow it tasted better now as they ate in this man's home. He also offered them his ragged blankets, which they accepted happily. He owned a pair of thick gloves, and he gave them to Duperry as a special gift.

Then he asked them if they had cigarettes. They shook their heads. He spoke briefly with Duperry, who responded enthusiastically, and the Frenchman pulled on his overcoat and walked out into the darkness.

"Hey, what's he doing now?" Jones asked.

"He's going to get us some tobacco. There's another prisoner on the other side of the field who sells the stuff black market. He'll be back in no time, just relax."

"He'd better hurry, it'll be light soon," Turner said, a nervous edge in his voice.

"What are you worried about? We've got an easy hour and a half before the sun comes up," Duperry snapped, and they began to talk enthusiastically about their trip. They spoke of their previous nautical experience, of which they had basically none, and discussed the trip with high spirits. After an hour had passed, Jones fed the fire in the stove and pulled out his tattered deck of cards. They played to distract their minds. Within a half hour the door swung open, and the Frenchman came in with an icy wind.

"Thank God, we were gettin' a little worried!" Jones exclaimed, then hesitated as he noticed the somber look on his host's face. The three Americans watched in silence as the door opened wider and four members of the Gestapo marched through the narrow doorway. Jones froze, feeling the sudden and utter ruination of all his hopes. His horror could only be matched by that of his two companions, staring with bloodless faces, their eyes and mouths frozen with shock and fear. The Frenchman stepped aside with a silent and pale face, and the Gestapo rushed forward, pulling the men from their seats. They moved swiftly and quietly, saying nothing to the fugitives as they prompted them forward. Without speaking, the three prisoners walked out the door and into the snow, which had begun falling in the earliest morning light. The Gestapo followed and shut the door behind them softly, with little more than a word to the French informer inside.

Cold-blooded, the Germans now stood facing the three captives, aiming burp guns at their heads. In a calm monotone, the man in charge ordered the prisoners to march toward the road with their hands on their heads. The Germans followed on motorcycles.

The prisoners walked fast, stumbling in their fear. They walked with open jackets and bare hands, oblivious to the cold. Their mechanical skills had so completely failed them that they repeatedly tripped and fell in the ice. They were forced back to their feet with a brusque warning and hurried on at a grueling pace.

Several miles down the desolate road, the Gestapo ordered them to stop and handed each man a lighted cigarette. After several shoves, the prisoners stumbled forward on the road while the Germans watched. The Germans barked another order, and the men came to a stop in a reluctant row. They knew now that they were going to die. Why the Germans had waited to kill them here they didn't bother to consider. They stood cowering and waiting, breathing their last breaths. The German men spoke among themselves, watching the three prisoners' terror-stricken eyes. All Jones could see was the guns swung casually over their shoulders as the Germans took their time, looking them over, exchanging a few words. He spoke a small prayer in the back of his throat, unsure if it was the prayer or a swallowed scream that gurgled to his mouth.

One of the Gestapo members finally made a decisive move and climbed on his motorcycle, motioning with his gun for them to continue marching. Sheer terror had stiffened Jones's joints, and he moved even more awkwardly, his mouth dry and immobile, his hands gripping each other on the top of his head with vise strength, whitened to the wrists.

"I just shit my pants," Duperry commented under his breath as they marched on. Now they were unsure whether they had been spared to be questioned then executed by the proper authorities or to be punished in some other, more unspeakable manner. Jones tugged at his jacket, wrapping it around his body, which now convulsed in violent tremors, suddenly overwhelmed by the cold. The Gestapo knew who they were and from where they had escaped, and the prisoners didn't question this, guessing that the Frenchman had explained everything to the Germans, including where to find the rowboat. He felt no resentment toward the Frenchman; it was their own stupidity he now cursed.

The four men, who escorted them to an unknown German headquarters, began to push the prisoners impatiently as the day progressed into late morning. As the sun reached its high point, they came into a tiny, unfamiliar village, where the Gestapo threw the prisoners into a dark, sealed room. They sat silently, their fear and misery unspoken. All three men stared ahead without seeing, so still and for so long that they seemed to have died in their spots. They saw now that they had no chance of escape left. Their last chance had been on the road, and with the heavily armed Gestapo behind them that had been unlikely. They awaited their fate without fear but with utter defeat.

Only hours later, they were dragged to their feet and moved back onto the road, into a jeep, and driven fast down the same road they had been walking. The scenery around them became unpleasantly familiar, and Jones realized that they were being taken back to 311/I.

It was late afternoon when they arrived at the compound, finding the sergeant in charge waiting impatiently for them. Other than the sergeant, the compound was silent and unoccupied, only the faraway noises from the bakery audible in the cold breeze. The other prisoners were out on the tracks. Duperry, Jones, and Turner remained in the jeep. The sergeant stared at them with contempt in his eyes. They had seen this sergeant in charge only a few times but recognized him with dread. They had to be shoved off the jeep, and they faced the sergeant with two members of the Gestapo standing behind them. The sergeant requested that he be left alone with his prisoners, and the Germans turned and walked away from sight behind the pig barn. Once alone with the three captured convicts, the sergeant let out a series of curses and threats in their faces, then turned on his heel and walked thirty feet ahead of them, a pistol in his hand. They exchanged looks in confusion as he stood with his back to them, smoking a cigarette with one hand and gripping the pistol with the other.

"He wants us to try to escape," Jones thought, but was afraid to speak or move. The sergeant smoked his cigarette casually, gazing off into the fields where Polish girls had been picking and bagging turnips less than a month before. As he dropped his cigarette and ground it down with his foot, the sergeant let out an expiration of air that they could hear clearly. When he turned, his eyes were alive with anger and hatred. He marched to stand before Jones and brought his pistol across the prisoner's face. He brought the pistol back to crack on the other cheek, and continued hitting him until he buckled to the ground. Then the sergeant began kicking, his pointed boot digging into his victim's empty gut. Jones was unsure when the beating was ended and directed on Duperry beside him. He felt the ice melting under his face and breath. His relief overwhelmed him, and he knew, even in his pain, that he wouldn't be executed.

When he saw the door of a root cellar swing open, his mind cleared enough to realize that he had traveled many miles from the compound again, with Turner and Duperry at his side. He was shoved forward and stumbled, reaching out for the frozen earth wall to steady himself before tripping down the worn steps. He wandered into the cellar toward a dark wall and curled into sleep.

CHAPTER 11

Jim Bruton pulled on his wooden shoes, the hard edges rubbing against new tender sores on his frostbitten feet. Since Jones, Turner, and Duperry had escaped, all the remaining prisoners had been forced to wear the German-issued wooden shoes, replacing their worn and comfortable combat boots. The wooden cloglike shoes spared their feet from the frozen ground and didn't wear out, but they also made movement awkward and running an impossibility. No one could escape in those shoes. They would never make it out of sight of the guards in the loud, cumbersome clogs. Since the threesome had escaped, the Germans also had moved the latrine forward so that should anyone attempt to sneak out the back, they would drown in human waste.

The bombing of the railroads continued steadily, and with the new, uncomfortable shoes, the prisoners worked slower than ever, laying an average of only four or five rails a day. Often the foreman would worry that there wouldn't be time to put together a new rail before the next train. At these times, they forced the prisoner crew to stand and do nothing for an hour or more, waiting for a train to pass before returning to work.

Bruton waited now with his shovel in his hands, banging it against the solid wood of his shoe as he watched Sylvester's antics on the tracks. He was sick to death of the Germans and their children, especially this bratty apprentice. It was a cold November day, and whether Thanksgiving had passed or not he was unsure. Stan Watsick came by to stand beside him, a tiny end of a cigarette butt between his fingers. He had burnt his fingertips down to a yellow, callused tissue from smoking these butts down to nothing. A frigid breeze had come up overnight, and they turned their collars up around their faces, strips of blankets wrapped around their necks. Bruton's large ears stood out red in the cold wind above his collar.

"Haven't you pinned down your ears yet? Hell, one gust from the Baltic and you'll be flying by those ears of yours right across Germany," Watsick joked.

"That's how I'm going to get outta here," Bruton returned with a laugh. They had heard from the guards that Jones, Turner, and Duperry had been captured the second day after their escape. They guessed they'd been shot on the spot; nobody had said anything otherwise, and the three had never returned. The news had sobered the already discouraged men, and they spoke less of escape, instead finding small ways to spite the Germans as their only means of defiance. They stuck needles in bicycle tires, stole anything they could get their hands on, whether they needed it or not, and generally set out to be an annoyance.

As they waited now, they heard the buzz of an engine above them, and looked up to see a World War I bomber sputtering overhead. The plane was ancient and decrepit compared with the modern aircraft of the forties, and it crawled across the sky at a pace that made Bruton and Watsick laugh out loud. Sylvester and several guards watched the plane and glared at the laughing prisoners. Bruton exchanged a look with one of the guards and pointed at the plane: "Luftwaffe!" He pretended to run for shelter in mock terror. The Germans began murmuring among themselves in annoyance. One new young guard moved toward him irritably.

Bruton bent and picked up a large rock from the ballast pile and weighed it in his hand as he watched the plane move over them. "Watch. I'm gonna bring down the Luftwaffe with this rock," he said to the guard, and Watsick let out a laugh. Bruton leaned back and hurled the rock up with his long reach, and all activity around them stopped as if, for a moment, guards and prisoners alike believed he could hit the plane. At that instant the buzzing engine choked. Their amusement turned to horrified disbelief as the engine gave way and the ancient aircraft began to lose altitude ahead of them. Its engines now had fallen completely silent, and it plunged groundward with sudden speed and disappeared behind a gathering of trees.

The new guard watched the plane's disappearance, then turned toward Bruton, who began to slink away nervously, incredulous at his bad timing. The guard lifted his rifle, shouting "Schweinhund!" He cocked his gun to shoot, but another guard placed a discouraging hand on his shoulder.

"You got one hell of a good arm," Watsick commented under his breath.

That evening as they trudged up the tracks toward the station, they passed the wrecked plane, staring into its smoking bowels, where it had run into a barn wall and lay in the snow burning slowly from the inside. Seeing the wreckage before them brought back the guard's anger, and he smacked Bruton on the head with the palm of his hand.

Even more prisoners had disappeared now, and new prisoners continued to take their places. A tall, blond man in his late twenties wearing an airborne uniform appeared among them one cold evening. The men questioned him about his capture and the progress of the war and listened skeptically as he stumbled for an answer. He spoke almost no English, and what words he knew were accompanied by a thick accent. The men summoned Watsick, who learned that the man was a Polish officer who had climbed into a dead trooper's uniform before capture. The Polish were not well treated now, especially the officers, who had little hope of being spared for a POW camp. The Germans had not noticed his inability to speak English. His name was Jon, the only name they were to know him by, and they agreed to keep his cover.

Rizzuto continued to work as he saw other prisoners come and go from the compound. He managed to ignore his illness when possible and idled his time at the tracks, working as much as he could and thinking about anything but his aching stomach and muscles. He helped the men sneak bread from the bakery and ate any extra bread and cheese with an appreciation he had never before had for food. Other days even a simple task like descending stairs became difficult, his head spinning. Old Pops spoke with him several times. "Bist du krank?" he'd ask, and Rizzuto would answer, "Ja, ja. Krank." But he continued working, knowing that there was no chance to leave the tracks in the middle of the day and that the Germans had no intention of allowing him to sit down and rest while the others worked.

While the snow fell in the subzero weather, the guards sat around a fire on crates and small benches, warming their hands as they watched the prisoners' progress. They were even more subject to the cold, since they were not active, but it was an easier life than the one most had come from on the Russian front. Many guards had come and gone since the prisoners' arrival in the fall, and the most recent were straight off the front lines. They were mostly wounded men, no longer fit for combat. They were amused with the complaints of the American prisoners, who repeatedly protested against their working conditions. It was too cold, the prisoners insisted.

"Deutschland nicht kalt, Russland ist kalt!" they would say with a belly laugh, ordering the men back to work. But for many Americans, who had come from the mild southern states, this weather was hell, and for all of them, it was too cold to work in. Unloading rails from the cars, they lifted them onto their shoulders with a "Hup hup HO." When they dropped the rails onto the handcar, their hands remained attached, and they ripped them free, leaving increasingly thick layers of skin behind.

Rizzuto wrapped himself up and tried to survive each day with the same numb apathy. He knew that Thanksgiving was close and tried not to imagine his family's turkey dinner, his parents and two sisters around the table, their prayers for his quick return. He had two other brothers in the service, and it seemed to him an eternity since he'd seen them. He had his doubts that he would ever see home or any of his family again. He knew that he couldn't survive the winter the way he was headed.

On the last day of November, after Pops woke the men, he watched Rizzuto crawling out of his bunk. He told the ailing prisoner to wait and hurried the other men out front for roll call. After the men had left for work, Rizzuto and Pops walked the eight miles to the doctor in Marlow. Rizzuto listened to the conversation between the doctor and Pops after his brief examination. The doctor declared that Rizzuto was well enough to return to work. He had a mild case of dysentery. He wasn't surprised at the diagnosis, and when Pops told him to get dressed he did so apathetically.

The following morning Stan Watsick climbed out of bed in a feverish sweat. He'd had dysentery for over a week and could hardly move without painful stabs in his stomach. He sat on the concrete at the train station, and Mickelson sat at his side, joking with him to keep up his spirits. A large beer baron passed, and Mickelson nudged his friend with a grin. With sober faces they watched the fat man wearing traditional suspenders and shorts, then exchanged a look and burst into laughter. The nearest guard gave them a prod with his rifle and they stifled themselves.

They worked for only an hour into the morning before Watsick lost consciousness. He found himself at the doctor's office lying on a stiff bed, awaking to a stabbing pain as the doctor gave him an injection directly into his stomach with a giant needle. With alarm he tried to sit up, but they restrained him until the needle was removed. He had suffered an ulcer attack, they explained. The injection should take care of the problem, and he would be fine for work the remainder of the day. He climbed to his feet without fully comprehending what had happened and pulled on his filthy gray shirt. The guard guided him out the door as the people in the sitting room glared.

He walked back to the railroad slowly and felt his stiff chest and stomach loosen. Once back at the tracks, he felt strong enough to lift a shovel. Mickelson looked him over carefully as he went back to work.

"You all right?" Mickelson asked.

"Yeah, sure, never better," Watsick answered, flexing his biceps.

"You bring anything back to eat?"

Stan shrugged and shook his head apologetically with regret. They returned home that night to eat beets and potato soup.

CHAPTER 12

Vaguely Jones became aware of men around him eating. The smell of barley soup was unmistakable, and he felt his hunger return as a desperate aching in his stomach. He realized he had to hurry if he was going to claim his piece of bread for the day. He'd missed his rations the first day, watching the light appear above the stairs without interest as the guard came down in his overcoat, bread and watery soup in tin cans. The prisoners in the small cellar clustered around, and each snatched his ration and returned to his place along the wall, to make it last for an entire day. This was not just their only sustenance, but their only entertainment as well.

Jones had little idea where he was or how many men were down there with him. It was so dark that he could see nothing but cracks of light between the upper wall boards, defining the level of the cellar aboveground. Some men stood facing the wall, the strain of light cutting a line across their faces as they watched the world through a half-inch crack in dim, narrow perspective. Jones had no interest in what they saw. His kidneys ached, and his jaw was so swollen and sore that he imagined it was probably broken. Turner and Duperry were down there with him, but he had no idea where, or if they were badly hurt. It was too dark to recognize faces on the dark forms moving or lying around him.

After several days, the pain gave way to boredom and anxiety, and Jones took a greater interest in what went on around him. Eventually he sought out and located Duperry and Turner. The three friends tried to cheer one another, wondering how long their punishment would last. There were at least ten and sometimes more than twenty men around them, most being punished for the same crime. Some of the men were allowed out of the cellar each day to be marched around a nearby field to stretch their muscles and to breathe the crisp air before returning to their damp dungeon. The cold nagged at the prisoners, and Jones huddled constantly in his coat, trying to draw warmth from those sitting beside him. Nobody spoke, nobody had interest in the others, and he was reminded of his miserable trip to Stalag XII-A.

After a week or so, Jones began to stand in front of the cracks in the wall, watching the activity outside. They were locked in the middle of a prison camp, mostly inhabited by Russian prisoners. He saw the faces of Russians only briefly, but he could clearly see the pen that they slept and dwelled in, the rags they wore, and the horrifying level of starvation they had reached. They seemed like the walking dead, their bones pressing through where they should have had breasts and thighs. It was a frightening sight, and he wondered if he saw his own future as he stared out at the bleak scene for hours, his only distraction.

Some of the Russian prisoners were still healthy enough to walk up to the root cellar where Jones now stood. They watched the Americans come out for their walks each day. He saw one Russian come and lurk before him several times on the other side of the wall, actually stooping and looking into the crack at him, and he stepped away in alarm, until he saw a hand-rolled cigarette slip through the crack and fall to the floor. Frantically Jones dropped to his knees to grope around the dark floor for the cigarette. He obtained a match from another prisoner and sat smoking with relish. He was touched by the kindness of a prisoner who clearly had less than he, and he wished he could walk out and shake his hand. He made the cigarette last for three days, which was long enough for the Russian to come up with another, placing it through the crack and holding it until Jones pulled it from his grasp with a thanks.

After more than three weeks in the cellar, Jones emerged for the first time into daylight for a supervised walk around the grounds. The light seemed almost blinding, although the winter German sun was dim. The snow had piled deep around the grounds, and the temperature seemed to have actually dropped even further since his escape. With a small group of men he marched along the perimeter, the guard shouting for them to stay together and move fast.

Now, for the first time, Jones got a close look at the Russian prisoners whom he had been watching at a distance for so long. They were being fed as Jones passed, and the brutal hatred the Germans felt for the Russians struck him with profound horror as he saw the treatment of the prisoners, a reflection of Hitler's policy toward Germany's greatest enemy. They were thinner and more wasted than he had guessed from a distance. Many of them lay in frozen mud, ignoring the feeding frenzy, their eyes sunken obscenely into their sockets, their faces glazed over and listless. It was a look Jones recognized, and he knew that they had given up on life. They would be dead within a day or two. Some looked to be dead already.

Those who still had the strength to fight for their lives hovered anxiously near the fence, where a German guard stood on the opposite side, throwing small pieces of bread one at a time across at them. The men fought over the first piece of bread with a desperate ferocity that shocked Jones. He had never seen anyone reach that level of desperation as they leaped for the bread, one grasping it and another knocking him down, forcing it out of his hand. This prisoner stuffed the bread in his mouth and tried to swallow but was knocked down and strangled by three other prisoners until he coughed it up. They ripped at each other's hands as they tried to get at least a chunk of bread into their throats, far enough down that no one else could retrieve it. As the performance went on with each piece of bread, the German tossed the chunks strategically and laughed as the Russians fought, clearly entertained to see his worst enemy reduced to this level. They were crazed dogs, no longer human, and had lost all trace of civilized behavior. Before more than ten of the forty or more men had eaten a piece of bread, the guard walked away, leaving the others to try again the next day.

When Jones was back in his root cellar, he was almost relieved that his imprisonment was so easy. But he grew hungrier every day, his arms and legs shrinking up, his stomach slightly bloated. He felt weaker with the passing weeks and had trouble doing his rounds of the camp. Any fleas were no longer a problem in the freezing cold, but lice persisted, and the rats that squealed and squirmed across the floor around him began to look tasty even raw, freshly strangled.

Boredom was his most persistent problem, and he sat fading in and out of coerced sleep to pass the time. He waited anxiously each day for his walks around the yard, but often he would be disappointed and the guard wouldn't come for them at all. Occasionally he talked to Duperry or Turner, but conversation always returned to the most painful subject—food. They thought back to the best dishes that their mothers had ever made, the food that they had eaten most when they were boys, the food that they would eat if they ever got out of Germany. None of them had much hope of that now, in their dark dungeon, far removed from their families, their country, and the war. The Russian prisoner who had passed him cigarettes didn't come over anymore, and Jones guessed that he had become one of the most desperate prisoners who could only sit with blank eyes, waiting for death.

The guards didn't speak with the prisoners. Jones asked when they would be leaving this place but got no answer. He had seen some men leave, but it was impossible to tell where they were being sent.

One morning, more than six weeks after the threesome's attempted escape, the guard opened the root cellar door, and instead of gathering up men for their daily walk, pulled Jones, Turner, and Duperry to their feet and put them on a jeep. It was late afternoon, and as the jeep drove along the rural roads, Jones felt exuberant to be in the daylight and leaving the hellhole that had been his home for so long. Whether he was going now to the Führer himself, to another work camp, or to his execution, he didn't care; he was satisfied just to be moving away from that place.

They drove for well over an hour before he realized that they were headed back into familiar territory. He recognized the small towns and roads, and then finally, with a sinking feeling, he watched them pull into 311/I. Leeps was there to meet them as they climbed out of the jeep and gave them each a cuff on the side of the head. He was not in a good mood. It was late and he was eager to get home. He unlocked the door to the pig barn and ordered them to hurry inside. The other prisoners already sat inside, the stove heating the loft half-heartedly. The single bulb lit a table that the men had erected for card games, and five men sat around it playing poker with broken matchsticks provided by Kalkreuth. While some members enjoyed winning streaks, others fell further into debt as time passed. Those unfortunates agreed to pay off their losses with Red Cross supplies, if they got any, or after the war—if they survived it. Other men lay in their bunks or sat near the stove talking about food. The room had the fresh smell of burning tobacco, and several of the men were smoking. They all looked up at the three men who came trudging into the barracks, returned from the dead.

Marlowe left the poker game and crossed the length of the loft to meet them. He now had a full beard that brushed his collar, and hair hanging over his ears. He stood before Jones and examined his wan, emaciated form.

Jones gave the tall soldier a sheepish grin before he spoke. "Well, we didn't make it this time, but next time we'll be gone so fast the Germans won't know what happened." Marlowe laughed with relief and pounded his friend on the back, then turned to welcome Duperry and Turner back to 311/I.

The prisoners had little to tell the three escapees, except that they had some new prisoners and others had gone. It was late December and only a week before Christmas. The work was the same, four to six rails a day, within a ten-mile radius of the town of Sanitz. They would be back to it the next morning. Leeps, Herbert, Pops, and the foreman, as well as Sylvester, remained with them, while various other guards seemed to come and go.

Jones was not happy to be back. His and Turner's bunks were waiting for them, thin straw mattresses covered with narrow blankets—the sight that had once made him want to risk death to leave. Several of the men looked worse than he remembered, their faces more swollen than before from the beets. He ate several of the vegetables they had stored but were now stockpiling for Christmas.

"You're going to celebrate Christmas?" Jones asked Marlowe with an ironic laugh.

"We're gonna do our best. We can't just curl up and die here," Marlowe answered, and Jones sat on his bunk, anxious and irritated.

The following morning, the German guards were in a celebratory mood. The Germans had recaptured a vital port in France with one well-planned offensive called the Battle of the Bulge and had slaughtered the Americans and British there. The city of Antwerp was now again in German hands, and the damaging loss could mean the beginning of the end for the Allies.

The men listened first with disbelief, then massive depression. They verified the news with a new prisoner who had the entire story. Montgomery had been badly defeated, and the war seemed to have changed direction. Hitler was no longer on the defensive. Jones had hoped in the back of his mind that the war might end soon, but now he had lost even that minute hope.

Work was more difficult than he had remembered it. His socks had worn completely through at the toes, and he turned them around and pulled them on upside down, leaving the ends loose over his toes to try to keep them warm in the wooden shoes. Although the men stole charcoal at every opportunity, it was not enough to heat the barracks, and they were cold at night as well as at work. Watsick had removed every other slat in his bunk for the stove and now slept on strips that suspended him precariously above Mickelson.

Sylvester still worked with the men, now a miniature tyrant. He stole tools from the men and watched them flounder around the tracks in search of a spike or hammer. If anyone showed anger against him, they were firmly reprimanded or beaten. The degradation of being lorded over by a little boy reached Jones's very core, and he sank into deep depression. Even the hunt for food did not interest him.

CHAPTER 13

B ruton straightened from his labor over the rails as sheets of pain fired through his frozen hand. He dropped the hand drill in the snow to examine his swollen and discolored thumb. The pain throbbed upward through his wrist and lately made his work excruciating. The nail was cracked in several places where the rail had crushed it more than a month earlier. Besides the bruise, he could see dried blood gathered under the dead nail.

As the weeks had passed since the accident, his thumb had grown worse rather than healing. It swelled and pulsated in the cold weather, and the discoloration looked bad to him. He knew that it was infected.

Herbert, spotting a prisoner standing idle, wandered over to investigate. He peered at Bruton's thumb. Bruton tested the puffy skin under the nail and watched small drops of blood ooze free and then collect. The guard asked Bruton if his thumb slowed his work, and he replied yes. If he was lucky, he imagined, Herbert would send him to the doctor in Marlow. He hadn't been there before, but he'd shared the eggs and cheese of those who had and could now picture the doctor's pantry as clearly as if he were there. The guard made no comment and turned to walk on down the tracks toward the small bonfire where the other Germans were sitting.

Bruton grasped the large drill in his hands and went back to his work, when he saw Herbert striding back toward him.

"He's asked Flop Ears' permission. He's taking me to the doctor," Bruton thought enthusiastically, then noticed a large object in the guard's round hand. He backed away in sudden aversion as he recognized a giant pair of pliers.

"Nein, nein," he said, shaking his head as he took another step backward, but the guard clamped Bruton's hand between his two and turned it over. He grasped a piece of nail in the pliers and, with an iron grip, yanked it loose from his thumb. The resulting blood made it more difficult to find the other pieces, and Herbert wiped it off with a piece of cloth before going after another piece near the cuticle and heaving with a grunt. Bruton pulled his hand back in horror to see through the bleeding that his entire cuticle had been ripped loose. He looked at the guard, dizzy with horror, and Herbert again took his hand, wrapping a cloth tightly around his thumb and across his palm to secure it. Bruton understood him to say that the bleeding would take care of the infection. The guard returned him his hand and, as he turned to walk away, patted him on the back like a gruff father. The throbbing pain was at first unbearable, but as the cloth soaked up the blood, it seemed to subside. By the afternoon, Burton had little doubt that his nail would grow back without the cuticle, but gangrene would have been worse.

Jones went about his work methodically without noticing the troubles of his friend Bruton. His thoughts were focused on the Russian prisoners he'd seen while in solitary. He knew he should be thankful that his life was easier. He felt as if he were as thin as they had been but knew he couldn't be. The railroad made the difference, keeping him active and his muscles from atrophying. And the 311/I prisoners were comparatively well fed, to keep up their strength for the railroad work.

As the sun went down in the late afternoon and the freezing temperature again began to drop, Jones looked through the large snowflakes at the length of the railroad track, a desolate sight that seemed to stretch on for an eternity. He was surrounded by enemy territory, and he knew now that there was no mistake, the Germans had him for life. He felt that they had already taken most of him but the physical shell, and they used that to do their work for them. The only purpose he served was helping Hitler beat Jones's own people. It was a worse fate than he had ever dreamed in his most extreme fears going into combat. It was worse than being killed on the battlefield, worse than being ripped apart by German civilians. He even envied those who had grown sick and died. They were no longer working on the railroads; they had outwitted the Germans. Hitler couldn't get them anymore, and now they were heroes of sorts. He thought back to his capture for the hundredth time, wishing he'd killed that German sergeant while he'd had the chance.

His depression grew as the evening progressed and the work continued well after dark. He didn't care how long it lasted; the distraction of the work and the cold kept him from lying in the loft thinking and listening to his shrinking stomach groan. He had distracted himself for a long time with the thought of escape; now he had nothing but his hunger, and even that was in the hands of the Germans. He no longer felt like putting them on or seeming happy—it wasn't worth the effort.

He realized he wanted to die. He had considered it before but only as an abstract heroic concept buried in his mind and never taken seriously. He wished in earnest that he had been killed in Holland, but now he was ready to take the idea one step further. The thought of returning to the barracks was unbearable to him; even working, swinging the hammer one more time, seemed unbearable. He had one more chance at freedom. He could make one last decision on his own without the help of the Germans, a decision that would lead him out of the Nazi prison system. As the men put their tools away, he looked around him impatiently and stood at the train station silent and alone. He shrugged away companionship, and the men huddled together several yards away, shuffling their feet and jumping up and down in their wooden shoes. They recognized Jones's mood; they'd been in it themselves.

He watched the approach of the passenger train, the engine piling toward him at top speed. The prisoners and Germans stepped back to allow its passage. This train did not stop at the station. Jones remained on the edge of the platform, leaning out to see the engine more clearly. It seemed to slam toward him, nothing but a front light and churning black shadows of smoke in the dark sky. He could smell the coal and grease and hear its iron power, and he knew that his time had come. This was his only chance. He held his breath, prayers coming to mind and being rejected as the train came closer and he could almost feel its impact against his body. He willed it to hurry, before his courage failed him, before he questioned his conviction to die, before he would end up going back to the pig barn.

"I'm never going back there," he thought, his eyes squinting to a close as if to spare himself the sight of his own death, and he leaned forward at the moment the train reached a roar and passed through the station. As it hurled past, Jones realized he was frozen, standing on the platform, his wooden shoes at a dangerous angle on the edge of the cement. The cold wind blasted his shrunken body in the train's wake to remind him that he was alive. He took a step back and a breath of smoky air. He'd lost his courage. At the moment when he should have jumped, he'd gone into a state of paralysis. He stood on the station, shaking from the cold and his own horror. He had been too afraid to face death. He knew that he would never be able to take his own life. That had been his one chance, and if he couldn't do it then, he would never be able to. He would live each day as long as he could, as long as the Germans kept him alive, and there was nothing he could do about it. He took several deep breaths before Mickelson walked over to him in the dark.

"We're going to get us some bread tonight at the bakery. You want to help distract ol' Leeps?" he asked, digging his hand in his pockets and blowing bursts of steam between himself and Jones. Jones nodded. "Sure, leave it to me."

CHAPTER 14

Christmas morning began the same way as all the other days, and as Leeps hollered "heRAUS!" up the dark stairs at them, most of the men climbed out of their bunks and into their wooden shoes without giving a thought to the holiday. Fisher and Marlowe reminded the men by opening up with a round of "Jingle Bells" as they waited for the morning train. The others looked at them skeptically. As the prisoners stood at the cold Dettmannsdorf train station, they saw little around them resembling a Christmas holiday. With a shrug, Jones and then Turner sang along with half-hearted choruses, and eventually the other prisoners joined in. They gradually began to feel a vague and forced sense of festivity.

The German commuters stood on the platform staring at the prisoners in surprise. Although many of those in Nazi Germany celebrated Christmas privately, they observed the holiday little as a nation. It was wartime, and other concerns took priority. It was another workday for nearly everyone.

On the train the Germans listened to the men sing "Deck the Halls" and "I'll Be Home for Christmas," the guards standing by with condescending smiles. After several carols, the prisoners agreed that they shouldn't be working on Christmas, and as the train reached Sanitz, they rallied around Marlowe, encouraging him to talk to Flop Ears for them.

Marlowe, with Kleppe as interpreter, strode toward the foreman, who stood watching the men and the damaged tracks, his hands behind his back and his hat pulled down over his large ears.

"Tell him it's Christmas Day. Christian people don't work on this day," Marlowe said, and Kleppe gulped, speaking to the curious foreman in an apologetic voice. Hanukkah had recently passed, and Kleppe ignored it deliberately. The foreman let out a hiss of air between his yellowed teeth before responding with an unpleasant smile.

Kleppe translated: "He says this is wartime, and Christmas or not, the trains have to get through. Germans have to work—they're not going to make an exception for American prisoners."

"All right. Tell him we'll compromise. We'll work half a day and leave at noon." Kleppe stared at Marlowe silently, and he nodded at him in encouragement. "Go ahead." After the foreman understood the suggestion, he let out a throaty laugh, then abruptly turned his back and walked toward the fire the guards had started for their long day at the tracks. Marlowe and Kleppe exchanged a look and followed. Several prisoners wandered behind in curiosity.

"You say the trains have to get through just like any day? How about if my men lay four rails by noon, then you let us go home. That's as much as we usually do in a day. If we can't do it, you can have us all day." As Kleppe repeated the proposal in German, the foreman looked at Marlowe, and his face twisted into a smile before speaking.

"Acht Schienen," he said, holding up eight fingers.

"He says he needs eight rails laid today."

"I know what he said," Marlowe snapped. "Tell him we'll do it by noon, but then he agrees to let us go home." Those prisoners who were within hearing distance now spoke up their approval. They could lay eight rails in that time, easily. The foreman again smiled at Marlowe and nodded, wishing him good luck before turning away.

The prisoners were inspired by the contest and got to work with unfamiliar enthusiasm. Chasteen and Lindsey took the handcar down the tracks for the rails, pumping it so fast that Herbert braced himself to keep from falling off, his raised eyebrows expressing his surprise. The men worked their way through "The Twelve Days of Christmas," then started again with "Deck the Halls" as they secured the next rail. Sylvester stood in front of the tracks, his hands thrust in his pockets, observing them with uncharacteristic silence. The foreman and guards watched the work with expressions first skeptical, then dumbfounded.

As the morning passed, the singing grew louder and more jocular. The prisoners laughed out loud at the expressions on the foreman and guards' faces. This was their moment of glory, and they were now showing the Germans just what they could do. By the time they were laying the last two rails, German civilians had gathered to witness the dramatic transformation in the American paratroopers. The prisoners were enjoying themselves, and everyone could see it. Jones put all his weight into turning the swivel drill, while whistling "Santa Claus Is Coming to Town." He drilled in screws at a speed at least five times his pace of the day before.

At 11:35 the men started loading their tools with irrepressible excitement. The foreman stood with his hands on his hips, shaking his head in disgust and disbelief. The men could easily read his thoughts. Even the German rail workers couldn't work as fast as they had just done, these same prisoners who had been nothing but lazy and stupid for three months. With a resentful toss of his hand, the foreman acknowledged to Marlowe that the men could go home, and the guards moved them out to the train station. The men shouted with triumph, singing carols loudly and joking with seldom-seen exuberance. The guards were not displeased themselves. Once the prisoners were locked up, they also were free to go home for the day, and they listened to the prisoners' songs with tolerant smiles.

Several prisoners ran around the tracks as they pulled out with the guards, gathering up strips of foil American planes had dropped to interfere with German radar. The shiny strips seemed festive now and could make decent tinsel. They wiped off the snow and mud and stuffed handfuls in their pockets. Marlowe scanned the yard behind the station for a Christmas-sized tree, and not finding one, snapped a branch off a large pine. Leeps watched the men scavenging for several minutes before asking them what they were doing.

"Christmas tree—Tannenbaum," Marlowe explained, before walking past him to board the train.

That same morning, in the 311/I kitchen, Kalkreuth was putting together the Christmas pudding. The men had pilfered and saved up several loaves' worth of bread over the past few weeks, and he now soaked them in milk and honey stolen from the doctor's kitchen. The sawdust bread, which was hard and dry, he now molded easily. He monitored the straining of the potato soup, and when the baker's back was turned, he managed to sneak spoonfuls of potato peels from the pig's stock back into the soup. They had a Christmas feast planned.

Once back in the barracks, the men went to work with the tree, balancing it carefully on the poker table and draping it with tinsel. They paused to admire the war-tree. Rizzuto unclasped his paratrooper wings and fastened them to a small branch. Bruton removed his 82nd Airborne "AA" insignia, and Jones watched before commenting, "You know what AA stands for, don't you?"

"What's that, wise-guy?"

"Almost Airborne." The men of the 82nd let out moans of disgust as Jones and the 101st men laughed, and they all began taking off their pins and medals. Soon the tree shimmered with insignia, wings, dog tags, Purple Hearts, and photographs of wives, girlfriends, and parents. When they were finished, the men backed away and stared at the tree in silence. There was no doubt that it was the most beautiful Christmas tree they'd ever seen. They fell silent in personal reflection as they looked at the symbol of their perseverance, and the afternoon grew solemn and melancholy.

In the early evening, they ate their Christmas pudding with potato soup and all agreed that it was delicious, despite the 60 percent sawdust Kalkreuth said was rationed in the bread. They listened silently at afternoon feeding time to the grunts and squeals of the giant pigs below, fighting for their broth.

They were surprised to hear a visitor come up the stairs, escorted by the one guard remaining on duty. He was an American prisoner from another compound above the dairy. He brought with him a prayer book. The men of 311/I looked at him in amazement. They'd never had any idea that another group of prisoners existed right there in the barn, next to them.

"I thought you men might like a little service for Christmas," the visitor said. He seated himself by the stove, which roared with heat from the mountains of coal they had saved. They gathered in a circle around him silently.

Marlowe's dysentery worsened with the hours, and the men kidded him as he trotted off repeatedly during the service for the chamber pot at the top of the stairs. By evening, he sat on the pot for longer periods of time, unable to get up. As the other prisoner left, he grinned and nodded Merry Christmas to the sick trooper as he passed him on the pot.

While Marlowe sat this way, he heard the front door unlock again and swing open below him. He listened to voices and saw forms, realizing that the two people coming up the stairs toward him were Leeps and a woman. He desperately tried to get up from the pot but was unable. The German couple looked at their feet as they climbed toward him, Leeps talking in a low, guttural slur while the woman giggled. Marlowe realized, as they stumbled several times on the steps, that Leeps was dead drunk and was showing the prison barracks, as if showing off his office, to his girlfriend.

The couple reached the top of the stairs and both paused, looking at Marlowe where he squatted helplessly. Leeps ordered him to pull his pants on, finishing his sentence with a fit of giggles. The stocky German girl, in her twenties, laughed along with him. She hadn't done well to choose Leeps, a half-mad, retarded man with a badly maimed face and constant stream of spittle bubbling from the corner of his mouth. But men were not easy to come by in this stage of the war, a fact that some of the prisoners had come to appreciate from the glances of German women—especially Chasteen, who had even exchanged a flirtatious smile with the foreman's daughter.

Leeps put his arm around the woman as they faced the gathering of prisoners sitting by the stove. The prisoners stared back at the two intruders with bare hostility. They didn't appreciate the intrusion on Christmas Day, and their resentment would have been apparent to the German couple if they hadn't been drunk. Leeps spoke in an incomprehensible mumble as he pointed and spoke to the girl, frequently pausing to giggle and nuzzle her ear and neck. He attempted to introduce her to the individual prisoners, and his eyes caught Mickelson's as he announced, "Danski." She waved at Mickelson, who stared back at her without response, and Leeps combed the group with his eyes.

"Danski und . . . und." He brightened when he located Watsick. "Und Polski!"

She squealed when she noticed the Christmas tree. She hurried across the loft to examine the pictures, dog tags, and medals hanging from its branches. She removed a pair of wings and turned them over in her hand with an "Ooo" of approval. Suddenly she turned to Leeps and made a request that all the prisoners understood at once. Marlowe stood and pulled on his pants. She wanted the tree. Leeps nodded happily and stepped forward to reach for the tree with a gargantuan hand. He came up short as several men jumped in front of him. Within seconds every man in the room had crowded around the tree.

"Take that tree over every one of our dead bodies. We'll kill you first," Marlowe spoke behind him first in English, then broken German.

Leeps hesitated in drunken confusion, looking back at Marlowe as if he didn't understand. The men had never stood up to him before, and he was caught completely by surprise. The girl waited expectantly and looked from Leeps to the men as they stared each other down. After several minutes, Leeps put his arm around the girl and guided her toward the stairs, his face now serious. Marlowe stood in front of them and held out his hand. Reluctantly the woman handed him the wings that she'd wrapped in her fist, and the couple stumbled out in silence.

When the door shut, the men heard her complaining to Leeps in a high voice. The prisoners looked from one to the other, enjoying their moment of triumph. They sat around the tree for hours into the night, talking about their families at home, the food they used to eat at Christmas, the presents they'd received. It was the most memorable Christmas of their lives, and they went to their bunks late in the night with a feel of content perseverance that allowed them a sense of hope, if only for that night.

CHAPTER 15

Back on the tracks December 26, 1944, the men got to work at their usual blackadaisical pace. The slow ringing of hammers coming down on stakes with casual swings echoed across the tracks. The foreman stood watching them from his position near the large fire. He removed his hat and slowly scratched the gleaming top of his smooth head. Turning, he spoke first to himself, then the guards, pointing at several of the prisoners. The guards marched out toward the tracks, minus Pops, who stayed by the fire, his rifle lying near him on the ground as he warmed his hands. Pops had little interest in prisoner discipline.

Three guards crossed to stand before Dan Jones and Charlie Chasteen and shouted orders: "Today, you lay twelve rails or you don't go home," the prisoners translated from the German. "No work, no food."

The men shrugged, looking from the guards to one another. They didn't understand and returned to what they were doing. The guards moved on to the other men and gave several of them a sharp crack between the shoulder blades, but the men stubbornly prevailed in their feigned incompetence, deliberate in their inability to understand a word. The foreman watched the performance, his face flushed with anger. He was determined not to be taken advantage of anymore.

The beatings and harassment accelerated through the day, and the men realized that they may have made a mistake working as hard as they had the day before. Now all they could do was feign ineptitude once again, but this was no longer convincing. Despite their effort to keep working slowly, they began to pick up their pace.

Jones realized late in the afternoon, as the sun sprayed dreary light through thick fog, that he had somehow accomplished almost twice the work he usually did over the course of the day. He glanced at the huddle of Germans by the fire, even Sylvester now sitting quietly, subdued by the chill, tracing patterns in the snow with his small foot. No one was looking. Jones dropped his drill. He pulled a shovel off the ground and began casually tamping ballast under the track, although the section he worked on was already finished. With relief, he felt some circulation returning to his tired arms.

By the time he noticed Flop Ears, it was too late to retrieve his hand drill. The foreman strode toward him, his shoulders braced with stiff determination. His eyes, alive with rage, locked on Jones as he stopped fifteen feet from the prisoner. Jones had been through several beatings now and knew full well how much he wanted to avoid them. He also knew how much the foreman hated him, and resentful dread filled him as he tried to look unconcerned.

The foreman raised his rifle and cocked it. The prisoners and even the guards watched in horrified fascination. They had all seen the foreman's temper grow worse during the day, and none were surprised now to see him contemplating murder. He aimed the rifle steadily at Jones's head, and as Jones thought to himself, "He's bluffing," the foreman fired. Jones felt the bullet hit his head, and he collapsed on the tracks in silent terror. He lay curled in the gravel, gasping for air, then finally scrambled back to his feet. His hand tested the top of his head and found that the bullet had only skimmed his scalp, leaving a tiny trickle of blood where his new part lay. The foreman continued to stare at him, his rifle cocked, his face like stone, and Jones reached for his drill with heroic determination. He screwed at the closest bolt with vigor and enthusiasm, so much so that sweat poured off his face in the subzero temperatures.

The Germans kept the men at the tracks longer than usual but could not get twelve rails out of them. Another freight train, the last, was scheduled to come through at 7 P.M., and they worked, feverish and inept, under constant censure. Already the sun had dropped, and snow fell with a vengeance around them. Watsick and Mickelson tamped gravel under the new segment of track and exchanged few words as they went. They were tired and miserable. Mickelson dumped the gravel under the rails and pounded it down loosely and unevenly with the back of his shovel. Watsick watched him for several minutes before commenting, "What the hell are you doing? That ain't gonna hold the tracks." They exchanged a smile. Together they worked, leaving hollow pockets under the tracks. Several other prisoners joined them, filling gravel in such a way that even under casual examination the tamping would seem solid.

The train heaved by after 8:00, and it gathered speed as it passed over the newly repaired tracks, the engineer waving to the foreman. Suddenly the prisoners and guards fell back in panic as one rail collapsed under the immense weight of the giant engine, and the trail bolted from the track. It hurled forward forty feet on the ground and threatened to topple sideways before grinding to a disastrous stop, the two front cars completely derailed. The prisoners slunk quietly out of the way of the Germans, who converged in a huddle of frantic rage. But it was late and nothing could be done. The train would take hours to be backed onto the tracks. It would have to stay where it was overnight, and the prisoners were sent home. The men agreed, without voicing their fears, that they would continue to work slowly, no matter what the consequences.

They escaped the derailing of the freight train with no more punishment than a cut in their food rations. They now supplemented their rations daily with vegetables, bread stolen from the bakery, and a large ring of cheese one of the men had filched weeks ago, which still melted smoothly over their bread on the stove.

They had written letters home but had received nothing back, and the letters they sent were strictly censored. Their spirits were so low that the letters family members finally did receive from them were brief, hollow, and unpleasant, as well as uninformative, with maddening slices and blots by German censors.

"They treat us OK, food is good," Chasteen wrote home to his mother as he pulled fragments of a dead mouse from his soup. He wrote without emotion and with stoic blandness. She would know he was alive, and that was the most important thing. Dan Jones wrote to his mother, unwilling to lie but unable to tell her the truth, "I am healthy, but not as I used to be." He asked her to write to Caroline, and he signed off in the large block letters that the Germans insisted on.

Marlowe spotted a German officer visiting the compound the following night and, encouraged by his men, approached him to issue a complaint. Their interpreter, Kleppe, had returned to the hospital after a bad case of dysentery. Now they had little means of communication. Marlowe spoke a few words of German to the officer and asked for an interpreter. The officer lifted his hands in a gesture of futility as he shook his head. He spoke no English and was not going to hunt down someone who did. Duperry came to Marlowe's rescue, summoning the elderly French prisoner who worked in the bakery. This man, although he didn't speak a word of English, was fluent in German. Duperry, Marlowe, and the baker stood before the officer as well as their sergeant in command and an entourage of guards.

Marlowe began his case with direct displeasure: "We are living here under terrible conditions. Where are the Red Cross workers? They don't even come here to see the place. We haven't received one single Red Cross package since we got here. We work twelve hours a day or more, most weeks without a day off. As you can see, many of these men are sick and need medical attention. German prisoners in American hands are not being treated this way. We don't get enough rations, either." As he took a breath, he nodded at Duperry, who now turned to the baker and spoke to him in French, gesticulating wildly. The baker listened, nodding silently, then Duperry fell silent and all eyes fell on the baker. The German officer tilted his head toward the Frenchman with a condescending smile, as if waiting to hear a child's tantrum. The Frenchman flushed and looked from the Germans to the Americans. Duperry spoke to him again in French, and he responded in the same language.

"What's he saying? I thought he spoke German!" Marlowe shouted angrily.

"He does. He's scared to tell them what you just said."

Marlowe threw up his hands in exasperation and turned circles before looking back at the German group, who waited for communication. He took a deep breath as his face flushed and spoke again to Duperry.

"You tell that Goddamn son-of-a-bitch coward that if he don't translate what I just said, he's going to be in a lot worse trouble than he could ever be from these Germans. I'll kill him myself."

He continued cursing to himself as Duperry spoke to the Frenchman. The German officer let out a low rumble of a laugh, grasping the general idea of the conversation. The Frenchman, trembling unhappily, spoke hesitantly in German. Whether he translated directly, Marlowe couldn't tell, but they proceeded with their three-way conversation.

"We've got no soap, no towels, no blankets."

"Pas de savon, ni serviette, ni couverture."

"Kiene Siefe, kein Handtuch, keine Decke."

The officer nodded intently as he listened to the speech and agreed to look into it. Meanwhile, the sergeant in command glared at Marlowe vengefully.

The next morning, the prisoners received an extra piece of bread with their coffee, and their portion of soup seemed slightly larger. A few incidentals showed up, including a bar of soap, which Leeps handed over with an insolent leer, and they were promised a Red Cross package soon. But in a week the place had returned to normal, and the officer's promise was forgotten.

CHAPTER 16

The year 1945 arrived unnoticed by the prisoners. Only the growing harshness of winter and the replacement of guards affected their lives. Their work never seemed to end, and neither did the snow. Their hands cracked, peeled, bled, and became as clumsy from frostbite as their toes.

Jim Rizzuto looked up from his work as he shoveled ballast and caught Pops watching him. He had lost at least one quarter of his weight, and he could feel it, his uniform hanging loosely from his shoulders, his trousers knotted over his shrunken frame. He had quit eating lately; it only made him sicker.

Pops now spoke with the foreman, and they both looked at Rizzuto. The prisoner dug his shovel into the gravel and looked away from them nervously. None of the prisoners liked to be singled out. Pops returned to Rizzuto and told him to put down the shovel. They were walking to Marlow.

Rizzuto had been to see the doctor in Marlow twice, and he knew without a doubt that his third visit would generate the same response: "Send him back to work." But he left with the guard, relieved to put down his heavy tools.

As the doctor began examining Rizzuto, Pops grasped his arm and interrupted, "This prisoner is too sick to work on the tracks." The doctor looked at the guard and waited, and Pops ordered him to declare the prisoner unfit for work. To Rizzuto's amazement, the doctor nodded and obediently wrote the paratrooper's release, ending his career in railroad labor.

Jim Rizzuto was sent back to Stalag II-A in Neubrandenburg, where he remained for the duration of the war. Watsick and Mickelson noticed his absence on the tracks and then in the loft, not surprised, but unsure of his fate. They would not see their friend again for forty years.

With the passing of January, fewer German civilians came to watch or jeer at the Americans, and those who happened by had a more solemn, drawn look in their eyes, a look of want and discouragement. There was little doubt that the war was not as favorable for Hitler's Germany as the guards made out, and the men wondered occasionally if the Germans would run completely out of food. Many of the guards now ate little more than the prisoners did, and the men agreed to start stockpiling whatever food they could.

Occasionally, after working all day to piece together the German railroad, they would hear the familiar sound of American bombers buzzing toward them, and prisoners and guards alike would dive suddenly for cover. They would watch with incredulity as the bombers dropped their load on the rails that the 311/I internees had just repaired. Several prisoners jumped to their feet and cursed the American pilots, shaking their fists at the retreating planes. The railroad work was all they did, and as much as they hated it, they were proud of what they accomplished. They felt a twinge of satisfaction as they left for home each night, looking back at the straight and solid rails of their creation. After the bombing, they were forced to start the work anew, tearing up the rail, waiting for new supplies, waiting for trains to inch past, standing in the freezing weather, hating the pilots of those American planes.

One frigid morning soon after Rizzuto's departure, the guards left the men in the loft for the day without explanation. It was a Sunday, which they now occasionally had off, and they sat by the stove trying to stay warm and distracted with games of cards or conversation. They had heard all each other's stories and knew of each man's exploits in the army and in high school. They knew what kind of food their mothers used to make, and what girl was probably crying her eyes out every night for them at home.

Stan Watsick sat winning all the cigarettes as usual, then shared them with everyone as they sat around the table, wrapped in their long coats. The loft was dim, as the bulb had burned out several weeks before.

They looked up expectantly as they heard the door at the stairs open, and they waited as slow, heavy footsteps plodded toward them. Herbert came to face them at the top of the stairs. He was a man in his mid-thirties, but he now looked years older, and his Hitler-square mustache sank over his mouth. He stood looking at the men with a strange unnatural and defeated expression in his dark eyes. He walked toward the stove and knelt without speaking, holding his hands up before it, rubbing them slowly together in the dry warmth. The men fell silent, unaccustomed to social visits from guards. Marlowe and Fisher sat down beside him and spoke to him in German, asking if they had to work today after all. But Herbert shook his head silently, staring at the small stove.

"What's the matter? Is something wrong?" Marlowe asked. Herbert's eyes grew teary as he looked at the young American men beside him.

"Meine Frau, meine Kinder . . . sind umgebracht." He gestured his explanation, speaking slowly and repeating everything he said. His wife and children had been killed the night before in Berlin by American bombers. The prisoners listened in shocked silence. They thought they understood why he had come to them. He couldn't show his sorrow before his comrades. The German people had been changed by Hitler. They could no more show the weakness of sorrow or fear for their country than they could celebrate Christmas. It was unpatriotic. It showed a lack of faith in Hitler. They seemed hardened people who mistrusted each other profoundly. He broke into tears again as he spoke, his words slurring as his voice cracked in sobs. The men understood only fragments as he described what he'd heard, streams of tears now running onto his large coat. Fisher put his arm around the distraught man, and Marlowe spoke encouragingly, saying only those words he could express in German—that they understood, that war was hell, that what had happened to his family was a very sad thing, and that they sympathized.

Herbert warmed to their compassion and spoke freely, not caring that the men understood little of what he said. The men sat around the loft listening, struck mute by the irony of a war in which this man came to the enemy for comfort. A few men shrugged and returned to their card game or walked back to their bunks. He was still the enemy, and suffering during wartime was nothing new. They were all suffering themselves, but they sure couldn't talk to Herbert about it. Fisher and Marlowe stayed at his side for nearly an hour before the man regained his composure. He tugged a handkerchief from his pocket and wiped his face, then smoothed his hair with a damp hand. He stood and straightened his coat, nodding good-bye to Fisher and Marlowe. As he left the barracks, he paused, giving the men a final sweeping look while raising his hand in an enigmatic salute.

Lindsey waited until the door shut, then spoke up from the card table: "That guard is going to be trouble for us, just wait. He's already thinking about takin' it out on all of us." Some disagreed, but the general consensus among the men, even Fisher and Marlowe, was that he was a man to avoid.

Herbert would prove to be the least of their problems, however, as a rage fueled by frustration was germinating in many of the guards. The Germans now feared that they might be losing the war.

The next day, the prisoners were surprised to be told that they would not work on the railroad. They were assigned a new project. They would be digging a large clearing near the tracks and laying out cement in a round block. The foreman explained their task and walked off with young Sylvester at his side to sit by a fire nearby.

Marlowe followed behind them speaking in a blend of German and English. "What is this? What are we building?" The foreman looked him over irritably, waving him off with his gloved hand. Young Sylvester imitated his gesture and threw in a few insults. Marlowe squared his shoulders. He was a bigger man than Flop Ears, and he straightened himself above him and walked back to the work site, suspicion in his blue eyes.

The men worked on the project grudgingly, none happy to be building something they didn't understand. They worked as slowly as they could, and when a young Polish prisoner walked by, looking at the men curiously as he passed, Marlowe asked Watsick to speak with him. Watsick walked over to the prisoner, who stopped and waited, while Jon, the Polish officer, watched silently. Jon didn't dare speak to the Polish prisoners. His fluent Polish would give him away. Watsick, who spoke decent Polish, knew most of the Poles well, being one of the most personable of all the Americans. Even the girls in the field would straighten and wave to Watsick as he called out salutations in their language. He called all of them Sophie—a good Polish name. He had learned from these women that they worked in the fields in the day and were taken into town to service bored German soldiers at night. Watsick hated the thought, and his heart went out to the Poles, who had been in this war and suffered here, miles from their home, for so many years longer than most Americans.

He now asked the Pole what he knew about the project they were undertaking. The Polish prisoner looked over Watsick's shoulder at the men who stood expectantly around their work. It was already the end of the day, and a clearing was laid for the cement. The prisoner turned to Watsick and began explaining. Soon Watsick marched back to Marlowe, his face set in anger.

"It's a Goddamn gun emplacement," he said, and all the men looked up, dropping their tools. The guards, not understanding what had just been said, could sense mutiny, and they stood over the men with their rifles ready. They shouted at the men to return to work, and reluctantly the men obeyed. Within an hour the guards returned them to their barracks, where the men clustered around Marlowe for instruction.

"It seems to me there ain't no way we should be working on a gun emplacement," Marlowe began, and the men all voiced their agreement. "All right, so what do we do? Refuse to work?" The men again concurred. "Are you all sure?" They nodded unanimously. "Then I'll tell them first thing tomorrow, we ain't working on it any longer."

The next morning, the men stood around the work project in a tight, defiant group as Marlowe spoke to the foreman: "It states right in the Geneva convention that we don't have to work on any gun emplacements or weapons of any kind. We ain't going to lift another finger to put that thing up." The foreman looked at him, a vein rising above his ear. Marlowe waited, wondering if the foreman would catch his bluff. He had no idea if such a clause was stated in the Geneva convention, but he knew it ought to be, and he'd brought it up for added weight.

The foreman let out a sigh and left Marlowe to request the presence of a German officer. When this man was located, Marlowe repeated his speech to him. The officer paced angrily and the day stretched on as the men sat down and waited. One thing they had learned since their imprisonment was patience. The foreman and the officer argued in strained tones. Charlie Chasteen watched two young German women pass by and smiled and waved. They looked away, but not before he noticed a friendly light in their eyes, and he almost believed he'd seen one of them wink.

At noon, with a tight expression and raspy voice, the foreman called the guards over to him. Marlowe knew that he had triumphed, and he grinned at the men without speaking, cautious of annoying the Germans any further. Within minutes, they were back at work on the tracks. The prisoners took a handcar down the tracks for rails and sang American folk songs loudly as they went. They worked at their usual slow pace and had laid only two rails by the end of the day.

As they stood waiting at the train station that evening, several German commuters eyeing them suspiciously, Jones slid his foot along the icy platform lightheartedly. "I'll bet you could slide quite a ways on this ice," he said to Turner. Jones stepped back on the platform experimentally and slid toward Bruton, who gave him an encouraging shove. Some of the others followed suit, and taking a running start, each slid across the station. They started lining up for turns, skating toward the German civilians, stopping several feet short and returning to stand in the lengthening line. The civilians and guards alike watched them in amazement as if the prisoners had lost their minds. They seemed at that moment more like schoolboys than enemy prisoners.

Spivey said he was New York jitterbug champion in 1943–44, and he now did a few fancy steps on the ice, noticing the eyes of German commuters on him. "Come on, Spivey! Let's see you dance," the prisoners encouraged, and he began a few simple jitterbug steps, then danced faster, taking one of the other men as a partner. They showed off for a German audience that was now a large crowd. The people pushed closer to see him dance, as the prisoners cheered him on. Several of the German men and women began to smile. Two small German boys watched, fascinated, and tried to imitate the steps. The guards moved toward the prisoners threateningly. The German people were warming now toward the small, good-looking American kid who performed shamelessly for them, enjoying the attention while other Americans continued sliding across the station around him. The guards looked at each other with a nod and stepped forward, one to grab Spivey, and another to stop Bruton, who was skating backward with his hands raised dramatically above his head. They shouted gruff warnings at the prisoners, effectively dampening the excitement, and forced them into a tight, quiet group. In the sudden silence, the civilians lost interest and turned their concentration on the tracks as the train approached.

CHAPTER 17

The prisoners learned quickly just how much they had humiliated and infuriated their captors by refusing to work on the gun emplacement. By winning that battle of wills, they had set themselves up for increased punishment and harder work. They now traveled to Sanitz in a boxcar known as 40 & 8, set behind an open car carrying an 88 antiaircraft gun. They would no longer travel with German civilians. As they climbed out of their car, they passed the gun emplacement project and saw work back under way. They recognized the men who worked on it as French prisoners.

The foreman appeared at the tracks with his usual lunch briefcase, along with a foul expression. He set the men to work immediately, barking at them continually to hurry up. Several of the men were severely beaten for little reason, except as examples and as recipients of the Germans' anger.

As Charlie Chasteen pumped a handcar, a guard stood above him casually tossing a large rock in his hand. Chasteen's eyes followed the movement of a young woman walking near the tracks, casting sideways smiles in his direction. Suddenly the guard hit Chasteen full force across the forehead with the rock. Chasteen reeled and fell off the handcar, then stood, shaking his head and feeling for blood. His fingers ran across a bulbous swelling, but the skin was unbroken. He picked up his hat and pulled it down over his forehead. He didn't mention the incident to the other men.

Unprovoked attacks became commonplace over the next few weeks, and as the men worked, they tried to see 360 degrees around them. Even Sylvester had become more malicious, shouting abuses or throwing fistfuls of gravel in their faces. Anything he could think of to provoke them, he acted upon with precocious ingenuity.

Incredibly to the Americans, the temperature continued plunging daily, and they stuffed their coats with newspaper they found discarded along the tracks. They took as much coal as they could from the station to keep the loft heated, until the Germans caught on. In mid-January the American prisoners were accused of stealing over a thousand pounds of briquettes. Now they could only pick up the occasional piece of coal that fell off a passing train. Food was more difficult to steal because there was less of it for the Germans, but the men were so adept now at stealing that they had a healthy-sized stash in their loft. Men took turns playing sick and going to the doctor's office. Duperry was the most frequent visitor, disregarding Marlowe's warnings that the guards were running short of patience.

Several days of consistent hard labor and beatings took their toll on the men, and they became increasingly irritable and clumsy with their work. Chasteen felt the foreman watching him more closely than most of the others, but after a few days he no longer cared and took his time at his work, pausing several times as the snow that fell on them warmed to slush.

The temperature had reached its lowest and now worked its way suddenly upward. While it hovered above freezing, the men again cursed the German weather as snow turned to heavy rain. Chasteen, Lindsey, and Spivey stood trying to wrap themselves tighter to keep off the rain, as the guards shouted at them to work. Several men dropped their tools and went to Marlowe. "Let's stop working. They can't make us work in this," they said, and Marlowe shook his head. He doubted that they could push the Germans any further.

They shouted back and forth to each other over the noise of the rain, and Chasteen joined the group of rebellious men who informed the guards they refused to work in the downpour. The foreman approached the group swiftly, and without negotiation pulled Chasteen away from the others. Chasteen realized that he was in trouble, but even in his helplessness he still wondered if he could turn the situation to his benefit. As Leeps came to stand on his other side, the two Germans dragged him toward a small shack that was commonly used for beatings, away from the curious eyes of the townspeople. Realizing what was happening, Chasteen frantically began to put together a plan for an escape. If he could get them both on one side, he could let them get in one good hit, then pull the weapon loose from Leeps and strike him in the groin, smash the skull of the foreman, then head out the back of the shack. He knew he would be killed if he was caught, but he had to try.

They dragged him into the dark shack, which rattled with the urgency of the heavy rain, and shoved him forward. Immediately, as he stumbled for balance, the foreman hit him full force in the back of the neck with a forcing rod. As the foreman bludgeoned him again with the heavy piece of metal, Leeps stood in front, holding him by the shoulders. Staggering under the blows, Chasteen realized that with Leeps in front of him he was completely helpless. He soon lost conscious thought as the foreman continued to strike him across the back and shoulders until he could no longer stand, then tossed him in a heap outside of the shack, an ugly example for the other men. The prisoners looked at his limp form; they were sobered by the act of violence and rendered silent in their fury. After the day's work was over, several men came to his assistance, gathering up the injured prisoner. They helped him stand and half carried him to the station, oblivious to the rain in their resentment—resentment that seemed to keep resurfacing no matter how hard they tried to control it. Each time they won a small triumph, they once again were beaten down. Chasteen said nothing more than, "That son of a bitch Leeps got right in front of me. There was nothing I could do."

Chasteen was back at work the next morning, bent nearly in half and staying as far from the foreman and Leeps as he possibly could. It was hard for him to control the murderous thoughts that now ran through his head, and he eventually gave way to them, growing obsessed with thoughts of torturing and killing the bald foreman who had tormented him for so long. Snakes of knotted skin and welts ran across his back, and he guessed that he had fractures of some kind in his back. The pain was excruciating, and he worked feebly throughout the day, fueled only by his fantasy of killing Flop Ears. Although he accomplished little on the tracks, the other men covered for him, doing his work when the guards weren't noticing. He was not the only prisoner with deadly hatred welling up inside him toward the foreman. The prisoners shared a general understanding that if the opportunity arose, they would kill him.

Within a week the rain finally gave way to sunshine, and it warmed the men's backs as they worked. Spivey and Chasteen set themselves up along the outskirts of town, working a distance from the guards and foreman and even from the other prisoners. Chasteen's back was healing but permanently damaged, with stiff kinks that caused him to tire quickly. He moved at a relaxed pace, not unhappy with his work there on a warm day, away from the constant abuse of the Germans.

Several townspeople walked by on the road fifty feet above them, and a few glanced in their direction, but the two friends paid little notice until they heard feet stepping lightly down the gravel slope toward them. Chasteen looked up to see the two young German women he'd waved at in the past smiling down at him. The women knelt in front of the two men, who were hunched over their work, and Chasteen looked them over in appreciation and disbelief. They were both pretty, in their early twenties, one a willowy blond and the other slightly older and smaller with red hair and brown eyes. They spoke to the men softly in German, asking them their names.

Chasteen and Spivey introduced themselves eagerly, and the girls told them who they were, the blond calling herself Anna, and her friend, Merta. They said they were both officers' wives who were all alone since the war and could use some men to help them around the yard. They lived together in a house nearby. Charlie wiped his face and smiled at them winningly, overwhelmed with his good fortune. He would rather have one of these girls than even old Flop Ears' head, and he spoke with a generous smile and the little German he knew, offering to help the women out any way they wanted. He and Spivey glanced around them repeatedly for German witnesses, but the girls paid no attention, smiling at the two men smoothly. They left within minutes, winking and laughing melodically as they climbed gracefully back to the road. Spivey and Chasteen stared after them transfixed. It was the best fortune they'd had since their capture, and they now exchanged a look and laughed, certain that they would see the young women again soon.

A middle-aged guard had joined the men several weeks before. Too old to fight on the front, he had replaced Herbert, who wasn't. More than a week after the two friends had met the officers' wives, Chasteen noticed the guard staring at him with a wry grin. The guard took Chasteen aside and told him that he and Spivey would be helping two civilians with some yard work later in the week. He looked Chasteen over, up and down, before grinning unpleasantly and shaking his finger at him as if he had known their purpose.

Chasteen had seen the women around the tracks several times since meeting them. They watched the two prisoners or spoke with this guard. Chasteen noticed that the guard spoke with special interest to Anna, the young blond. He now only stared at the guard blankly, as if in ignorance, hoping to avoid any jealousy. The two friends had told the other prisoners about the girls, but the men were scornful. They needed proof. Most of them were now far beyond any interest in women. Food was their only interest. Only occasionally a prisoner lay in his bunk recalling the soft feeling of a particular woman in his arms and his loneliness would become momentarily unbearable.

When the two men were called off the tracks on a Friday morning, some of the prisoners cheered them. Chasteen straightened his clothes, while Spivey ran his battered comb through his hair. He'd recently had his hair cut by one of the other prisoners, who had trimmed it with dull shears, if not expertly, at least generally straight. He still washed his hair and body every chance he got, often using the ice water in ponds and meadows, and was considerably cleaner than the other prisoners. While others drank their water rations, he washed in his. The two friends now joked in nervous anticipation on their way to the house, Pops guiding them to their place of work.

They found the German girls watching for them from their kitchen window. The women came out of the house as the three men approached the step. They gave the prisoners only a vague glance, then thanked Pops, telling him that they would be fine with the two Americans if he would just come for them again in the evening. Pops, who had removed his hat, smiled at the young ladies and nodded his head in response. His house was not far away, and he was pleased to be spending the day at home with his wife. If he had any idea that anything unusual was happening, he showed no sign of it and walked away briskly.

The women put the prisoners to work on a stack of dry wood behind the house. The woodpile was immense, but the women urged them not to hurry— it didn't have to be finished in one day. They retreated into the house as Spivey and Chasteen watched them. When the door was shut, the two men blew on their hands and got to work, wielding the axes easily, well toned from their work on the railroad. Frequently they paused and glanced toward the house, where a thin line of smoke rose from the chimney and occasional movement could be seen through the windows. As the morning progressed, Chasteen found himself becoming bold with enthusiasm. He had expected more than chopping wood, and he now asked Spivey if maybe the women wanted the men to make the first move. Spivey laughed and lifted his shoulders in a question mark. "What's it going to hurt to wait? We got time on our side." But Chasteen could work for only another five minutes before setting down his ax, resting his hands on his hips as he watched his friend swing at the wood.

"I'm goin' in," he said, his voice determined. Spivey watched him walk up the steps and tap lightly on the door, then turn the handle and disappear inside without waiting for an answer. Seeing the door remain shut for several minutes, Spivey returned to his work, determined to wait for his friend's report.

Chasteen walked into the house and paused inside the door, looking around him. He stood in a small kitchen, more modest than those he'd grown up with in South Carolina but comfortably furnished with flowers and baskets and a table in the middle of a hard tile floor. Both girls watched him from where they stood chopping vegetables. He hesitated only momentarily, as the look they gave him, if surprised, was not annoyed. Anna gestured for him to take off his coat, and he did so, hanging it on the chair, watching her blue eyes in anticipation.

It was red-headed Merta who laughed and spoke encouraging words to her lighter-skinned friend. Anna picked up a basket with a smile and moved past Chasteen toward the basement door. She stopped and looked back at him with an inviting smile. Would he like to help her choose some potatoes from the basement? Chasteen nodded wordlessly, his German escaping him suddenly, and Merta called out good-bye as he followed Anna down a narrow set of stairs.

In the dark chill of the dank basement, Anna turned to face him and put down her basket. Without speaking, he pulled her into his arms, feeling her compliant against him. The feeling and smell of a woman was so intoxicating he was aware of nothing at first but his immediate exhilaration. When she kissed him, her lips expressing as much desire as he felt for her, he let out a groan of pleasure and smiled against her mouth as his hand slid down her skirt, then back underneath it.

"Prima, Prima," he whispered, her makeup smudging his face with a sweet, sticky smell that further aroused him. His hands roamed her body freely, sliding loose a collar, then a stocking, trying desperately to get her clothes off, in a fury of anticipation. As he slid his hand underneath her blouse and then her brassiere, squeezing the soft flesh of her breasts, she squirmed free and rested a small hand on his pants, pulling at the zipper. She wore no panties, and loosening his pants, he found himself violently in the grips of his excitement. Within moments, moving hard and fast, he released long-suppressed desires, and they both collapsed on the cold floor happily.

She was back on her feet within seconds, straightening her clothes and gathering potatoes to put in her basket. He watched her with a wide smile, then followed her back up the stairs. Merta offered a teasing glance, and he climbed back into his coat, walking out into the icy cold, where Spivey now waited impatiently.

CHAPTER 18

Spivey and Chasteen continued their work with inattention, Chasteen savoring what was a memory still warm, and Spivey anticipating anxiously. Merta stuck her head out the door long enough to invite them both inside for lunch, encouraging them to leave their work until later.

"So dedicated!" she cooed in her language as they passed her. She was smaller than Anna, and several inches shorter than Spivey. The two exchanged smiles as she shut the door. Clearly Spivey and Merta were well matched, and as Spivey sat down next to Chasteen at the table, she rested her hand on the back of his chair, watching him eat attentively. They had prepared a bowl of vegetable broth that tasted delicious, the generous chunks of potatoes soft and nourishing, with turnips and carrots and cabbage. The men devoured their food, and already as Chasteen wiped his bowl clean with a hard piece of bread, he looked at the folds of Anna's skirt around her hips and warmed in excitement. Now that he had been with her once, his lust was inflamed tenfold. They walked hand in hand to a sitting room in the front of the house, leaving Spivey alone with his new girl.

As Anna dressed for the second time, Chasteen watched with admiration. She climbed to her feet to discover in horror that in his enthusiasm he had ripped her stocking. She found the hole with her finger and ran her hand along the length of it, then looked at Chasteen for an apology. He stared back, shocked at the apparent anger on her face. He told her that after the war he would buy her ten pairs to replace them, but she waved his offer aside with her hand. As he stood and climbed back into his pants, she sat naked, staring forlornly at her stocking, completely devastated.

"Hell, it's only a stocking," he blurted in English, frustrated by her sudden mood change. He slid the silk out of her hand and pulled her to her feet and against him, kissing her passionately. To his relief, she smiled grudgingly, then with the dimples that he was now accustomed to.

After dressing and sharing a cigarette with him, she showed him a picture of her husband. He was a Luftwaffe man, a high-ranking officer, and she hadn't seen him for years. She reflected, as she stared at the picture blankly, that she could no longer be sure that he was alive at all.

When Spivey and Chasteen returned to 311/I, they couldn't control their smug grins. Chasteen told the men that the food had been great, the work easy, and as far as the love . . . he didn't want to make them sick with envy, so he'd spare them the details. It took only a few minutes of coaxing before Chasteen told them the general events, and that night he and Spivey slept in the filthy and cold quarters less hungry and less alone. They dreamed through the night of softer beds and warmer places.

The next morning, as Leeps hunkered up the stairs, Duperry let out a groan and winked at his bunkmate. He had played sick several times since Christmas, and some of the guards believed him to be very unhealthy, while others were more skeptical. He was an expert at his play acting, gripping his stomach as sweat broke out on his face and neck, his eyes rolling unnaturally back in his skull. He began his performance again this morning, while the other men climbed to their feet and began marching down the stairs single file. Leeps approached Duperry and stared at him without comment for several minutes.

"I'm krank. Krank," Duperry said, rolling slightly from side to side. "So don't just stand there, get me to a doctor, you dumb son of a bitch," he added, his face twisted suddenly in his contempt for the half-wit guard. Leeps had been with the men since they had arrived, and most of the men knew him as an unpredictable danger. The guard now understood clearly that he was being insulted, and his face screwed up in childish anger.

"What the hell are you wai . . ." Duperry continued as Leeps swung out an arm as big as a tree trunk and lifted him up from the bunk by his collar. The guard kept a bayonet loosely in his hand, but he gripped it tightly now and suddenly plunged it into Duperry's face. The remaining prisoners in the barracks recoiled in horror, realizing that the bayonet was penetrating the man's eye, and his terrified screams filled the loft and the barn, drowning out the squealing pigs below.

Leeps dropped the man to the floor after pulling his bayonet loose and wiping the blood on his trousers. He looked at the horrified crowd around him and shouted, "Los! Schnell!"

"Oh, my eye, my eye! My eye!" Duperry screamed in a strange roller coaster of sound, his pain and fear raising his voice then lowering it. He held his hand over his face, blood pouring between his fingers. The men remained where they stood, unwilling to leave their comrade there on the floor, and Leeps stepped back to him, yanking him to his feet and shoving him toward the stairs, which he stumbled down, screaming even louder.

Duperry went to work with the others, under the orders of Leeps and agreement of the other guards. Marlowe helped wrap the young man's eye with several strips of clothing over the cavity, donated by the other men. He whimpered now quietly, asking Marlowe if his eye was gone.

"No, it ain't gone. He got you on the side. You'll be all right, but just keep it covered and press on it some. You have to stop the bleeding." Duperry trudged to work with the other men. Some of the guards looked at him skeptically as the cloth over his eye went from dirt gray to scarlet and blood dripped down the prisoner's cheek. An elderly German man stopped to stare, and Watsick looked up from his work.

"Haben sie Tabak?" he asked. The man started in surprise, looking Watsick over, then reaching in his pocket to hand the prisoner a cigarette. Mickelson gave his friend a congratulatory pound on the back, and Watsick lit it and shared it with him.

CHAPTER 19

Jim Bruton heaved with all his weight on the handle that he pumped to budge the heavy handcar. It moved more slowly than usual, and he and another prisoner groaned as they struggled with the heavy load. The two men were transporting the tools and six full-length rails, as well as themselves, a guard, and Sylvester. The guard stood at the rear of the cart, balancing his bayonet while securing the loose rails. Sylvester sat in front, humming loudly, his hands buried in his pockets and his foot sliding along the track in front of them.

The rattle of the aged car was a familiar sound, and Bruton heard it only subconsciously as they neared the work site, the prisoners coming into view. They picked up speed, now within a hundred feet of the work site, then felt the wheel lurch, the entire cart jolted by the impact of an object underneath. An ear-piercing shriek followed, and the prisoners grasped the handles and brake, bringing the handcar to a sudden stop. Sylvester rolled off the cart onto the ground as he screamed in agony. The boy had slid his foot too close to the moving parts, and it had been pulled under the front wheel. He now lay on the ground, his hand clutching his ankle, his foot bent at a bizarre angle.

The guards and prisoners surrounded the boy at once, in a giant mass, and the foreman shoved through them to examine the foot, his face uncharacteristically pale. He was ultimately responsible for the boy. The foreman tugged at the laces of the small boot, but the level of Sylvester's screams reached a new high, and he pulled away. After several aborted tries, the foreman agreed to leave the boot on the mangled foot. Bruton watched silently, sympathetic despite himself as he saw the little troublemaker now so helpless and pathetic. The foreman stood and looked around him at the crowd that had formed and ran his hand across his bald head. He instructed Pops to take two prisoners and the boy into Marlow by handcar, where the doctor would be able to help him. Pops selected Jones and Marlowe, and they loaded Sylvester on the cart, wrapping a stiff cloth around his ankle. Pops seated himself on the back.

Since their internment, neither Marlowe nor Jones had been to the city of Marlow or any other town of more than a few hundred people, and they were almost excited to be headed somewhere new. Sylvester shrieked in his pain as they went, but when the car came to a stop near the station and curious people turned inevitably to look, he quieted to a forlorn whimper. Marlowe and Jones took turns carrying the boy as they proceeded through town toward the doctor's office. As they walked they spoke soft encouragements in his ear, offering him a few jokes and distractions from his pain.

He brightened slightly, wiping the tears that had collected under his eyes and attempting a few smiles as they told him how they'd always wanted a cast when they were his age. Jones demonstrated how Sylvester would look when he walked, staggering on ahead of the group, drawing stares from the towns-people and a grin from Sylvester.

Marlowe and Jones stood in the waiting room, leaving the seats for Ger-mans, while Pops and the boy hurried into the office. They had little doubt that the foot was badly broken, and the two prisoners spoke together quietly, sur-prised by their own concern for the boy.

When Pops returned, he smiled for the prisoners. Sylvester's parents were on their way. The foot was broken but would heal well, the doctor had prognosed. Now, as they left the doctor's and Sylvester, the sun had brightened the streets of the small town, and they wandered through, looking at the sights with curi-osity. Pops took them through town at a leisurely pace, enjoying the first warm sunshine after a long, miserable winter. Jones and Marlowe watched the people pass, surprised to see so many who still seemed to live normal lives regardless of the war.

Pops stopped in a tobacco store, and they waited out front. Even Pops was pleased to be in town. He shared a piece of sausage with the men as they strolled back to the tracks.

By the time they were back at the work site, the day was nearly over, and they helped load up the tools, although the tracks remained in disrepair. The tracks were increasingly more difficult to rescue as time passed and the Ameri-cans bombed more and more frequently. Often after a day's work the tracks were in almost the same state of chaos they had been in when the men arrived.

At the station that evening, Spivey danced again for the other train passen-gers, his steps more enthusiastic as his fellow prisoners encouraged him. Sev-eral of the men took turns dancing and performing for the Germans. Heartened by the changing weather, they joked and clowned in front of the staring Ger-mans. Many of the civilians laughed outright, enjoying themselves as much as the prisoners, but the fun was immediately squelched by the guards. The last thing they needed was German sympathy for American prisoners.

Jones watched the German people greet each other with their customary and obligatory "Heil Hitler." They used it as a replacement for good morning, how are you? or good-bye, and every German citizen was required to say it. Jones looked at Leeps and held his hand up, saying "Heil Hitler!" in a mocking voice, the grin on his face derogatory. Leeps looked around him in confusion and responded, "Heil Hitler." Although he knew he was being teased, he didn't dare respond otherwise, should other Germans be watching.

From the guards they continued to hear that Patton and Montgomery were getting a resounding thrashing, but the Poles and French told them otherwise. As their guards were replaced by older, weaker, or more severely wounded men and the others disappeared to the Russian front, the prisoners guessed that the Germans were fighting a losing battle, spreading their soldiers thinly across Europe.

CHAPTER 20

When the guard came for Chasteen and Spivey the following Friday morning, he looked the two over with a scornful smile before wagging his finger in Chasteen's face. He faced the prisoner with an unshaved and wrinkled face, his bloodshot eyes examining him with distaste. "Ja," he said thoughtfully, with an accusatory nod. Chasteen shook his head with a hasty jerk. "Nein," he assured. The guard seemed not to hear. "Ja, ja, ja, ja," his finger stroking the air beneath the prisoner's nose. Chasteen imagined that sexual relations with a German girl could be punishable by death, and he answered as many times with a negation. He was sure now that the guard was involved with at least one of the same girls.

They worked in the backyard of the small house for only an hour this time before entering the door. The rest of the day they spent with the women, talking and eating but mostly locked in embrace. Chasteen was well accustomed to his blond lover, and they lay together naked, relaxing in each other's arms. He knew nothing of the girl except that she was the wife of an important officer, an officer that he suspected was dead, although she still hoped for his return.

The four of them ate together at the small table and joked and laughed as the prisoners struggled with their German. The men had no misconception as to their role in the women's lives and asked for nothing more than these days of pleasure, away from the mundanity of their work. As the day reached an end, the men hurried out to the backyard, busily chopping wood when Pops came for them. The guard smiled pleasantly, oblivious to the unusual grins the men flashed at him despite themselves.

Food was scarcer as each week passed, and the men found even fewer solid remnants of potato in their soup. Kalkreuth, who worked in the kitchen each day with the French chef and several German guards, informed them that most of the giant hogs penned below them had been slaughtered under Hitler's orders. Their soup was thinner now, he said, because there were fewer potatoes available for the compound. Even the guards were forced to eat increasingly smaller portions of what had already been inadequate nourishment. The pork from the hogs had been sent off by train, and none had enjoyed as much as a bite of it.

The men were surprised when Kalkreuth suddenly lost his job in the kitchen and was sent out on the railroad with them. They had hardly seen the man previously. He told them with disgust that he had been fired from his job of privilege for their sake. The German guards had brought in a dead horse, he had no idea from where, and the smell had spread throughout the kitchen swiftly and sickeningly. The horse had been dead an indeterminable time, partially frozen in the winter snow. The front end was unrecognizable in its state of decomposition, but the Germans got to work sawing off the hind end while Kalkreuth watched, incredulous. They pushed the putrid hunk of meat toward his pot of water, which was heating over a large stove, and instructed him to cut up the meat and throw it in the soup for the prisoners. The prisoners hadn't had meat for months, because the Germans had little meat to offer, and now they honestly felt that they were treating the Americans. Kalkreuth looked from the meat to the guard and shook his head in disbelief.

"I ain't putting that meat in their soup. It's rank, spoiled, you understand? It's gone bad, foul. They will be *krank*," he told them, putting his hand over his nose to express himself. The guard was not only irritated, he was insulted. The meat was not bad, it had been frozen. "This is a war, they're not here on vacation. Put the meat in the soup!" Kalkreuth shook his head, and the guard grappled around him for something to hit the insolent prisoner with. Generally the guards liked Kalkreuth. They knew him better than they did the other prisoners, and he interacted with them on a familiar basis. He rarely suffered the beatings or verbal abuse that the others did. Now, as the guard came at him threateningly with a soup ladle, Kalkreuth stood his ground in front of the horse that lay reeking on the kitchen floor. Rather than hit the prisoner, the guard paused and allowed him one last chance. He ordered Kalkreuth to cook that meat. If he didn't, he would be out working with the other men on the railroad. Kalkreuth folded his arms stubbornly and with finality, and the guard shook his head, grabbing him by the collar and dragging him out the door to be locked in the loft until the men returned. Kalkreuth refused to eat the soup for the next few evenings, but the other men did, assuring him that it was just the usual potato peelings. If they were sick from it later, they couldn't tell, with all their other ailments.

The morning after Kalkreuth's incident in the kitchen, as the men marched down the tracks in their usual prison cavalcade, Jones nudged Marlowe. Limping at the foreman's side was the small figure of Sylvester. He walked with a crutch, his foot wrapped in plaster. The boy looked up and caught the prisoners' stares as he and the foreman met the group, and Jones turned away, not in the mood for the boy's pranks or obnoxious jeers. He heard nothing and looked over his shoulder in curiosity at the boy, who watched him now with a blank expression. Leeps ordered Jones to work, and Jones turned his hand sideways, saluting first in front of him, as he clicked his wooden heels together, then over his groin. "Heil Hitler!" he said in the typical German shout, and as usual Leeps irritably answered the rude salute, knowing that he was being watched. Jones was surprised to hear boyish laughter and turned to see Sylvester giggling over his trick on the half-wit guard. Marlowe and Jones exchanged glances and shrugs as the boy fell silent.

At midday, the Germans huddled around the fire, pulling grease sandwiches and cold coffee from satchels. Jones worked nearby, turning his hand drill with slow heaves and groans. He started when a small object fell heavily in the gravel beside him. He glanced up to see Sylvester watching him out of the corner of his eye. Jones moved to the object casually and picked it up; it was part of Sylvester's sandwich. He shoved it into his pocket and turned away, unable to control a wide smile. That night he offered to share the small corner of sandwich with Marlowe, but the group leader grinned and pulled a piece of bread from his own pocket. Sylvester had undergone a change of heart that they agreed could make their lives much easier.

The same evening, as Watsick passed the bakery, he reached in the window in the darkness and ran his hand over the tender backs of six loaves of bread. He fumbled anxiously, trying to grab them all at once. He intended to hand three of them out to Mickelson. "Mick?" he whispered before he heard the voice of a guard approaching and saw Mickelson wave to him in warning. In alarm, Watsick shoved all six loaves under his coat and shirt and moved on with the other men, Mickelson staying between him and the guards as the loaves slipped and shifted against his chest.

At the door of the barn, Mickelson and Watsick hurried through, but the guard called them back: "Danski! Polski!" Watsick turned nervously to face him. Several bulges in his clothing stood out plainly, and as the seconds passed, a loaf fell from his coat onto the ground with a thud. The guard grasped Watsick by the arm and tugged at his coat, pulling the bread out of his clothes. He smacked the prisoner across the face with a loaf before sending him up the stairs. Once inside, Stan let out a cry of relief. He had managed to save one loaf of bread, incredibly still trapped in his clothing.

CHAPTER 21

As Chasteen and Spivey left the tracks for their fourth weekly visit to the German women, Chasteen caught the middle-aged guard staring after him with contempt. It was clear that the guard was somehow involved with Anna, Chasteen's girl. As they walked toward the town, with Pops behind them, Chasteen mentioned it to his friend.

"I could be gettin' myself in trouble if Anna's sharin' herself with me and that guard."

"I know. Don't worry. If anyone asks, we're just chopping wood," Spivey assured him, but Chasteen was not confident. He had endured more than his share of beatings and punishments as it was, and now he wondered if the pleasure was worth the risk. He couldn't very well refuse to see her, but he wondered if he could send someone in his place.

This morning, in the early spring drizzle, the girls invited them into the kitchen almost immediately for some coffee. As the four young people sat around the kitchen, the women's eyes danced with excitement. They had been pondering the situation of the two American prisoners, they explained. They had decided now (and they looked at each other and paused, giggling with excitement) that they would help Spivey and Chasteen escape. The two prisoners looked at each other, leaning forward in their chairs, suddenly nervous to even hear the implication from Germans, as if one of the guards would come walking out of the closet when the word "escape" was used. They shook their heads at the women. "No. Not possible." But the women leaned forward, undaunted by the two prisoners' reluctance.

"It would be easy. You come here next week, we hide you at a friend's house. She's already agreed to do it. In a few weeks, we'll meet up with you and disguise you in German clothes. We'll leave town, to my mother's," Anna explained. Now Chasteen was intrigued. The two women had spent days working on the perfect plan, and their enthusiasm was intoxicating. Spivey and Chasteen began to smile, considering the ramifications of escaping the country in German uniform with the help of SS officers' wives. They listened to the plans in detail and tested them for any possible weakness. But the plan held up. Anna slipped a narrow arm around Chasteen's shoulder and bit at his ear as she whispered that she loved him. The subject of escape was dropped for the time by unspoken agreement, and the two men spent a quiet day in the house, never raising an ax.

That evening, as they waited in the front garden for Pops, they discussed the possibility of escape. They knew they would have no trouble breaking loose, but staying hidden in such a small town where many of the civilians now knew them by sight would be challenging. Very few Germans would be as sympathetic as these two girls were.

Chasteen finally brought up the question that hovered in both their minds: "Can we trust those girls?"

"I don't know why they'd want to frame us. They're nuts about us, you know."

"But they're German and they're officers' wives."

"That's true."

"And Anna's been with that guard, and who knows who else they might have over to 'visit.' This whole thing could have been planned by the guard."

"And we don't know this person they say is a friend of theirs and will hide us. Even if we can trust them, can we trust her?"

They agreed to say nothing to anyone at the barracks and shook hands on it, putting off the decision.

Marlowe and Jones had by this time become close allies with Sylvester. The boy slipped them food as often as possible and actually made their work more enjoyable. He stopped picking on the other men and occasionally helped them when he could. He gave up his crutch and hobbled with a stick that the prisoners cut for him. The general amiability between them did not go unnoticed by the foreman, although the boy did his best to hide it.

By now those at the train stations and in Dettmannsdorf were familiar with most of the prisoners, and the novelty of tormenting them had worn thin. They were drained by the war, more concerned with their own hunger and want than with these young Americans who became grubbier and somehow less pathetic all the time. The men were growing accustomed to their illnesses, dysentery making large sweeps through the compound. They now knew it wouldn't kill them. They had learned to do the work without much effort and joked and sang throughout the day whenever possible. The guards constantly disciplined them, but even this they had grown somewhat accustomed to. They all wore scars on their backs and occasional welts on their faces where they had been hit, but they

healed quickly and were soon back to work again. They had become so resource-
ful with their stealing that many nights they ate as well as or better than the
Germans did, or so they believed.

The weather continued to change with the local mood, and the frozen ground
softened, while small plants and flowers began to poke upward, oblivious to the
suffering around them. The men once again tossed their overcoats on the side
of the tracks in the middle of the day, and eventually the large fire that had served
to warm the guards and foreman remained unlit.

The German people still lined up before the prisoners and watched them,
sometimes for the entire day. The look in their eyes was ominously blank and
fascinated, as if transfixed, unable to look away from the prisoners they hated.
Several times Bruton paused and commented to Jones, who worked beside him,
"That don't look good." They tried to shrug it away. They couldn't be responsible for Hitler losing the war. Whatever the Germans heard from the Führer
now, the prisoners could only guess.

Their first Red Cross package was a shock to them. The guards left it in
the loft and watched as the prisoners went through it in ecstasy. It contained
cigarettes—American ones, chocolate, Spam, fruit preserves, chewing gum, and
to Pombano's delight, two pairs of boxing gloves. The cigarettes were divided
up first. They had all developed raspy voices and racking coughs from smoking
tobacco rolled in newspaper. Now they sorted through the goods with relish,
with plans for high-stakes poker games and setting up a black-market trade
system with the guards.

The work on the tracks reached a new level of futility, and Jones and Turner
were sent temporarily to a small farm to help plant potatoes. They worked hard,
happy to be away from the tracks, and at midday the farmer's wife left two plates
of steaming potato pancakes on the step for them. The thick pancakes were
stacked high and drenched in sticky maple syrup. Jones had never tasted anything like it and ate with rapt enthusiasm. He cleaned the plate and glanced back
over his shoulder to see if the woman might be back with more. It was the best
food he had ever tasted, and for the next week he could think or talk about
nothing else as he bit off more of the dry sawdust bread that was his tiresome
staple.

The following week, Spivey and Chasteen met with their girlfriends and tried
to distract them from their plans of escape. The women constantly brought it
up, and the men as many times changed the subject. It was hard for them to say
no to the plan, but instinct told them to avoid it. The women finally gave up
and pouted irritably. Chasteen tried to console his lover by pulling her into his

arms, but she pushed him away in annoyance. By afternoon, Chasteen and Spivey found themselves in the backyard chopping wood.

Pombano began taking both pairs of boxing gloves to the tracks with him and put them on as the men waited for trains, badgering other men to spar with him. Bruton had the most impressive athletic background, and Pombano asked him if he knew how to box. Bruton shrugged. "I did a little boxing in high school."

Pombano tossed the spare set of gloves to him. "Let's go a round. I'll be easy on you."

Bruton picked up the gloves reluctantly. "No hard punches, then; you got to give me a handicap."

"Yeah, sure. Don't worry about it," Pombano replied, dancing around him with his gloves poised in front of his face. Bruton and Pombano began their fight with a cluster of prisoners and German civilians watching. They circled each other, tossing their uncut hair out of their eyes. Pombano held his gloves down at chest level, letting Bruton tap him with a few test punches, then hauled off and hit his opponent in the jaw.

The spectators laughed, and Bruton stopped, feeling his lip for blood.

"Goddamn you anyway, Pombano," he said. "What happened to my handicap? Now I'm going to have to hit you with a Goddamn shovel." Pombano laughed and began to dance and weave again.

"OK, I'm sorry. I got carried away. I won't even touch you. Come on, one more round." Leeps and the other guards stood together leaning on their rifles as they watched, laughing at the performance until the train came through and took the men back to work.

Watching Duperry's eye continue to bleed, the guards removed the prisoner from the railroad tracks by midday. He was taken to the same hospital where he had hoped to be sent originally by playing sick.

The men worked now along the fields of a turnip farm, and a cluster of Polish women in large, potato-sack dresses picked turnips along the tracks. The men laughed as the women, who suffered from dysentery as badly as they did, would just stop in the middle of the fields and squat, smiling good-naturedly at the American prisoners while they relieved themselves under their immense dresses.

Jones fell in love with a dark-haired girl working alone beside the tracks. She was young, not more than eighteen or nineteen, and even under the dress and the unwashed, uncombed hair he could see she was strikingly attractive. She noticed him staring and looked up at him with a smile, pulling a strand of dark hair out of her eyes. Her hands were covered with mud, and she periodically brushed them off on her dress. Her arms were thin and sinewy from heavy work and lack of food, but not more than his own. He said hello to her in Polish, coached by Watsick, and she smiled again, answering him shyly. He asked her name, and they exchanged a few words of introduction as they worked, while he moved casually closer. The guards of both her camp and his were well out of sight. They could hide themselves easily from the foreman as well, who stood on the other side of an empty boxcar. She practiced saying his name, Danny, with a giggle, as if she hadn't laughed for some time, and he asked her if she was married. Again she giggled with her answer, no. As the day came closer to an end, Jones asked if she would go into the boxcar with him to talk alone. He spoke through gestures and a few faltering words of German and Polish. She understood and nodded impulsively. He reached for her small, worn hand and they climbed into the boxcar and closed the door. Several of the prisoners including Turner had seen the quick exit, and they exchanged silent laughs.

In the dark safety of the boxcar, Jones put his arm loosely over her shoulders and kissed her gently on the face and mouth. As they kissed, she moved toward him and he wrapped his arms tightly around her. They stayed locked this way for a half hour. He pulled his small, green address book out. He had a tiny worn-down nub of a pencil, and she used it to write her name and address in Poland. He watched her attentively as she wrote carefully in the dark, then pulled her to him again. He heard the shouts of one of his guards, but only twitched a muscle when the door burst open and the winter sun shone on them, framing them like a picture. The guard and several prisoners stood watching, and the guard almost laughed before he pulled the young people away from each other and out of the boxcar. He cuffed Jones on the side of the head with his rifle and sent him to work on the opposite end of the rails. Jones looked back at the young girl as he was dragged away and blew her a kiss, while the other prisoners cheered and whistled.

Throughout the distraction of Jones's escapade, Chasteen noticed the middle-aged guard glaring at him, as he had ever since Chasteen's last trip to Anna's. The prisoner looked away, trying to ignore him. He was aware of the guard moving toward the foreman, who stood with crossed arms, watching the slow progress of the prisoners. They spoke together, their heads bent in collusion as their eyes focused on Chasteen.

Several minutes later, the prisoners were startled by a ruckus several hundred feet down the tracks. Jones straightened and dropped his hammer instinctively to see what was happening.

The foreman had grown increasingly exasperated with the men and the war as the train system became less and less efficient. Over the past weeks, he had stood silently watching and stewed, allowing his anger to grow and intensify. Now he had reached the breaking point, and Jones saw him and a guard mercilessly beating a prisoner on the tracks. The other men had stopped their work, and Marlowe exclaimed, "The Goddamn Krauts have Chasteen again. That's it!" The finality in his tone, which carried in his loud, booming voice, was not lost on any of the men. In succession they left their work and marched in the direction of the assault. It was another of many unprovoked attacks, and they had reached their own breaking point. They surrounded the foreman, guard, and Chasteen, forming a tight circle. Marlowe pulled Chasteen loose. The prisoner immediately straightened up and faced his assailants with unmasked hatred, his face swollen and deadly.

"You're going to have to kill every one of us to hit this man again," Marlowe said to the foreman, leaning down and shoving his finger in the bald man's face. The other guards had joined the group, their rifles trained on the prisoners, but they were now a tired and ailing lot, and they held their weapons as if unsure whether they wanted to use them, or how, and on whom.

The foreman squirmed away from Marlowe and told the guards to step away. Chasteen and the rival guard faced each other with venomous hatred. Chasteen was ready to fight, now that he had an even match. Reluctantly the guard stepped back, and the foreman looked around him at the men. A brief look of horror passed over his face as he saw their expressions. He gruffly ordered them back to work and sat down beside the tracks, badly shaken. Sylvester watched the exchange silently from the tracks where he had been playing. He gave no response when the foreman called him. After the third attempt, when the foreman's voice cracked in exhaustion, Sylvester slowly went to the man and sat silently beside him.

The men felt the change of atmosphere as well as the foreman did. Even the German people who had paused to watch could now feel it. The mood had changed, the winds were no longer blowing in Germany's favor, and the prisoners were not scapegoats anymore.

CHAPTER 22

One April morning, Chasteen came down the stairs of the pig barn to find another new guard waiting for the men. He looked for the guard who had given him so much hell over Anna but saw him nowhere. His antagonist, despite being in his late forties, had been sent to fight on the Russian front. This new guard was well over seventy and stared at the men without interest as they filed out into their rows. His face seemed to hang loose from his head, creased and dotted with dark, sootlike stubble. An elderly farmer of Dettmannsdorf, he was too old to have fought in the First World War. He was a fat man, but his sallow face gave the impression of one who had recently lost a great deal of weight. The prisoners had noticed that even the guards at the tracks each day no longer ate their grease sandwiches or sausage, but instead chewed on pieces of bread.

The men now slowed to avoid trampling the old guard. He hobbled beside Leeps as they led the procession to the train station at a sluggish pace. His ancient legs were severely bowed, leading Jones to comment to Bruton that he could drive a bowling ball between them with complete clearance.

Even at the leisurely pace, the elderly guard had a difficult time walking the two-mile distance. He traveled with an arm held securely by another guard, stopping occasionally to cough and spit before catching his breath. Leeps and Pops, the only two original guards, supported and cajoled the older members among them, trying to help them through a day in which they should have been at home before a fire instead of monitoring a group of young prisoners at hard labor.

The beatings had ceased since the day the prisoners had rescued Chasteen. Even Leeps had changed his attitude, treating the men with more respect. Duperry watched him with death in his one good eye. He had returned from Marlow several days after his altercation with Leeps. His vision was intact; his hatred of Leeps was palpable. Leeps now avoided Duperry, and fear often flashed across the guard's disfigured face.

Fewer trains passed each day. They tangled along the damaged tracks nearly every mile. Food and supplies came through to the small towns in decreasing quantities, and the people became more desperate.

The ponds, which had been frozen for so many months, now thawed. Several prisoners wandered out to them, washing a few items of clothing and their upper bodies in the frigid, murky water. They now had every Sunday off, and they fought boredom as the long days crawled by. Marlowe asked a guard one Sunday morning if they could play a game of baseball out in the field, and he agreed, bored himself and curious to see the American game.

They set up a diamond in the muddy compound, and Marlowe and Fisher chose teams. Bruton wadded a piece of oilcloth and tied it together with string, while Mickelson polished a board from his bunk to take the place of a bat.

The game started slowly, as the men watched the ball plummet to the ground with a limp thud after each swing. Jones threw the ball from third base, and it unraveled before landing. They adjusted their swings to compensate for the rewrapped wad of material, and Watsick finally hit a fly ball that earned him a home run. Gradually their enthusiasm grew along with their skill. They hollered back and forth as Watsick ran the bases while the other team fished for the ball in a shallow pond.

"Foul ball! Foul ball!" Bruton shouted, as Leeps and the other guards laughed at the performance. The noise attracted German passers-by on the narrow road toward the train station, and they walked into the compound and stood among the guards. The crowds grew larger as the game progressed, and Marlowe's team pulled ahead by four runs. Stan Watsick ran to third base after a fly ball that had been dropped by Jon. The Polish officer knew little about the game. Watsick stopped and brushed off his pants, looking around him at the crowd that had formed. A warning chill ran through him as he stared. At least forty Germans had gathered while they played, without his realizing it, and he was shocked to see that, instead of the amused smiles he had grown accustomed to when the prisoners played games, they wore venomous looks in their eyes. A middle-aged woman wrapped her arms around her son protectively and cursed at Watsick, her boy's eyes reflecting her own livid rage. The other Germans were not cheering with the prisoners either and seemed more to resemble a lynching mob. Women, old men, children, and a few badly mangled ex-soldiers glared at the jovial Americans. The German civilians moved in a half circle enclosing the baseball diamond, some of the more aggressive ones shouting loudly over the sound of the players and picking up fist-size rocks and sticks, ready to attack. They outnumbered the prisoners, who were little more than twenty now. The guards watched, reluctant to witness a mob scene but also hesitant to interfere.

Watsick was not the only prisoner to notice the mob now, and the game came to a silent halt as the young men faced their aggressors nervously. The German people were circling in a huddle around them, and the men realized that their fate looked bad as their eyes met the angry faces with apprehension. Individually they were stronger than the members of the crowd, and they imagined they could outfight them or at least kill several of them if necessary. But as a young man moved in with a rock toward the nearest prisoner, Pops shouted a warning and the guards took action, ordering the people back, training their weapons on the crowd. The German civilians moved away like skulking stray dogs, circling back then forward, reluctant to leave the fight, then finally disappearing along the road, muttering to themselves.

The Americans looked around them, profoundly disturbed. Mickelson took over as pitcher, throwing hard to the next hitter, Pombano, who swung with a boxer's short punch. They returned to their game, subdued.

They were unsure of the date or even the month when Leeps brought them an announcement: The American president was dead. Roosevelt had finally died. America had no leader, the army would fall apart.

"That's a lie," the men responded, annoyed at even the insinuation of such a thing.

Leeps walked away, not caring whether they believed him. They marched off to work and disregarded his announcement, sure that it was a last desperate act to break them down, when the war was clearly reaching an end. Roosevelt couldn't die now.

Throughout their internment, the prisoners had been paid a token sum from the German government for their labor, which, having no use for it, they had saved. Each man had earned little more than a few dollars, Marlowe and Fisher earning the most because they were over twenty-one. Now the men agreed to pool their money and buy themselves some beer. Marlowe collected a handful of deutsche marks and presented it to a guard, asking him if they could buy some beer. The guard shook his head and pushed the money back at Marlowe. He wasn't taking any prisoners to buy beer.

Marlowe refused to be turned down. He asked if the guard would be willing to buy it for them. He threw in a pack of American cigarettes, and the guard agreed, heading into town at the end of the day. He brought back a small tankard full of beer.

As the men waited at the station, Duperry spoke with the Frenchman who worked there. He returned to the men pale and disturbed.

"Leeps was right—Roosevelt is dead," he said, and they fell into brooding shock. They marched back to the compound in silence, walking slowly for the guards and even helping some of them along. One guard carried the beer for them, hardly more than a few pints, and turned it over to them at the barracks.

They took the small tankard of beer up to their barracks along with their apprehension, and listened to the door lock behind them. They sat together by the stove, which they kept fired low now, and passed the container around for a swallow each as they remembered their homes and families. Together the men composed a letter of condolence to Mrs. Roosevelt and asked the Germans to mail it for them the next day. The men assured each other that Roosevelt's death would have little impact on the war. Truman could take over, and Eisenhower was the commander that kept the military alive. He was its driving force.

The following days proved the prisoners to be correct. Fewer and fewer trains passed, until an entire day would pass without any. They worked slowly and the foreman no longer cared. If the trains didn't come, there was no point in repairing the tracks. When Jones and Turner took the handcar with the elderly guard, they offered to hold his rifle for him as he tried to heave his feeble body onto the small cart. He gratefully handed the weapon to Jones, who held it with a surprised laugh as the old man used both hands to hoist himself up with tired arms.

They often spent hours sitting along the tracks, Jones pulling out his deck of cards and playing along the ties as the worried and haggard foreman hovered around the area talking with the guards. His young, dark-haired daughter visited him often as his own work dwindled to nothing, and Chasteen looked her over with a blatant appreciative grin.

The men began exchanging home addresses. They agreed to join for a large meal as soon as they got home, meeting somewhere in the Midwest, or New York as Spivey and Pombano insisted, to eat a feast.

Chasteen and Spivey had not been invited back to Anna and Merta's house since refusing the escape plan. Now Chasteen's thoughts were almost entirely focused on killing the foreman. Duperry wanted Leeps, and they sat glaring at the Germans as they played cards or talked. The foreman still tried to keep the prisoners working, ignoring the futility of it. He spotted Chasteen, Jones, and Duperry seated idly along the tracks, staring at him as they spoke. He crossed the rails to join them, ordering them back to work. They sneered in response. There was no more point in working. He asked them just what they were talking about.

"We're sittin' here trying to figure what your ugly head would look like on my mantel at home. After this war, I'm going to kill you, you son of a bitch, and then I'm going to find your daughter, and I'm going to get as much of her as I can before I leave this place," Chasteen answered, his angry eyes trained on the foreman as he spoke in a combination of German and English that made the general meaning clear.

The foreman clenched his teeth, and his face burst a dark red as he stared at Chasteen without response. With considerable effort he turned his back and walked away. They realized that he was afraid.

It was the following morning when a young guard, recently off the front, told Mickelson that Hitler had ordered the Germans to kill all American prisoners. Hitler was desperate now and capable of anything. Mickelson kept the story to himself, believing it only skeptically. He watched the Germans carefully, unsure whether the guards would be afraid to turn their guns on all of them. It would not be hard to do, and unknown to him it was happening in a few other work camps. The guards often sat in tight circles conferring, about what the men did not know.

It was impossible now for the prisoners not to notice the movement of people along the roads and train tracks. People were traveling into the town from the east, carrying suitcases, trunks, boxes, and sacks, riding bicycles or horses, or pulling carts and wagons. They came into the town with nothing to eat and no place to stay and camped along the roads. At first there were only a few isolated parties, then gradually the number grew to the point that at any time the men could see refugees moving along the road, their valuables on their backs. The propaganda machine had fallen silent; the people no longer cared about the handful of American prisoners.

The Polish prisoners told Jon and Watsick that the Russians were moving in on Germany at breakneck speed. There was no question in any German person's mind that the Russians wanted revenge. They had suffered at the hands of the Germans for many years. Now they moved across the country in a swift rampage of murder and destruction.

When the American prisoners sat waiting on the tracks one warm spring morning and the foreman never appeared, they knew the end had come. Bruton sat on the steps of the train station with two railroad stakes, driving one with the other into the cement, carving his name and the date carefully between his feet. No one stopped him or glanced in his direction.

Within days they noticed military men coming back from the front, shedding their uniforms along the way, trying to find any scrap of clothing that would disassociate them with the German army. They dropped guns and various weapons on the ground as they fled.

Watsick and Mickelson watched the parade before them and looked at each other as a deep roar groaned in the distance.

"What was that?" Watsick said.

"Thunder?" Mickelson shook his head as he spoke, knowing the source of the sound was not natural.

"That's artillery! The Russians are almost on top of us." They scrambled to their feet with the other prisoners, staring into the distance at the rising clouds of smoke they had not seen since combat, burning across Germany toward them. The guards uttered curses under their breath as they stared transfixed and horrified.

The cannons pounded continuously throughout the day, growing closer almost by the hour. Citizens of the town began to pull out in a panic, as rivers of people passed through with their few belongings and children on each hand, moving as fast as they could along the roadways, scrambling desperately to keep ahead of the Russians.

The men sat on the tracks the following day and watched the movement, staring silently. Only Leeps and the young blond guard were still with them.

The following day, no one came for them, and they sat locked in their barracks, watching through the window, no sign of the guards around them. At night they lay awake listening to the pounding of firearms growing alarmingly close. It was the old sounds they recalled from their days in Holland, and the prisoners became increasingly anxious to escape their barracks.

"We can't go back that way and survive," Jones said, and Marlowe agreed. They would be crazy to head straight for the lion's jaws. They sat through the morning, determining whether they should try to break the door down, when they heard it unlocked and opened. The young blond guard came up the stairs to meet them, his eyes haunted with terror, his breathing loud and raspy with panic. He spoke to them in rapid German, and they strained to understand the words he sputtered.

The Russians were all around within a few miles of town and past them to the south. They all would be dead by the end of the day, he assured them, he and the Americans alike. When it came to the Russians, everyone was their enemy right now. The prisoners listened to him and glanced at each other, unsure of their next move. Marlowe asked him how close the Americans were on the west side. He replied that it could be as close as fifty kilometers, and they were moving fast with the British and Canadians, scrambling for their share of Germany. He explained that the German people were headed for the western lines to avoid being captured by the Russians. All the other guards had fled, he said. He was the only one left.

Marlowe fell silent in thought as those around him waited; then he offered a suggestion. The guard could lead them south toward the Russians as if he were turning them in, that way passing through the remaining German strongholds. Once safely away from anything German, they could cut west, taking him with them toward the American line. The men all agreed—it was a reasonable plan, and they would begin the journey immediately.

As they stepped out into the compound yard, they determined to head straight across the fields, ignoring the open roads, the better to reach the Russian lines and then west toward the Americans. They would be moving against traffic, but with a German guard escorting them, no one would think twice about it. As they began their journey, Chasteen stopped.

"We can't leave here without Flop Ears," he said.

"Forget Flop Ears, we got our lives to worry about. We got to get out of here before we're overrun. Flop Ears must be long gone," Marlowe assured him.

Chasteen shook his head. "I swore to myself I'd kill that son of a bitch and take his head back with me. I ain't leaving without him. He lives just a quarter mile from here. Who's coming with me? We can catch up with the others by tonight."

The men shook their heads and looked at the ground, and Chasteen glanced from Lindsey to Spivey.

"Not you, Spivey? You won't come with me?"

Spivey shook his head uncomfortably. "No, Charlie, I just don't see any point in it. It's like Marlowe said, he'll be gone by now."

Chasteen shook his head and started off on his own with a shrug. He called out behind him, "I'll meet up with you all in no time." They watched him go, then turned and began to strike out across open country.

PART IV

CHAPTER 1

E ast of 311/I, at Stalag II-A in Neubrandenburg, Jim Rizzuto had become aware of the Russian liberation of Germany weeks earlier. He had been at the stalag for close to four months and now awaited the liberation with unmatched enthusiasm.

For several months, Rizzuto had worried about remaining in East Germany forever; from inside the compound, there had seemed no sign of an end to the war. His health had returned to him gradually at II-A, although food was scarce and he weighed only ninety pounds. The stalag was located next to a German marine camp, and often Rizzuto worked with the marines, building temporary housing around the base. It was nothing like the hard labor of the railroad tracks, and although he continued to lose weight, he slept through the nights and was relieved to have escaped the loft of the pig barn and the German rail system.

With April, the atmosphere around him had begun to change. He heard that the Russians, moving through Poland, were only miles from Neubrandenburg. They seemed to move into the area overnight, accompanied by the sound of cannons and heavy artillery. By April 28, all work ceased in the marine base, and the American prisoners sat in their quarters listening to the shelling and waiting, while the Russians came within forty kilometers of their compound.

The following morning, the Germans unlocked the doors of the camp and ordered the men to go. They would all be fleeing the area—the Russians were within a few miles from their door. The men sat in confusion as the German guards who had regulated their lives for so many months disappeared forever, having issued their final order: Leave. The prisoners determined not to obey. The Russians would liberate them; they had no reason to flee. The American lines were hundred of miles to the west—too far to walk.

They played cards and sat smoking impatiently as the clamor of war sounds around them grew nearer. By evening the Russians reached their compound, and at midnight they flung open the doors to liberate the prisoners.

When the sun rose the next morning, Rizzuto walked out the doors, cautious with his freedom, and instinctively wandered toward the German marine base. The smoke that rose from behind its walls spread a rancid odor through the cool German air, and he continued forward in reluctant fascination. Inside the walls of the base he found nothing but remains. The base had been burned to the ground overnight, leaving charred bodies and foundations of the houses he had once labored over, choking in their own smoke. Near the gate, he glanced at the body of a German soldier, his head blown off and no sign of it, but a bloody burnt stump of a neck and brains five feet beyond. He hurried back toward the other American prisoners, eager now to begin a plan of action, to finally leave this country.

The Russian mission was retribution for the agonies they had suffered under the Germans, and they had little time for Americans. They advised the prisoners to pack up and begin walking toward American lines near the Elbe River. The lieutenant colonel and prison leader for the prisoners shook his head skeptically. It would take them weeks to walk that distance; very likely they would never even come close to their own lines. The men agreed to wait until the Americans reached them. They guessed that it wouldn't be long. The Russians looked at the prisoners, shaking their heads. As far as they were concerned, these Americans could do whatever they wanted.

A week passed as the men waited, and Russian soldiers moved through in greater numbers, marching in their units toward the east-west lines. Several American men grew impatient and set out to walk. "You're crazy if you think the Americans are coming out here. This place just gets more Russian every day. We got to get the hell out."

Rizzuto watched them leave, knowing instinctively that they were right. The prisoners were running out of food and time as the war spread out in confusing directions with less clear-cut enemies. The best thing they could do was to get out while they could.

On the morning of May 6, Rizzuto and a dozen more men began their trek across Germany, which led them to American lines. The war had not ended, but Russian troops were flooding west toward Berlin. Rizzuto was lucky to be in the midst of the spearhead west, which concentrated on fast movement. Rural areas, such as Dettmannsdorf, maintained German control longer before being besieged with peripheral Russian troops. A Russian truck offered Rizzuto transportation to the Rhine, where he caught a barge to the American line.

CHAPTER 2

The men of 311/I moved across the field with the German guard in front, as rivers of people worked their way in the opposite direction, trying to reach the road leading west. It was still early, not yet 9 A.M., and the people stumbled past them with vacant, tired expressions as if they'd been walking all night. The men moved quickly for miles, working their way through the hordes. It was a warm day, and they discarded their overcoats as they went, tossing them into ditches, glad to know they wouldn't need them anymore. Those who had saved their combat boots wore them now for the first time in months, while the others struggled along in their wooden shoes or even walked barefoot. Despite the numbers of people, the air around them hung strangely silent, a foreboding pregnant aura that made everyone move as quickly as they reasonably could.

The numbers of fleeting Germans decreased as they worked their way farther south until eventually they saw only a few solitary travelers. They had reached an area of farm country and small towns that seemed completely evacuated. The German guard now became nervous and climbed into a prisoner's discarded coat and jacket. He tossed his own uniform into a field, and they continued on more cautiously. He was concerned that the Russians were no more partial to Americans than to Germans, but the prisoners disagreed. They had gotten along well with Russian prisoners and couldn't imagine allies turning on each other before the war was finished. They were still unified by their hatred of Hitler and Nazi Germany.

Coming over the crest of a hill, they now looked down at a wide and vacant highway that stretched beyond an expanse of hilly pastureland, leading north to Rostock. They saw several bodies lying on the side of the road, but the silence seemed to signify peaceful resolve. They ran down the side of the hill to the highway in a large wave. Once standing on the silent road, they considered following it for several miles, hoping to run into Russian soldiers and test out their relations with them.

Then they heard with surprise the unmistakable sound of hooves approaching them. From the sound on the otherwise somnolent road, they guessed it to be several dozen horses. They backed instinctively away into the ditch and eyed the southern turn in the road. It was several minutes before movement could be seen, and they watched figures come around the corner. An entire army of unfamiliar-looking soldiers in dark uniforms came toward them on horseback, some horses carrying two men, several tanks rumbling between them. All were drinking from tall bottles, lifting them high above their heads and pouring a clear liquid down their throats, laughing and shouting as they went. They noticed the cluster of American prisoners and looked them over curiously, then seemed almost immediately to disregard them. Jones realized that these were the Russian Mongolian soldiers, who were famed for having helped thwart the German army. Now they were not only fierce and imposing but stone drunk, and as the huge cavalcade passed, a soldier fell off his horse as he took a large swig from his bottle. The man behind marched his own horse across the soldier without so much as a glance. Several Mongols met this fate as they lost their balance, and those who could pulled themselves to their feet and hurried after the group. Marlowe had been prepared to step in front of the group to ask directions and introduce himself, but now he thought again and stayed safely in the ditch. One Mongol soldier raised his rifle at the Americans with a laugh but began to lose his balance and dropped the weapon.

After the Mongols had passed, several men darted into the road to pick up the Russian rifle. Then they discussed what to do next. They heard a single engine approaching from the same direction the Mongolian troops had come from, and they paused, now unsure if they should remain in the open. This time a motorcycle with a sidecar came around the corner. A Russian soldier in full uniform rode with one hand, swigging from a bottle. In the sidecar, another soldier sat with a teenage girl of indeterminable nationality in his lap. He played a squeezebox loudly and tunelessly in front of her. All three whooped and shouted along with the music, and when they saw the group of Americans, the soldier in the sidecar reached for his rifle and shot it straight into the air. The motorcycle roared to a stop before Watsick and Marlowe, and the soldiers asked in slurred Russian which way to Rostock. Watsick tentatively pointed up the road. The soldier saluted him with the bottle, and the motorcycle roared off, the music from the squeezebox accompanying their drunken singing. The men watched the group disappear around a corner, then heard the ear-bursting crash of a mine. Debris scattered from the motorcycle, and the men shook their heads in astonishment.

They guessed now that the Russians would be little help to them, and reconsidered their plans. Soldiers streamed by in increasing numbers, stragglers passing between larger units. The men watched masses of German soldiers taken prisoner march by with their hands on their heads, even some civilians caught in the stampede. Several tanks passed, and a Russian woman stuck her head out of a turret, looking around her with intent eyes. She wore a military uniform and was large enough to pass for a man but for her large breasts and long, blond hair. She glanced at the American group and pulled a machine gun out of the tank, aiming at a light pole and firing rapidly, her shot shaky but direct. She let out a drunken laugh and turned the gun, firing indiscriminately at any object that seemed a good target. She saw several bodies lying in the ditches, and she fired several rounds at them, shouting what sounded like a Russian war cry as she did so.

"These Russians are Goddamn lunatics," Jones said, and the men now turned questioningly to Marlowe. They were not happy with their original plan to stay along the road north. They were deep in Russian territory now, and it was clear that the Russians didn't care whether they helped the Americans or killed them. The Russian soldiers were war-weary. Many who passed along the causeway had been fighting in the war for as long as six years, and life or death meant nothing to them.

Marlowe determined that they would be better off crossing the road and heading in a generally westward direction across the fields, where they could reach American or British lines without much interception in Germany. They noticed a large, sprawling farm on a hill and instinctively moved toward it. Jones picked up a revolver and holster, then glanced behind him as a figure galloped toward them on horseback. It was Charlie Chasteen. The group paused, watching his approach and looking for a head dangling from the horse's side. When he was within a hundred feet, they saw that he was empty-handed. He told them his unlucky story.

He'd discovered the horse near Dettmannsdorf and ridden it back to Sanitz. The city of Sanitz was silent. He easily found Flop Ears' house and walked in the unlocked door. Finding no one in the front room, he shouted Flop Ears' name and then his daughter's as he strode through each room, sticking his head out the back door and seeing no one. Whether Flop Ears had fled from the Russians or taken Chasteen's threat to heart he couldn't determine, but the entire family had vanished. Disappointed, he rode around the town streets on the unlikely chance that the foreman was still somewhere thereabouts.

The Russians had already begun to march into the small town. Determining that he would never find his enemy, Chasteen turned his horse southward and rode directly into a regiment of the Russian infantry. He was surprised by their hostility and lack of respect for him, an ally. Repeatedly Russian soldiers shouted at him. They liked the looks of his horse, and a few aggressive infantrymen reached for the reins. He was forced to slow the horse to a walk as he fought his way through the soldiers, and two Russians grabbed the reins and pulled it to a stop. Chasteen tried to pull the reins free again, while another soldier grasped his sleeve and tried to pull him off the horse. With his free hand he desperately reached for a pistol he'd found in Sanitz and aimed it at the closest soldier. After hesitating, the men released the reins, and Chasteen galloped the horse through the soldiers. He'd spent the rest of the afternoon second-guessing his fellow ex-prisoners, until he finally caught up with them here.

The men now picked up their speed toward the farm, which appeared to be one of the most luxurious mansions they had ever seen. It was a luminous white structure, with the barn built into the house as an annex. The rich land that stretched around them boasted of healthy crops and clearly belonged to the owner of this opulent home. They walked up the step and through the giant front door, which hung open, an invitation for all those who passed by. They stopped in a foyer lined with mirrors. A giant chandelier hung above a luxurious curve of wide, velvet-covered stairs. Voices could be heard from unseen rooms in many languages, and they intercepted a young Pole walking through the door with a bottle of cognac in his hand.

He explained to Watsick and Jon that the owners of the house had disappeared in the middle of the night as the Russians closed in. Now he and the other indentured servants, who were prisoners of war from Russia and Poland, were ransacking the place, keeping for themselves everything they could possibly find. The German family had left everything.

They watched a young Polish girl stroll by in a mink coat, smoothing the soft fur against her cheek as she walked up the stairs. The men scattered immediately to join the souvenir hunt.

Jones wandered up the stairs and into a large den, where a young Polish farmhand crouched before a safe. He turned to see Jones and asked for his assistance as he wrapped dynamite explosives around its steel walls. He seemed to accept Jones's presence without question. Jones eagerly hurried to his aid. The German family couldn't have carried anything valuable with them, so he had little doubt that the safe contained most of the estate's wealth. The two men wrapped several layers of dynamite with heavy rope around the safe. Jones lit the fuse, and they lunged under an oak desk across the room, hugging their heads.

The explosion was more violent than they had intended and shook the desk where they crouched. When they crawled out, they squinted through the smoke and dust around them and realized that they had done more than blow the safe.

A hole in the wall, large enough to walk through, faced them accusingly. The two safecrackers laughed slowly, and found that the safe had burst into several pieces. They raced for it, bracing themselves on their knees as they pulled treasures from the wreckage. It contained mostly jewelry, string after string of heavy diamonds and rubies, pearls, and emerald rings. The farmhand rolled them across his callused fingers in fascination. Jones found a heavy metal box and opened it to see millions of marks. He counted through them and guessed that there was over a million dollars' worth of German currency. He proposed that the farmhand keep the jewelry while Jones took the money. He grinned to himself as the Polish servant agreed. With the German money, Jones imagined he could buy that much jewelry for Caroline and his mother and still have enough left for a house and a car. Maybe several cars. He stuffed the money inside his clothes. He would learn later that the postwar mark was worthless.

Jim Bruton led several men up a narrow and lengthy set of stairs to the attic. "People always keep their valuables in the attic," he explained. As they shuffled through old furniture and memorabilia, Bruton discovered a set of prints of Africa, apparently taken by a member of the family and framed professionally. He examined the pictures up close, leaning forward as he lifted one carefully between his hands. Suddenly he was thrown backward, dropping the print as an explosion erupted on the floor below. He headed for the stairs, then paused, distracted by a rack of antique guns.

Watsick and Mickelson followed two Polish girls into the basement. The girls smiled at them, offering their names in response to Watsick's Polish. In the basement, they found a party in progress, a wet bar sprawled against one wall and a Russian officer pouring liquor out of a large bottle. He'd brought his own vodka; even a home like this had run out of alcohol toward the end of the war. He laughed and greeted the two Americans hospitably. Where he had come from they had no idea. At least six women were seated around the bar, most of whom were forced laborers, maids, cooks, or personal servants. They lounged on the bar stools and chairs sipping vodka, while the Russian gulped his drinks from the bottle. Two more 311/I refugees followed the two friends into the basement. The Russian officer counted them, four altogether, and pulled glistening crystal glasses out of the cabinet, lining them up and pouring four large drinks. Watsick and Mickelson reached for theirs first, as a gesture of goodwill to the Russians, and toasted their impromptu bartender. The vodka tasted strongly of the potatoes it was made from and was so fiery that they both choked, then gasped for air as the fluid bubbled and burned its way down their throats. The Russians let out a hearty belly laugh. Watsick held out his glass, more confident this time, and the man with the vodka refilled it. Soon the party atmosphere got the best of them and they sat on the floor, singing and giggling, drunk for the first time in a year, and without food in their shrunken stomachs the alcohol made a mad rush for their heads.

Marlowe wandered around the main sitting rooms and then the kitchen in search of food. A servant girl rushed by him carrying a stack of linens, and he shook his head in wonder at the mayhem around him. He turned when a young housekeeper came up behind him, addressing him in English.

"Mister! Mister? Your men drink very much. You go see them." She had a worried expression on her young face, and he hurried off after her without hesitation. Looking out for the other men was second nature to him now. He came down the stairs to find six of his men, including Watsick and Mickelson, laughing loudly as they refilled their glasses from a jug of vodka. Several empty bottles lay on the floor. The Russian greeted Marlowe with the same amiable camaraderie that he had the others and poured him a drink in another crystal glass. Marlowe took the glass, instinctively suspicious. He had fostered an increasing distrust of Russians over the course of the day, and now seeing the first openly friendly one, he was leery. He took the glass and held it to his lips, smelling the strong vapors that burned up his nostrils. As the Russian lifted the bottle to his own lips, and tipped his chin up to drink, Marlowe tossed his head back with the glass, pouring his drink out on the floor. Nobody in the basement was in the condition to notice, least of all the Russian officer, who let out a cheer to see how easily Marlowe had finished his first shot, and now poured him another.

Chasteen and Spivey wandered off looking for souvenirs. They roamed from room to room before finding what they had hoped for, a large, round combination for a steel safe set into the wall. They found tools in the barn and returned to begin chipping at the wall, tearing out plaster, then hacking at the hinges of the door. More than an hour later, the door fell loose with the final swing of an ax, and they plunged their hands eagerly into the safe. They had found even more than they had hoped for. Diamonds, myriad loose stones, gold coins, even gold teeth were tucked away in the vault. They spread the valuables out on the floor, looking behind them at the door and the hallway, then shutting the door carefully. They made two even piles of treasures, taking great pains to divide the riches fairly.

There was a shiny Mauser pistol with a wooden holster, which Chasteen offered to Spivey, but his friend refused. He'd found one in Normandy and had already sent it home to his mother. He now carried a Russian pistol that he'd scavenged along the causeway. Chasteen placed his share of the treasure lovingly in his Red Cross bag, which he'd carried in his back pocket since February. He tucked the bag into his jacket, and they walked up the stairs in search of comfortable beds.

Dan Jones found a bottle of whiskey hidden in a flask in the oak desk and shared it with his Polish partner in crime before wandering toward the stairs. He was hungry, desperately so. He imagined that if whiskey could be found, so could food, and he decided to search out the pantry. As he descended the circular stairs, he looked down through the railings to see, reflected in the large mirror lining the wall, a Russian soldier standing at the foot of the stairs, steadying himself to begin his climb. The Russian held a rifle in front of him as he reached for the railing. His eyes suddenly froze as they met Jones's in the reflection.

Jones reacted suddenly, alarmed by the gun. "Americansky!" he shouted, startling the confused soldier. The Russian fired point-blank at Jones's reflection, and they both froze, staring at the shattered glass, before the soldier wheeled and faced Jones. He ran up the stairs toward him, and Jones bolted back up the remainder of the stairs and down a long hallway, until he found a back set of stairs and lost his pursuer.

On the second floor he ran into Turner, who told him that Russian servant girls were sleeping in the bedrooms. Jones turned the knob of the first door and walked in. A large Russian woman of his own age lay in the bed, blankets pulled modestly up to her neck as she watched the American approach. He ran to the bed without diplomacy and climbed under the blankets with her. Before he could snuggle comfortably against her warm, soft shape, she had grasped him by the neck and thrown him out of the bed. He hit the floor five feet away with a resounding thud, and he reevaluated the situation. He made a move toward her again, but she sat up threateningly, and he slipped back out the door to find his own bed.

Spivey and Chasteen found a comfortable bedroom at the head of the stairway on the third floor, with two down beds and an immense window behind. Chasteen opened the door to a walk-in closet and ran his hand over the row of Nazi uniforms hanging there. The man of the house was an officer, and an important one, he guessed, as he pulled a hat down from the top shelf and called out to his friend, "Hey Spivey, take a look at the braid on this hat." Spivey had seated himself on one of the beds and was now looking over his own share of jewels. Chasteen lay back on his bed and let out a sigh of satisfaction.

"Hell, I don't remember ever lying on a bed like this," he said. He held the hat up in front of him as he reclined comfortably, examining the workmanship of the braid. He had never seen anything in the military with so much intricate handcrafting, and he turned it over with fascination. He heard a step in the hallway before the open bedroom door, but before he could react, Spivey leaped to his feet and fired two rounds at the doorway. Chasteen dropped the hat and looked at the limp figure of a Russian soldier lying in a spreading pool of blood in the doorway.

"Shit, Spivey! What the hell did you do?" As he spoke he saw the rifle lying next to the dead man. He guessed the truth before Spivey told him.

"He saw that hat, you crazy asshole. You looked like a German Gestapo with that hat in front of your face. If I hadn't shot him, you'd be dead now. There was nothing else I could do."

The two Americans looked at each other in the horror of what they had done. The Russian was more than just a soldier, they realized now as they approached the body. He was an officer. Various Russians roamed the house at this moment. Spivey and Chasteen would surely be shot down in retribution. They slammed the door shut. Without discussion, they quickly stripped the man of his clothes, wadding up the uniform and throwing it in the back of the closet. They wrapped the naked body in a quilt and rolled it under the bed. They now stood examining the blood stain. No one had responded to the gunshots; enough shooting was going on around them that apparently no one had paid any notice. They scrubbed at the blood with a shirt, and it easily came off the polished floor. They tossed the shirt in with the Russian's uniform, and then they waited. The house quieted as the sun set, the occasional shouts and singing surging from far reaches of the house, then dying as fast. Spivey stuck his head out the door and saw no one. He motioned to Chasteen, and the two grabbed the body, sliding it into the hall and toward a back set of stairs. They stopped several times to rest but saw no one, and they dragged the body down the stairs.

The two friends came to a stop at the bottom of four sets of stairs in the boiler room. The furnace was easy to find, brewing with hot coals and cinders. The men threw piles of coal in the furnace and waited as they slowly ignited. When the stove was hot enough, they looked at each other with a nod and opened the furnace door, lifted the body one last time, and shoved it inside. Chasteen looked at the giant package in the furnace as Spivey headed for the stairs.

"It won't burn like that, Spivey," he said to the back of his reluctant friend. "If anything, it'll put the fire out." Chasteen picked up a shovel and began digging into the hot coals, dropping them over the body. Spivey returned to watch and finally advised, "That'll do the job. He'll burn just fine." The coals were already eating through the quilt where some flames had erupted, and the men slammed the furnace door on the smell of burning flesh. They hadn't been happy with what they'd done and now returned to their room in sour moods.

Marlowe had spent several hours "outdrinking" the Russian sergeant and now sat among his drunken men, who were sprawled happily around him. He still dumped the drinks out when the sergeant wasn't looking but was offered fewer refills as the Russian slowed down. Marlowe was relieved when the sergeant passed out behind the bar, several bottles of vodka still unopened beside him.

"Mick, Watsick, help me out with him. We'll leave him in one of the beds upstairs," Marlowe said. The men only looked at him and laughed, their minds comfortably drifting.

He badgered and shoved at the men until they agreed noisily to help him, and the group dragged the sergeant up the stairs and into the closest room, leaving him to sleep away his vodka. Marlowe and Fisher, who had now joined them, looked for a place to sleep and found a servants' bedroom with comfortable beds. They climbed under the covers, leaving their boots on out of nervous habit. It was late now, well past midnight, and despite themselves, they slept heavily.

Marlowe and Fisher leapt out of their beds in horror, their hearts rapping painful beats against their ribs, when a volley of bullets flew over their heads and smashed into the wall behind them. A Russian soldier had mistaken them for Germans, and now as they pleaded "Amerikansky, Amerikansky!" he nodded with a wave and walked away, his gun cocked, to roam the house for remaining Germans. He was drunk, and six years of hatred of the Germans burned outrage on his face. Marlowe and Fisher followed him into the front lobby. The soldier stood poised, unsure whether to climb the stairs or scout the rest of the servants' floor. Marlowe pointed at the narrow set of stairs leading to the basement. "There's girls down there," he said, gesturing with his hands a shapely female form. The Russian hesitated, understanding the universal gesture. They held up their hands to count out, many girls sleeping in the basement. Russian girls. The soldier grinned, and they realized suddenly how drunk he was. They had to help him down the stairs and left him there. Glancing back, they saw him doze off as they climbed the stairs back to the main floor.

CHAPTER 3

When Marlowe awoke, the sun was beginning its ascent toward the window, casting an opaque dawn light across the floor. He had slept for an hour or two at the most. He bolted out of the soft bed, still in his uniform and boots, then realized that Leeps was not climbing up the stairs toward him. There would be no more "heRAUS" in his mornings. After a brief moment of exultation, he reviewed the situation.

The grandeur of the house was clear in the early morning light. As he wandered through the foyer, he looked around with new appreciation at the chandeliers and the giant shattered mirror. The noise and merrymaking within the house seemed to have died, and the immediate silence around him was punctuated by the faraway rumble of artillery. Curious about his surroundings, he strode toward a door that led to the parapet. The towers stood fifty feet above the house, and he realized that from the top he would have a panoramic view for miles. He climbed the dark, narrow spiral stairs, walking softly without knowing why. Reaching the top, he moved swiftly toward the open windows to see if he could identify Rostock, or Russian troop movement. He started when he heard a thin whimper from the small space not more than ten feet behind him. He turned to see a woman huddled on the floor in a shadowy corner, regarding him with terrified eyes. She was well dressed and well fed, clearly a German, in her late fifties, and a member of the family that had until the day before reigned over this land with regality. But it was not her that he had heard. Clutched to her chest was a tiny lapdog, squirming against her as it whined and sneezed. He couldn't imagine why she had been left behind. He stepped toward her and in German asked her name. In response she started crying, dropping her face to the furry back of her dog. He waited, and within seconds she looked at him again, her face streaked with tears.

"Please kill my dog," she said to him in clear German, and he hesitated, staring at her without comprehension. He shook his head and held out his hand to her, telling her to come downstairs with him, no one would hurt her.

"I don't care what they do to me. I don't want my dog to suffer. Please kill him."

"The dog will be all right," he assured her. "No one will hurt your dog. Come on downstairs now." She ignored his outstretched hand but climbed obediently to her feet, dabbing a handkerchief under her eyes with a restoration of dignity. She walked down the stairs with him and stopped at the foyer. Whether she paused to look at the shattered mirror or the general state of looting, he didn't notice. He left her there, standing with her dog, as he headed up the stairs. The Russians seemed to have pulled out of the house, except for a few sleeping ex-prisoners, and he now determined to round up his own men. It was time for them to move on.

Chasteen awoke to sunshine and lay for one moment savoring the luxury of his bed and freedom. He stretched, then sat up and reached under the bed covers for his bag of jewels. He felt nothing. He stumbled to his feet and tore apart the bed, then his own clothes, before he accepted the truth. Someone had stolen his treasures during the night.

"Spivey!" he shouted, waking his friend in agitation. "Do you have your jewels?" Spivey looked around him in confusion, then pulled his small parcel out of his coat pocket.

"Son of a bitch!" Chasteen fell to his knees and began searching under his bed, around his bed, lifting up the sheets and dropping them repeatedly. "Didn't you hear anything? Anybody? I lost the whole Goddamn thing, every piece of gold, the pistol, everything." His anger built on itself as he looked around the floor again, knowing for certain that he'd been robbed. He believed it was one of his own group, and he named several names to his friend, who only shook his head, saying, "Hey, you got to have proof." They left the room as they heard Marlowe calling them, and they walked down the stairs, Chasteen silent in his outrage.

As the group gathered together in a tired and drunken cluster, Marlowe tried to organize a plan. Jon, the Polish officer, was their greatest help now. He had spent several years in Germany and knew the geography well. He convinced them that the best plan would be to head straight west, bypassing Rostock. That large city would be overrun with Russians by now. They agreed, and the group began making their way away from the house across the fields, beating the path of the sun.

Several of the men pulled a wagon out of the garage, stealing a horse to pull it. Dan Jones and Jim Bruton volunteered to seek out more horses. Jones had riding experience dating back to his childhood. Bruton grinned as he added that he didn't have much experience with horses, but since he was from Kentucky, it was in his blood.

Other men stepped in front of two German boys riding by on bicycles and grabbed the handlebars, forcing them off. As the Americans rode away, the two boys trudged off on foot.

Jones and Bruton helped themselves to three horses grazing in a nearby meadow, riding two while Jones pulled the third behind them. They turned to ride back toward the road, where they could expect to find the cavalcade of Americans, but stopped short when they saw movement in the next field. A German farmer was plowing his field, moving at a determined pace, oblivious to or unperturbed by the chaos and upheaval throughout his country. They pulled their horses up short and watched the powerful horse pulling the weight of the plow. Jones turned to his friend. "Take a look at that beautiful horse. It's a Thoroughbred, I'll bet."

"Let's go get it," he declared, and Bruton shrugged. They rode out toward the lone farmer. Jones nodded a greeting to the man, who watched them nervously. Jones looked the plow horse over before climbing off his own. Bruton stayed back several yards, watching from his own mount. Grabbing the reins, Jones brought the plow horse to a stop, then ran his hand across its flank. "This is quite a horse," he said.

The horse he had dismounted was little more than a nag, of advanced years and useless for long journeys. He now brought it forward, unharnessing the farmer's horse and leaving the nag in its place. He walked a few paces with the Thoroughbred, then climbed on bareback and rode off to join Bruton. He turned to wave to the farmer, but the old man stood with his back to Jones, his shoulders hunched, as he regarded his new horse in despair.

Bruton soon found a saddled horse that had lost its rider and climbed on, opting to pull the other horse. His legs had been rubbed raw without the comfort of a saddle. He rode behind Jones, who was moving fast on the Thoroughbred, trying to keep it in control as it bucked and jerked underneath him. As Bruton rode his tamer horse, he felt the saddle shift, and he moved his weight, trying to pull it straight underneath him. The horse picked up its pace now, and suddenly the loose saddle slid sideways on the horse. Bruton landed on his side in the damp field.

Meanwhile, the other men proceeded through clusters of tiny towns in a parade of horses, bicycles, and wagons. Several other Americans had joined their group, mostly POWs, from where they didn't know, but their number was now close to forty.

On a grassy hill above the road stood an institutionlike building. From its doors, hordes of people came running, streaming down the hill toward the men. They shouted as they came, loud unnatural screams that sent shudders through the men now watching in fascination. The crazed figures dispersed, making paths in all directions, many of them straight toward the road. Most were completely nude. The men realized now that they were running loose from an asylum. The Russians, who were everywhere around them now, had opened the gates and released or chased the inmates out into the chaotic countryside.

The number of dead along the road was alarming. Women, babies, people of all ages and nationalities lay discarded in the ditches. There seemed to be no pattern, no reason for their deaths. Whether they were prisoners shot by Nazis in a moment of panic, German civilians shot by Russian soldiers, members of the Nazi party shot by other Germans, or Germans shot by liberated prisoners, there were no witnesses left to the killings. There was no crime. The time for revenge and purging had come.

As the Americans stole bicycles and horses from the Germans, the Russians, almost within an hour, stole the same from the Americans. An object of value never remained with anyone long and tended to end up with a Russian soldier. The horses that Jones and Bruton had delivered lasted only a short time before they were taken from the Americans at gunpoint, sometimes traded for a drink of vodka. Spivey's treasures soon found their way into Russian hands.

As they passed the asylum, Watsick approached a Russian soldier, asking him for a drink from his vodka. The soldier handed the bottle to him, staring blankly at a naked teenage girl seated on the ground before them, rocking a battered doll in her lap as she hummed tunelessly. Her lips trembled, and her vacant eyes attested to her insanity. How long she had been free from the asylum he couldn't tell. The Russian soldier nodded toward her as Watsick returned him the bottle. He told him that the girl was his if he wanted, as a gift of goodwill between two allies. Watsick looked at the girl and shook his head sadly. He had been staggeringly drunk since the night before, but he still felt nothing but sympathy for the girl and said no. He walked away, afraid to turn back and see what her fate would be now.

They continued through another town, passing a group of Russians who stood beside their motorcycles as they drank and laughed. One of the soldiers approached the Americans, carrying a gas can in his hand, and he held it out to Mickelson, inviting him to drink.

"Vodka," he assured the apprehensive American.

"Nyet, benzine," Mickelson responded, pushing the can away from his face with a nervous hand. The other Russians watched the exchange, laughing boisterously. The Russian insisted several times that it was vodka and soon became annoyed, his voice turning menacing. Mickelson exchanged a look with Watsick before taking the gas can. The eyes of all the Americans and Russians were on him as he took a quick and cautious swallow. He felt the liquid burn down his throat and momentarily panicked. The vodka the Russians drank was harsh, burning almost as painfully as gasoline, and he recognized the flavor of potatoes with a sigh of relief. Seeing the change of expression, the Russians laughed heartily, and the men passed around the gas can, each taking a long drink.

They were now in a fair-sized town of more than a thousand people, and Russian tanks and motorcycles sat in all the intersections. It was early evening and the men were hungry. Marlowe suggested they split up, two men each taking a German house for the night. The pairs wandered off in different directions in hopes of finding food and beds.

Turner and Jones located a modest white house that sat quietly off the main street as if in hiding. They walked in the door without knocking and stood facing the round, startled eyes of a family of four. The two intruders announced that they would be staying for dinner and the night.

The family consisted of two middle-aged parents and two teenage girls between thirteen and fifteen. They seemed almost relieved to see the two young men. The once-quiet town was filled with the noises of drinking and shooting, and they had chosen to remain with their home. They were glad to have the slightly more sober companionship of the two Americans. Jones and Turner ate with the family at the kitchen table, consuming more than the four Germans ate together. After leaning back comfortably with a bowl of watery soup in their stomachs, they retired to the front room to sleep, stretching out on cots set up by the mother. The family retreated demurely as the American intruders settled down to catch their rest.

Sometime in the night, the two men leapt from their cots as a half dozen Russian soldiers burst into the house. They slammed the door open and marched in, looking at the two Americans curiously. They had come to investigate rumors that the house contained young girls. The parents came out of their bedroom and, guessing the intent of the soldiers, began to plead with them, offering them food and then money to leave. The soldiers pushed the couple aside and began trying doors. They found the two girls cowering in their beds in the room directly behind the living room. Turner and Jones tried to stop several of the men as they passed through the bedroom door but found automatic weapons in their faces. Helplessly they watched as the door shut. They sat down in the living room with the parents, all four in a row on the couch as they listened to the terrified shrieks of the young girls. The husband and wife clung to each other, completely hysterical. Jones and Turner would not look at the couple or each other, miserable with their helplessness. They sat this way for what seemed hours, listening to the noises from the bedroom and trying to somehow calm the parents, who sobbed uncontrollably. After an hour or more, the sun crawled up the side of the house and peered in the window at the miserable family.

In the early morning hours, the Russian soldiers walked back out the door, talking loudly as they wandered out of the house and down the street, their chatter sounding innocent and boyish. The parents rushed into the bedroom, and Turner and Jones now heard the crying of the entire family as the parents clung to their daughters, wailing in horror and sorrow. The men tried to sleep but were unable to, both feeling sick. They'd eaten too much and the alcohol now left them tired and irritable. Soon they walked out of the house without speaking to the family.

The American ex-prisoners met in the center of town in their usual way, joining instinctively without plans or organization. Those who'd had bicycles or horses the night before had since lost them. The group set out on foot toward the American-British line, which was now within a few miles. They reached the outskirts of Wismar, a small industrial city, by midmorning and looked at a small prison compound more securely enclosed than theirs had been. It was surrounded by dozens of milling people. The smell emanating from the compound awoke unpleasant memories of their experiences in combat, but many of them moved toward its gates with morbid fascination. Jones passed through the doorway, where groups of Russian soldiers stood in sober clusters. They were not drinking or celebrating now but spoke in deep and angry voices, their faces pallid and disturbed. People wandered through the gates dressed in shapeless, tattered uniforms like pajamas, striped black and white with large Ps emblazoned on their backs. They looked at the Americans inquisitively with large, haunted eyes sunken into their skulls. Their eyes expressed a listlessness that Jones likened to the dying Russian prisoners he'd seen while in solitary. The skin hung off their faces and necks as if they were wizened old men and women, but he realized as they moved closer that most of them were not much older than he and his companions.

Jones continued in through the gate, which was ripped open from its lock with outraged violence. The smell overwhelmed him as he staggered back with the realization of burning flesh.

The sight he saw froze him to his spot. This was the Germany that the Russians were avenging, that they sought to destroy, to burn to the ground, as Hitler had tried to do to them. German soldiers turned prisoners stacked the dead in large piles as the Russians shouted and hovered over them with guns, forcing them to finish their grisly detail. The actual officials and guards of the concentration camp had been shot dead when the Russians arrived, and now the German POWs were left to suffer for the horrors that their people had forced on others in this concentration camp for Jews and political prisoners. Several paused to vomit as they worked. Two men pulled bodies out of ditches and off the ground one at a time, to throw them into piles, while others took bodies off the tops of the piles and fed them into a hot stove designed for such a purpose. The dead prisoners were so thin and some dead so long that they were inhuman in appearance and were tossed easily to lie or roll down the piles like potatoes. Jones covered his eyes with his hand, then looked again before quickly turning away and walking out of the camp, nauseated. Outside the gates he paused to catch his breath and looked up to see a wizened man of his age standing several feet away, regarding him curiously with sunken eyes.

"You American?" he asked in English.

"Yes," Jones answered, gulping at the fresh air.

"I'm a prisoner from this place. I'm a Dutch Jew." Jones nodded without a response. The prisoner fumbled suddenly through his loose clothes and pulled out wads of brown paper, holding it in his clawlike hands excitedly.

"I wrote this while I was in there. It was how I stayed sane. Everything that happened is right here on this paper. Will you take it back to America?"

"Take it to America? Why?"

"Publish it. I want everyone to read what happened here."

Jones shook his head and turned away from the man. "No, I'm sorry, but that's not for me. You can do it from your own country. It's your book, not mine. You keep it." The prisoner nodded, stuffing the pages into his pants. He would find someone else, while Jones would regret his decision for years.

The Americans listened to the sounds of the Russian soldiers as they forced the sickened Germans to continue working. The Russians were so visibly disgusted by the sight that, for the first time, the Americans understood the rage of these avenging soldiers.

Marlowe and his men continued on through what were now huge masses of soldiers, mostly Russians. They were very near the lines where the Russian and Canadian troops met, and they struck out westward excitedly. They walked across the countryside now to speed their progress, and paused when they came across a large group of Mongolian soldiers camping in the field, cooking food on a large fire and drinking from a community bottle as their boisterous voices carried across the field. They spotted the Americans and called to them cheerfully. They didn't speak a word of English but communicated with the men that they were welcome to join them by the fire and share in their drink. The men exchanged glances, and first Watsick, then Mickelson, and finally all the Americans seated themselves beside their Russian allies.

CHAPTER 4

Chasteen and Spivey sat between two of the Mongols who made up part of a large circle around a bonfire. They accepted the bottle as it was passed around and laughed with the Mongols as they drank. They shared the triumphant feeling of these soldiers, and the group seemed united in its celebration. All felt good, and the party became more raucous and jovial as each hour passed. Although they didn't share a language, they managed to communicate through gestures and broken German and Polish. Some of the Mongols began dancing, crossing their arms in front of them and kicking their legs up in the traditional Russian dance. Several Americans tried to imitate the dance, and everyone laughed together as they fell in the dirt. The ex-prisoners coaxed Spivey to try, and they cheered as he managed a couple of steps before stumbling backward. Now he began to jitterbug, and the Mongols watched in fascination. Several of them began to join him, and he taught them a few steps. Marlowe left the party in search of food and located bread and cheese not far from the fire. He helped himself as the other men drank.

As they laughed and sang along with the Mongols, Jones watched one man pull a pistol from his holster and fire it in the air. He laughed with them, drunk and unconcerned. The dark Russian then spun the cylinder in the gun and handed it to the Mongolian seated beside him. The man laughed as all eyes fell on him. He held the gun to his temple, grinning at the Americans as he did so, squeezed his eyes shut, and pulled the trigger. It clicked, and he held the gun up triumphantly as the men broke into cheers. He spun the cylinder again and handed it to the man beside him. Chasteen and Spivey exchanged a look of alarm.

"Don't worry, it's not loaded. They're just havin' fun with us," Spivey said, but they suddenly jumped to their feet as the gun exploded and the man who held it slumped into the fire. The soldiers pulled his body from the flames, dragging him to a pile of rubbish ten feet behind them, a pool of blood bubbling in the fire. Now they handed the gun to Spivey, having reloaded and spun the cylinder. Spivey shook his head and backed away from the gun. They cajoled him good-naturedly, and he took the gun and handed it down to the next Mongolian. The game continued for several hours, and the Americans watched, now drunker than they wanted to be, silent and nervous as the party that they had been enjoying so much turned into a brutal game of chance. Another soldier shot himself in the head, and the others laughed before dragging off his body. The Americans looked at each other for a signal to leave but were apprehensive about standing and walking away.

As the day stretched out, several men left one by one, slipping away from the fire as their hosts began to drop off to sleep, and eventually the entire group stole away to continue their journey.

Within two miles, they reached their destination. Rows of tanks, jeeps, and soldiers swelled toward a center line where the Canadians, British, and Americans met the Russians. Check posts and blockades already formed a barrier, with fences erected and soldiers posted on each side. The men took their first look at the Cold War. They walked toward the fence that separated them from home and were immediately intercepted by a Russian officer. Although Rizzuto, several days earlier, had crossed the lines to his own troops without being questioned, it would not be so easy for the remaining men of 311/I.

Stan Watsick spoke for the men in what he knew of the language. He explained that they were American POWs trying to return to their regiments. The officer shook his head and motioned them toward his jeep. On its hood he spread open a map of Germany. Marlowe found Dettmannsdorf and pointed it out to the officer, who nodded, scratching his chin thoughtfully. He set his finger on the town, then made several comments to Watsick in Russian. Watsick translated. "He says we shouldn't have left 311/I. We should've stayed for the Russian army to come get us. He says we'll have to go back and wait. No one goes through this wall."

The men reacted in an explosion of fury, shouting their refusals to the non-English-speaking officer. "We didn't come all this way to turn back. All we have to do is cross the lines. Tell that son of a bitch we'll skin him alive if he don't let us across," Chasteen said, as the other men shouted their agreement. Watsick attempted to protest in the man's language.

"If you want to leave Germany, you will have to do it our way. This is Russian territory now," the officer told them bluntly. The men sat for some time in the midst of chaos, soldiers and jeeps buzzing around them as they stared ahead of them, despondent.

"Hell, it took us three days to get here. If we walk fast, we ought to be back in less than two. If we stay here, we'll end up being taken prisoner again," one man said, and several others agreed, climbing to their feet.

Marlowe remained seated, watching them. "After what you saw in the last few days you're going to trust the Russians? What makes you so sure that they'll turn you over to the Americans? I'm not walking back—it's crazy to walk away from your own lines. I'm staying right here," he said.

"And do what? We don't have any choice but to trust them!" someone else insisted, and they argued back and forth until the two sides inevitably divided. Watsick, Bruton, Chasteen, Mickelson, Spivey, Jones, and several other men seated themselves beside Marlowe and Fisher.

"Billy, you ain't goin' back, are you?" Chasteen asked his old friend, Lindsey, as the other group began to pull out. Lindsey gave him a nod and walked away with the small group, turning back once to wave. "Good luck," he called out. Chasteen was never to see his friend again. As far as Chasteen knew, Lindsey and his companions never returned to the United States.

The small group remaining along the west-east German line now decided to fall back until they came up with a plan. They walked a quarter mile to a barn and climbed into its warm and musty loft. Marlowe had already prepared a plan. He would sneak across the fence at the most weakly guarded point. With the help of another man, he knew he could make it.

"I'll go," volunteered a young man named Jim Novak, an 82nd Airborne from the baker's section of 311/I. Novak was someone they knew only from recent acquaintance, but Marlowe nodded in agreement. Novak was a healthy, sturdy-looking kid of nineteen and the men trusted him. The others agreed to wait, and the two men set out. Watsick and Mickelson were each carrying a bottle of vodka with them, and they began drinking as they settled into the hay for their wait.

Marlowe and Novak walked back to the lines in high spirits. Once they neared heavy Russian activity, they stood at a safe distance and watched the movement from fifty feet away in the trees. At this distance they were not noticed, but if they moved toward the wall, they would have had several guards on them instantly.

The war in Europe had just come to a close. Hitler, finally conceding his loss, had taken his own life that morning.

The two paratroopers followed the fence farther down, looking at the Russian uniforms everywhere. Once away from the road, the military seemed less concentrated, and they hunkered down, waiting for the sun to dip lower on the horizon. As they waited and the hours crawled by, their impatience ate away at their nerves.

"If we run fast we could both be over that fence before the Russians shoot, and they wouldn't try to shoot once we were on the other side," Marlowe said.

They agreed to try. The opposite side of the fence was everything for them, and they both knew they could make it, even with the unlikely odds.

"All right, when I say so, we'll make a run for it." Marlowe whispered.

Back at the barn, Dan Jones and Jim Bruton played a game of cards as they waited, while others watched absently, drinking from the bottles that Mickelson and Watsick passed around. A few shoved piles of hay under their heads in an attempt to sleep. Jones tried to concentrate on the game. He would not allow himself to consider the hopelessness of the situation. It could be no worse than it had been in the past. Now he could think of little but Caroline. As hard as he tried to control it, his mind bore a new glimmer of hope, and it carried that hope through a lifetime of fantasies, with his family, his wife, his children and grand-children. He tossed a card down, abruptly rejoining the game.

"I want you all to know, whatever happens now, you're all the best group of friends a man could have," he said suddenly.

The men murmured their agreement at once, suddenly somber and earnest.

"You're right, I can't imagine ever knowing better friends, when I think what we been through together," Bruton commented, taking a drink from the vodka and passing it on.

"We got to stay in touch if we make it back. I don't want to lose track of any of you all," Chasteen said, confirming that each man had written his name and address in his small book.

"That's if we make it back," Jones added, staring at his cards. The men fell silent, each thinking his own thoughts.

Conceding Jones's caution, Chasteen took a long drink from the bottle and bared his teeth against the burning in his throat. As much as he drank, he couldn't feel drunk. His nerves were stretched taut and nothing would relax them. He recalled the smell of the Wismar concentration camp, as well as that of the Russian officer he and Spivey had stuffed into the furnace. He'd long since had more than he could take of this country, and his jaw twitched as he compelled himself not to shove his fist into the wall. His anger and frustration had screamed at him for months. He'd almost grown used to the shrill sound in his ears, but now the noise was deafening, and he jumped to his feet to distract his thoughts. Spivey looked up questioningly from where he sat in the hay.

"I'm goin' out front for some air. This Goddamn loft reminds me too much of that pigpen we lived in." Chasteen hurried down the steps and stood in the late afternoon light, gasping at the fresh air. Above all the noises and destruction of war, he heard the twittering of new spring birds, and he felt his nerves loosen just slightly. He hadn't eaten in the past three days, and now he thought for the first time of food. He walked into a bevy of trees in hopes of finding fruit, then paused, listening to the sound of an approaching truck.

Suddenly he sucked in his breath as an engine churned miles away, but closer. He recognized a familiar sound that he hadn't heard for what seemed years, and he listened more closely, his mouth dropping open as he confirmed what he heard. It was the shifting, the double clutching that he remembered so well from his training. Only American vehicles had that sticking clutch that required several grinding attempts to shift gears. He heard the truck shift, grind and shift again with a sob of relief and joy. Running into the clearing, he watched a truck become visible, two American GIs driving toward him with Marlowe and Novak standing in back, waving and shouting his name.

Jones dropped his cards as he heard Chasteen whooping joyfully out front. The men leapt to their feet at once. They all knew instinctively that for them the war was finally over, and they crowded to the door in exaltation.

CHAPTER 5

A s Caroline's sister, Maude, sat on the front step in her Ireland home, she
breathed in the warm, sweet air of early summer. This was to be a summer she had anticipated without daring to expect. The Germans were defeated,
the soldiers were home. Production would slowly begin again as Great Britain
started to patch itself together. In a sleepy, faraway manner, she heard the songs
of sparrows over voices talking several houses away. She closed her eyes, turning her face toward the warm sun and feeling it burn pleasantly against her face
and neck.

"Maude?" Her eyes snapped open as she recognized not only the voice but
the accent, and looked up in shock at Caroline's American beau, Danny Jones.
The voice was more familiar than the face, and she shuddered as she met his
eyes. She remembered him as healthy, boyish, and jocular. The pallid, somber
face that looked down at her now was barely recognizable.

"Is Caroline inside?" he asked eagerly. His anticipation provided the only
light in his tired eyes. Maude hesitated. Her older sister was working at the
factory. Caroline had changed since Dan had gone off to the war, as much as
he appeared to have changed himself. She had waited, and she had grown impatient. Maude wondered now if her sister had ever really known that she loved
the trooper or had only been caught up by his energetic personality and American enthusiasm. Without his presence, her own interest waned, and other boys
again pursued Maude's popular older sister.

"I'll fetch her at work. You wait inside. I won't be more than a minute."
She led him into the house eagerly. She liked the young American and hoped
now that he would marry her sister, despite her fears of losing Caroline to a
place thousands of miles away.

Dan waited in the familiar house with anxious anticipation, his thoughts
rushing through the ceremony and beyond. He tried to recall her face, having
lost her photograph so long before. He knew that he was a sad sight. A former
brawny football player, he now stood five-foot-ten and weighed less than one
hundred pounds. But he was sure she would understand. He rushed toward the

door several times, thinking he heard her approach, before she finally entered the house behind her young sister.

His heart seemed to pause as he faced the dark-haired girl he'd thought of every night for so many months. She seemed very little changed, her clothes modest and simple, her young face naturally pretty without makeup, her hair pulled back from her face in dark brown combs. As he extended his arms out toward her, however, she looked at Dan with a hesitancy he didn't recognize. He saw her eyes fall on his hands, and he shoved them in his pockets self-consciously. The work on the railroads had worn his frostbitten fingers to gnarled and discolored stumps, only vaguely similar to the normal hands he'd once had. Most of his nails were nothing but nubs.

"Hello, Danny," she said politely, without closing the space between them.

"Hello, Caroline." He glanced at Maude uncertainly, and she quickly left the room with a smile. "Did I surprise you?" he asked when they were alone.

"You certainly did that. I didn't know you at first when I saw you. I wrote your mother and told her you were free."

When Jones had been released to a hospital in France, he had wired Caroline of his safety before contacting anyone else.

"She wrote me while you were a prisoner," she added.

"She's going to like you a lot. I suppose by now we've waited long enough to marry. When I go home to my family I'm going to have you with me as Mrs. Jones."

Caroline paused, then turned her back and asked if her sister had offered him tea.

"I don't want any tea," he answered sharply, confused by her aloof attitude. He watched her pace the room. "Have you missed me, Caroline?" he asked softly.

"Of course I missed you. Don't you know how worried I was when you just disappeared? I thought you'd been killed or gone off with some other woman, changed your mind about marriage maybe."

"Is that what's botherin' you? I haven't thought of a single woman the way I have you. You know I wanted to be married before I ever went off to Holland." He moved toward her and wrapped one arm around her stiff shoulders, but she didn't respond.

"Danny, things have changed. I waited a long time . . . too long. I don't think we should be married. You've changed. I just don't think you are what I thought you were."

"What are you talking about? What about our plans? Weren't we happy before? Things haven't changed since then, except that the war is over and we can live the lives we always wanted now. Together." He watched as she pulled free of him and fell into her father's chair with a frustrated sigh.

"I just don't think . . . I don't think that we are right together."

"Why not—we love each other, don't we?"

"I don't love you anymore," she exclaimed, standing to face him before running out of the room, her eyes full of tears as she disappeared from sight. Dan stood looking around him at the quiet and mean living room for the final time. He had never considered that Caroline would not be part of his future, never expected to have such a homecoming. He had spent the last year waiting and planning, and now he suddenly had nothing.

He had taken his new jacket off while waiting for her, and now he pulled it on over his emaciated body. He straightened his cap and let out a breath as he walked out the door, shutting it behind him. The late afternoon sunshine now surrendered to a light evening rain shower, and he pulled his collar up around his neck with an involuntary shiver and walked away from the house. His boots made a light and familiar tap on the cobblestones that had once seemed exotic and exciting. He turned his face up, oblivious to the Irish rain that ran across his cheeks and collected on his uniform, dousing his hopes and chilling his undernourished body.

*

EPILOGUE

July 1984

D anzley Jones pulled the last unopened box toward him through hot, dusty attic air. For several years, he had promised his wife, Irene, he'd clean the attic. It was a chore he had put off as long as he could. But he never had expected the accumulation of trinkets and mementos to be so overwhelming. Already he'd spent a long day sorting through boxes that dated as far back as the forties and fifties—piles of crates full of the boys' clothes, toys, baseball mitts, trophies, and BB guns, as well as gadgets and tools of his own that he'd forgotten he had ever owned.

The July heat had collected in the airless attic, and he paused, removing his glasses and wiping his damp face. This last dust-covered box was badly damaged, the cardboard crushed and torn. He sliced it open with his hunting knife. The weak cardboard fell open, and he peered into what was a nearly empty box. Several photos were scattered inside with forgotten letters and a tired-looking medal, his Purple Heart from World War II, the only medal he'd received. He shuffled through the papers impatiently, wondering if they were worth saving. The box clearly had not been opened since the war.

Groping around the bottom one last time, his hand met with a small, square object, and he pulled out a tiny, weathered green address book. As he turned it over in his hand, he saw that it was so battered and aged that the script on the cover had long since worn away. Dan remembered the address book with an unpleasant jolt that momentarily stunned him. He hadn't thought of that part of his life for forty years. His memory of the time in which the address book had been his only possession had been buried deep in an inaccessible vault of his mind—a vault he had hoped never to open again.

Suddenly oblivious to the dry heat around him, he opened the tiny book. The brown pages, as brittle as onion skin, snapped and creased as he turned them. But he could see names and addresses scribbled faintly in various forms of ink or lead. Some were completely illegible, but many weren't, and as he squinted through his glasses in the dim light, he saw names of people who had meant more to him at one time than anyone else in the world. Doug Turner, Stan Watsick, Jim Bruton. Recalling the circumstances around each name, the faces and voices, he saw the past reveal itself before him like a movie, too strange to be a part of his own life. Putting the book in his pocket, he brushed himself off and climbed down the attic stairs to the kitchen, where Irene was preparing supper.

For several days Dan Jones mulled over his finding, removing it from the bedside drawer where he had stuffed it, flipping through the faded names, then sighing and putting it again out of his sight. Irene watched him with a quizzical expression, but he found himself unable to properly express what the names meant to him and why he had never before mentioned that part of his life. The occasional nightmares he had, screaming out in anger that was contradictory to his jocular nature, were all that she knew. Now, forty years later, he couldn't explain to her why this small address book meant so much.

Monday afternoon in his office, Dan took his first step. Reaching for the phone, he flipped through the address book, and opening the page with "Earl Mickelson" scrawled in a familiar hand, he dialed the number he saw written there. The automated operator informed him bluntly that he had reached a disconnected number.

He next tried information in the same town and scrambled for a pen as a number was given to him. He dialed immediately, feeling his nerves tighten as he tapped his pen impatiently on the desk. The phone rang unanswered, and he hung up, discouraged. It was a mistake to bring back old memories, he decided. He could accomplish nothing by digging up that which he had struggled for so long to keep buried. No one else concerned themselves with the past. Why should he?

But that night after Irene was in bed and he sat up too restless to sleep, Dan found himself dialing the same number, holding his breath as it rang six, seven, eight times.

"Hello!" The voice was tired and startled, as if the speaker had been awakened from a deep sleep, but was instantly recognizable.

"Earl! Do you know who this is?" Dan asked, excitement surging into his voice.

There was a pause, and he wondered briefly if the connection had been lost before Mickelson responded, "Yes I do. It's Dan Jones, isn't it?"

Dan was incredulous. "After forty years you can recognize me just like that?"

"Well, your voice hasn't changed at all. How could I forget? How the hell have you been?" The conversation flowed in an uncontrollable rush, and they immediately began recalling their lives together, that part of their past that neither of them had ever discussed with anyone. After hanging up several hours later, Dan was unable to remember the conversation, but he was gripped with a feverish excitement. He had never imagined it would be so easy to talk with one of his old cellmates, and now instead of wanting to bury the unpleasant past, he suddenly wanted to call everyone in the book. He wanted to trace everything and everyone related to his imprisonment. He flipped through the pages and began to dial the phone again, then reconsidered, realizing for the first time that it was extremely late. He climbed into bed beside Irene and stared at the ceiling, waiting and watching for the sun to come up, until he dozed off, sleeping fitfully and waking himself from a bad dream.

At sixty years old, Dan had lived the majority of his life in North Dakota with Irene and his two sons. As owner of a plastering firm, he had secured a comfortable home and life for his family. Irene was a small, animated Swedish-American whom he had met shortly after the war. He had fallen in love with her then and still loved her as much now, after nearly forty years of marriage. The elder of his sons was now a doctor, the other his partner at the firm, both married with several children. He was a healthy, robust two-hundred-pound man who was recognized everywhere in town by his cheerful disposition and unmistakable laugh. He seemed a man with few problems, rarely taking life too seriously and always ready with a joke or a smile. Only the occasional nightmare plagued him with a world of corpses, violence, and gore. He slept little after such dreams and spent a day afterward silent and disturbed. Often he was horrified by the violence of his imagination, for these dreams seemed certainly more gruesome even than his experiences in the war, or at least his memories of them.

He never discussed his nightmares with anyone. He had always been silent about his past and what he had done and seen in the war. He knew few men his age who would talk about the war freely, especially those who'd been prisoners. It seemed natural to put those memories behind him, to attempt to live a happier and more productive life in recognition of his war buddies who hadn't survived at all. That was something he owed them.

So the following morning, as he sat at the kitchen table with the address book in his back pocket and a piece of toast in his hand, he found himself unable to explain to Irene or himself this sudden interest in recapturing the past.

"I just don't understand why now, after forty years, you want to talk. Why not two weeks ago, or twenty years ago? Why now?" she asked, sitting across from him at the table.

Dan reached for the butter with his knife and spread it mechanically over his toast. He studied his plate, wondering the same thing.

"I just wish I could answer that, Irene. I guess it's been building for all these years, and now it's finally surfacing."

Once back in the office, he pulled out the address book again and began dialing the phone. He tracked down three more friends—Herbert Marlowe, Jim Rizzuto, and Charlie Chasteen—and by the end of the week had been in touch with fifteen men from Work Commando 311/I. It was enough men for a meeting, and he began calling them back one by one, arranging a central meeting place and common free weekend. Surprisingly, none of the men had contacted any of the others for forty years, but most were interested in opening the doors to their friendship again. Others would speak with him about their families and jobs but had no interest in bringing back old memories. Dan respected their wishes and continued with his plans with those who shared his enthusiasm.

He approached Irene cautiously with the news. He was eager for her to meet his old friends but unsure that she would agree to join him.

"It might just be curiosity," Dan said to Irene, and she smiled.

"I'm curious myself—I always have been," she said, and the date was set for the first weekend in August in Cleveland, Ohio.

August 1984

Dan Jones sat on the corner of the hotel bed as Irene rummaged through the suitcase, the television blaring monotonously with the local news. He carried a list of the men he had contacted and their times of arrival at the hotel, and he now examined this list through his glasses.

"Danny, why aren't you in the lobby? You said you were meeting someone at 4:30."

"I am, Charlie Chasteen."

"Well, it's twenty to five. What are you waiting for?" she teased anxiously, and he glanced at his watch. He was anxious himself and hadn't realized it was so late.

"OK, when I find him I'll bring him up to meet you."

"If you find him and he hasn't given up on you," she scolded with a smile.

Almost forty years ago she had met her husband for the first time, just returned from prison camp. She was a young girl of nineteen, in love with a sailor, and he, brokenhearted over a lost love in Ireland. She had been rooming with his mother in Bremerton, Washington, for the previous eighteen months, and she had heard a great deal about the youngest son, who was away at war and missing in action for so many months. Irene had been a comfort to Mabel, who was both anxious about her missing son and mourning the recent death of her husband.

Dan and Irene had paid little notice to each other when they met. Their hearts were far away, heedless of those around them. But they had gravitated toward each other over time, at first reluctantly, despite Mabel's constant encouragements. Eventually they began going to movies together on double dates, meeting with friends, progressively falling in love. They married within a year. They had never regretted their decision over the years, even throughout the hard times. The fact that Dan, who had never mentioned his war experiences, was suddenly so eager to stir up the past baffled her, and she realized now that she was meeting a side of her husband that she had never seen a glimpse of before.

Dan walked into the lobby and saw several unfamiliar faces milling around the large room. He imagined Chasteen would tend to be late, and he stood waiting, watching anxiously, as each figure entered through the wide glass doors. He didn't know what he was looking for. He remembered clearly what Charlie had looked like in Germany, with his slow southern drawl and easy swagger. He recalled his agreement with his friends in a barn loft as they waited to be rescued. They had vowed never to lose contact with each other if they made it back. Yet once back in the States, the friendships seemed to disappear, and for many years even Mickelson and Watsick had lost touch with each other. He had never even tried to contact his friends, and he remembered now a letter from one of the prisoners, addressed to him in 1946. It had made little reference to what had happened to them in the past, yet he found the letter so painful that he stuffed it out of sight and never responded. He was a heavy drinker for many years after the war, and only by forgetting his experiences was he able to regain control of his life. He owed much of that to Irene, and he thought with a smile of her waiting patiently in the hotel room.

He scanned the lobby again, seeing no one who resembled Charlie, and tried to imagine how he would look today. But placing that face in this modern environment wasn't easy. As time passed, he became at first irritated, then disappointed, realizing that he wouldn't see his friend. He didn't wear a watch, and instead of looking back at the large clock above the elevators, he turned to a man standing near him.

"You got the time?" he asked.

The man looked at his watch and glanced in his direction briefly. "Five to five," he responded, and gave Dan a sudden second glance. The man who had spoken was about sixty, his face tan and weathered. He wore a short-sleeved, button-down shirt and brass string tie. His voice and accent were unmistakable. His face was one of character, alluding to a life full of excitement, of hardship, and of challenge. His eyes gleamed with a mischievous light that Dan had seen only once before.

"Charlie Chasteen! Why you old dog, you been standing here next to me all this time!" They stopped to stare at each other again. Dan Jones's hair had thinned and turned gray, he'd put on weight, he wore heavy glasses, but he had changed little. They moved toward each other and fell into an embrace as they faced, for the first time, the life they had deliberately forgotten until this moment. In shock they both wiped impatiently at tears rolling down their faces, as people moved around them with curious glances.

As they waited for the other men, arriving later in the evening, they sat together, baffled by their sense of timelessness, and they spoke in loud excitement, oblivious to the world around them. By 9:00, seven men sat together at a banquet table with their wives.

Jim Bruton grinned widely with a cigar in his hand, pumping hands and embracing the men with his warmhearted Kentucky manner, telling jokes and charming the wives.

Jim Rizzuto arrived with his familiar handsome and intelligent smile, his memory of the events so sharp the others fell to him for their information. He had youthful good health and enthusiasm for the new reunion and had determined to jump again with forty war veterans in Taiwan.

Earl Mickelson flew from his home in Colorado. He listened to the men talk and nodded his head, laughing and joking with his open and honest expression, little changed after forty years.

Stan Watsick was still a wiry man, and his face shone with a boyish friendly grin that seemed to reflect to a happy and unregretful life despite the hardships he had suffered. He and Mickelson marveled over the coincidences in their lives, even though years had passed without keeping in touch with each other. Now Watsick was the father of three grown daughters, and Mickelson of three grown sons.

Herbert Marlowe was still tall, still somehow the leader as he smiled with his warm-hearted, generous, and always responsible manner, one arm on the table, legs crossed in an unaffected manner.

After forty years they were together again, and they spoke not only of themselves but for those who couldn't be there, of Duperry and Spivey, Lindsey and Kalkreuth, Kleppe, Novak, Pombano, Fisher, and Turner. Some of these men would join them in the following years; some had passed away; and others, like Turner and Lindsey, remained missing.

They didn't know if they were proud or ashamed of their past, bitter or forgiving; whether they had been affected by the experience permanently; whether they had ever really recovered. They suffered similar physical problems with their kidneys, their eyesight, their teeth, and the scars they carried on their backs, as well as unexplained fits of depression. They shared their feelings, and that was all they could do, and forty years after their separation, it was all that they needed.

BIBLIOGRAPHY

Hastings, Max. *Overlord: D-Day and the Battle for Normandy*. New York: Simon and Schuster, 1984.

Hubbell, John C. *POW: A Definitive History of the American Prison of War Experience*. New York: Readers Digest Press, 1976.

Keegan, John. *Six Armies in Normandy*. New York: Viking Press, 1984.

Longmate, Norman. *The G.I.'s: The Americans in Britain, 1942–1945*. New York: Charles Scribner and Sons, 1975.

Myers, Debs, Jonathon Kilbourne, and Richard Harrity, eds. *Yank: The GI Story of the War*. New York: Duell, Sloan & Pearce, 1947.

101st Airborne, ed. *The Screaming Eagles*. Albany, GA, 1949.

Ryan, Cornelius. *A Bridge Too Far*. New York: Simon and Schuster, 1974.

———. *The Longest Day*. New York: Simon and Schuster, 1944.

Additional information about POW and concentration camps gathered from:
East German Consulate, New York, New York, 1990.
Jewish Community Association of San Francisco, 1990.
U.S. POW archival research by assistants to Congressman Thomas Foley, Washington, D.C., 1991.